DISCOVER YOUR PASSION RELEASE YOUR POWER

How to Fulfill Your Purpose in the Power of the Authentic Self

Johnny Cavazos MD

Discover Your Passion, Release Your Power: How to Fulfill Your Purpose in the Power of the Authentic Self by Johnny Cavazos

Discover Your Passion, Release Your Power: How to Fulfill Your Purpose in the Power of the Authentic Self by Johnny Cavazos

Printed in the United States of America

ISBN (paperback): 978-1-7338213-4-6

ISBN (eBook): 978-1-7338213-3-9

TABLE OF CONTENTS

INTRODUCTION

Have you noticed there seems to be a pervasive lack of energy in our society? Why do we all seem to be so tired? Why is there so much job dissatisfaction? Do you have boundless energy? Or is it a chore to get up and go to work every day? If we examine our own families, some of our family members always seem to be busy working on a project or activity, while others seem to be sitting around listless. Are all successful people born with tons of energy? It stands to reason that successful people don't always feel like getting up early and going to work every day.

We can't all feel full of energy and excited about getting up and going about our daily lives. Something else must come into play. In my last book, *Brave the Wave*, I emphasized spiritual experiences and getting in touch with the spiritual side of who we are because it brings us closer to our authentic selves. This is the supernatural aspect of who we are. A distinction can be made between our physical, or natural, selves and our spiritual selves.

When we speak about the physical powerplant of the human body, the liver is known as the "furnace or powerhouse"; it is our source for physical energy. The liver is responsible for releasing stored carbohydrates, and it oxidizes fatty acids when they are needed to get the body going.

But where do we get spiritual energy? One source of spiritual energy is passion.

What is your passion? Do you get excited about anything you are involved in? Do you have infectious enthusiasm? Where does your passion lie? How much time are you devoting to your unique passion? Those were some of the questions I asked a group of friends just out of curiosity. Being taken aback by their answers was the impetus for this book. Two questions kept coming up in my mind:

- How many people are walking around with no clue as to what their unique passion is?
- How many people think that discovering or developing their passion is irrelevant to what they are doing in their lives?

Those two questions stuck in my head. It was the pebble—the boulder, rather—in the shoe. In other words, it never goes away.

When I asked each of my friends what their passion was, the responses were something along the lines of "I'm too busy working" or "I'm too busy being a mom" or "I can't worry about my passion. That's a luxury. I'm just trying to survive." But is it?

What do *you* think about your own unique passion? Do you think having a passion is important for what you are trying to accomplish in this life—assuming you are trying to accomplish anything?

From my own experience, I'd argue that ignoring our passion is a mistake—a mistake that will have a direct impact on the quality of our lives on this earth. Ignoring our passion could be something we will regret in this life and the next.

This book is about helping you discover your own unique passion. Discovering our passion is critical to reaching our authentic selves because it's a crucial source of spiritual energy. Passion brings energy and power. When we talk about discovering and developing our authentic selves, discovering our passion and pursuing our purpose are both integral to the process. If you're interested in energy, power, passion and purpose, then this is the book for you.

There's not a lot of research out there regarding our unique passion, but there is some science to help us identify it. Passions come in two varieties: harmonious and obsessive. Making the distinction between harmonious and obsessive passions is where the *action* is because of the impact they have on our relationships. We are definitely interested in action.

Looking closely at the difference between these two types of passion can be helpful in examining our own lives and can assist us in deciphering which passions we are currently engaging in. Are you engaged in any activity that involves your unique passion?

Passion is defined as a strong inclination toward a self-defining activity that one likes (or even loves) and finds important and in which one invests time and energy on a regular basis. Passion is something we engage in regularly. It is a *source of energy*. In the pages to follow we will get into the multiple sources of power and energy we can draw on when discovering our passion and purpose.

When we are going over these ideas, it's helpful to look at people who have been successful in their lives pursuing and developing their own passion and purpose, such as musicians, artists, businesspeople, writers, and athletes, to name a few. As we look at other people and how they came to realize and develop their passions, it's possible they didn't even think about these ideas. It's kind of like when you hear people say, "I just do what I do." The problem arises when we *don't* do what we do. In other words, we don't feel fulfilled or satisfied with the activities we're involved in.

If we take the time to observe our surroundings, it becomes obvious that a lack of enthusiasm or energy seems to be prevalent. Just walk through an airport or go to a restaurant or grocery store. It's everywhere. We're not satisfied in our daily lives, and we aren't happy with our careers or jobs. Most people aren't content in their jobs, as one survey recently reported:[1]

"It is not uncommon for working adults to consider one or multiple career changes," Dr. Bill Pepicello, the president of the University of Phoenix, said in a statement announcing the results.... Nearly 80 percent of workers in their 20s said they wanted to change careers, followed by 64 percent of 30-somethings and 54 percent in their 40s. Although the majority of workers said they had career plans when they were younger, 73 percent of them had not landed in the job they had expected."

If you feel tired and unfulfilled, it may be reasonable to consider the value you place on passion and purpose. Ask yourself, "Am I pursuing my passion or my purpose in this life? Could I be missing out on all the benefits that come from living a life in the power of my passion as I pursue my purpose?"

Purpose is useful because it brings two very important benefits that help us survive in a broken, fallen world: power and protection. Purpose protects.

We should also be instilling these ideas into our children because of the value they bring regarding a sense of power and well-being. We will get to these ideas in the coming chapters.

If you are interested in finding the answers to the above questions, this book will help guide you on the road to discovering your passion. Once you begin to engage in that passion, you will have access to power. Once you have tapped into that power, this will help fuel the discovery and development of your purpose. We all have a purpose. If you can believe that, we're in business.

From my own experience, the desire to find purpose and passion came from an uneasiness or an unsettled feeling. I had a sense of anxiety, a feeling of being uncomfortable, an emptiness, a hunger. I sensed there was something more to this life than just survival and distraction. If we reflect on our own lives, we can see that much of our time is consumed by those two activities: survival and distraction. So, this yearning came from within. It became clear to me that I was created for something more.

What I began to realize is that this hunger comes from our spirits, our spiritual selves, the self that we were created to be. This is the self that lines up with the blueprint or architectural plans God had in mind when he created us. When we pay attention to those types of cues, we are on our way. Those yearnings or desires are there for a reason. If you have that spiritual hunger or yearning, congratulations, you are on the right path to a sense of well-being and joy.

Exploration, adventure, and discovery add excitement, interest, and fulfillment to our lives. Being open to new ideas and new experiences leads to greater vision, clarity, power, and energy. When we gain these attributes, it is much easier to recognize our purpose. Fulfilling our purpose brings love, joy and peace. When we readily identify the value of these pursuits, we can be confident that we aren't wasting time, effort, or energy.

As we examine these ideas, it will become apparent that passion and purpose are linked. They are intertwined like a rope. Passion is the engine that drives the boat, and purpose is the compass that we need to get us to the destination. We need both.

Getting closer to our authentic selves will help us in this process of discovery and development of purpose. Discarding ideas or principles that yield no value and are inconsistent with our unique authentic selves is part of the process. If you are asking yourself, "Can I do better?" or "Can I be better?" then we are headed in the right direction. It is pursuing the idea that we were created for more.

True spiritual authenticity yields love, joy, peace, and fulfillment. When you get closer to true spiritual authenticity, you benefit, and everyone around you benefits.

Imagine being lost at sea in a rubber dinghy with only a small engine and a compass. Will a big screen television help you get to safety and civilization? What about a recliner? Sometimes we focus on empty or shallow pursuits and passions that are inconsistent with our authentic self, the self we were created to be. These kinds of pursuits are not only a waste of time and energy, they suck the life, joy, and peace out of our day-to-day lives. They're part of the problem, not part of the solution. It's hard to paddle a small dinghy forward with a big recliner and a sixty-inch television in the raft. We need to get rid of some of that extra baggage on this trip.

We're after power, energy, passion, and purpose. As we begin to spend time and energy working toward these, we will begin to discover joy, fulfillment, and peace—and most importantly, love. These will spill over into our family lives and into the relationships with the people who are closest to us, the people we love the most.

These are the first steps on a unique and exciting adventure. Let's roll.

1

WHERE IS THE POWER?

"Be fearless in the pursuit of whatever sets your soul afire."

– Jennifer Lee

LIKE MOST GREAT STORIES, this one started in a smoky bowling alley. It was a Saturday night, and a group of friends and I were at a place called Rockin' Bowl, where there was bowling in a dark nightclub-like atmosphere. There was rock music blasting over a large PA system, cheap pitchers of beer, and mostly teens and twenty-somethings. Everyone was having a good time, but I kept getting distracted by a group of fifteen to sixteen-year-old boys next to us who were effortlessly bowling strikes. Being in a group of couples, I was showing off by using brute strength to power my ball down the lane, hitting the pins as hard as possible. Pins were flying with plenty of noise, but that was about it. Strikes were rare. Meanwhile, these teenagers were rolling the ball in unusual ways to get spin and curve on the ball, and they were consistently knocking down all the pins.

Being somewhat competitive, I did my best to get spin and a curve on my ball. While trying to catch myself from falling flat on my face, I injured my wrist. Then I asked myself, "How the heck do you get a curve on your ball when bowling?"

When it comes to questions that pop into my head, this one was not that important. But it helped me to see that if you look at questions that are not really that important and you have an attitude of curiosity, and a relentless drive to answer questions, there is much to learn. Tony Robbins said, "Quality questions create a quality life. Successful people ask better questions, and as a result, they get better answers." Bowling a curve means nothing in the grand scheme of things. But asking questions about passion and purpose have brought value and understanding to my life that I want to share. The drive and desire to answer questions about passion and purpose have had an impact and influence on my way of thinking. My drive to understand our own behavior and what motivates us pushed me to ask many questions and seek answers. From my own experience seeing thousands of patients, I've witnessed firsthand that many people go about their lives in misery and with no excitement or enthusiasm. I was there too. Once I discovered my passion while moving towards fulfilling my purpose, that is when things changed for me. This discovery process was the entire impetus for this book.

The questions I want to answer in this book are:

- Why are we so tired?
- Why don't we have energy?
- Why do most of us not enjoy our work life?
- Where do we find the energy we need to go about our lives?
- Why do so few people feel like they are in their "dream job"?

We are going to talk about energy, pep, passion, and purpose in the coming chapters. The information and discussion ahead will give you plenty of ideas about where to start if seeking your own unique passion and purpose are meaningful to you. They are part of the supernatural power that comes from the discovery and development of our authentic selves.

A Simple Question

The whole premise of this book came about because of a simple question I asked my friends when we were at a sports bar having wings and watching a game: "What is your passion?" In other words, *What are you excited about? What activity are you most enthusiastic about? What brings you great joy and fulfillment?* By their silence and puzzled looks, you would have thought I asked them what the meaning of life was. If my few friends assembled here were in any way representative of the larger population, then significant segments of the population not only don't *know* what their passion is but don't even *think* about their passion.

A couple of my friends tried to come up with something on the fly: "Uh, my kids. Yeah, my family; that's what I'm most passionate about." Somebody else said, "Look, I'm too busy working and trying to pay the bills to be worrying about my passion." Another said, "Hey, anyone gonna eat that last wing? If not, I'll take it."

This is what I want to go over in the chapters ahead: passion, power, energy, and purpose.

So back to the bowling story. To answer my curve question, I rented a video at Blockbuster Video on bowling—which gives you an idea of how long ago my "learn to roll a curve" quest began. The video featured Earl Anthony, a famous professional bowler. He went over the technique on how to roll a curve and, more importantly, where you want your ball to hit in the "pocket" that enables the pins to fall in a way more likely to result in a strike. With this information and a little practice, I was able to bowl a game in the low two-hundred range. (I have witnesses.) I'm sure I'll never be able to do that again, but you have to admit, bowling a game in the low two-hundreds is not too shabby for an amateur. I grew up playing golf, and from my own experience, it would be impossible to shoot a round in the low seventies if you have never played golf before, even if you had the added advantage of watching a video by a professional and a few practice rounds under your belt. I don't mean to offend you bowlers out there, but I believe that's true.

Look around at all the things available to us to get us up and going—that triple latte in the morning or that can of soda to wake you up. Energy drinks or small bottles of caffeinated pick-me-ups sit at the counter of every convenience store. How many of us are excited when we wake up and are itching and raring to go to work?

One of the most common complaints I hear from patients is "Doc, I just don't have any energy at all. I feel weak and tired all the time." That should be on the medical record: *Weak and Tired All the Time*. I've mentioned WOTs (wastes of time) in my previous book, *Brave the Wave*, now its WATs—weak and tired. Are you part of the WATs? Why are we so tired all the time? Is it because of our jobs? Where can we find enthusiasm and energy?

Could it be stress? Are we more stressed than a family living on the Great Plains in the mid-1800s? They had to worry about not having enough food to eat or being attacked by wild animals, bandits, or hostile Indians. Think about trying to go to sleep in a small wooden shack and wondering if you were going to be attacked in the middle of the night. Shouldn't we be feeling less stress in our modern times?

We all have periods of feeling weak and tired, which may be caused by certain circumstances. Yet most of us don't have episodes of feeling weak and tired when we're on vacation, even though we're staying up late and getting up early most of the time. Could it have something to do with the kind of activity or work we are doing? Maybe we feel it's repetitive, mundane, boring, and not very stimulating. So, how do we get power? How do we get energy? We need to break these ideas down into the physical and the spiritual.

What's Driving You?

Let's look at how we get physical energy. In physics, *energy* is defined as the amount of work that can be performed by force, and *power* is defined as the rate at which work is performed. The dictionary definition of *energy* is "the strength and vitality required for sustained physical or mental activity."[2] We can see that we all need energy. Power is the rate at which we can perform sustained physical or mental activity. It is a measure of how long and how fast we can sustain this physical or mental activity.

Where do we get power? What is it that drives us? What motivates us to take on new challenges or projects? I believe that real power and energy come from our own unique God-given passion. The interesting point to make is that authentic passion that is at the core of our authentic self yields both physical and spiritual energy.

Imagine being on a rubber raft in the middle of the Pacific Ocean. You are the only survivor after the ship you were on capsized in a storm. You have access to food rations and water. You have no motor, sail, or paddle, so you are just drifting at the mercy of the ocean currents and waves. You are without a compass, and you don't know how to navigate by the stars—not that you could anyway. This could be a description of how you are living your life at this very moment, drifting without power, guidance, or direction.

But let's suppose that you have a compass and you know the direction you need to be headed. But you have no sail or motor, no sustainable power or energy. You paddle a little bit, and you try to head in a particular direction, but you lose your drive or energy, so you give up. Or maybe you're a dabbler—you paddle a little bit, then take a break. The definition of *dabble* is "to take part in an activity in a casual or superficial way."[3] In fact, if you are stranded in a rubber dinghy on the ocean and you only dabble, you die. In the same way, if we don't take our passion or our purpose seriously, we will dabble through life.

Now, what if we have a huge motor and plenty of power but no compass or rudder? We might start moving in one direction, but over time, we end up navigating in circles. What's most interesting—or disturbing, depending on how you look at it—is that we may have no idea we are wasting time, energy or money. If the power, or energy, is unfocused and not leading us toward any one point, then not only is that power wasted, it leaves us prone to exhaustion and frustration.

Another way to look at this scenario is picturing ourselves in a four-wheel-drive truck. You have plenty of gas and a big engine. You floor the gas pedal, but you aren't getting anywhere because you are in deep mud. You're spinning your tires, but not only are you *not* going anywhere, you're sinking deeper and deeper into the mud, spinning your wheels for the sake of spinning your wheels—lots of noise but no movement.

These examples make it clear that energy or passion are not very useful without purpose. Clearly, we need the power, but we also need guidance. We need the ability to steer and navigate. What people fail to realize is that they already have both. Passion lies within us, though it may be dormant. We already have a purpose that is programmed within us, we just haven't discovered it, or we see no need. Most people who don't see the value or need to discover their purpose will ignore it.

That's why this book is about discovering our passion and finding our purpose. The question I posed to my friends made me realize that it's very likely that many people aren't interested in discovering their passion *or* finding their purpose. They are content to row in circles or spin their tires, sinking deeper into the mud.

The problem with ignoring your passion and purpose is that you may be missing out on the huge benefits that come from living a life consistent with your authentic self, the real and passionate you that God had in mind when he created you. When you begin to get closer to your authentic self, you can tap into that innate power already within you. It's the self that you were created to be, and it's in that authentic self where we find real power, valuable energy, and true fulfillment.

Do you know where you are headed right now? Are you confident that what you're spending your time and effort on is worthwhile and has real value? We were born to ask questions and seek the answers to those questions. This leads us to find answers that we didn't know we were even looking for. That leads to more questions, like *Why did I find that out right now?*

Someone may be saying, "Yeah, this is all great, but I'm having a hard time just getting out of bed every morning. My job is drudgery. It's like a prison sentence. I feel like I'm trapped. I have no control or power to change my situation." Hey, congratulations, you are a part of the majority. Join the crowd, and be comforted in the fact that you are not alone. A survey of American working adults showed that "only 14 percent of U.S. workers believe they have the perfect job and more than half want to change careers."[4] By some estimates, there are *seventy five million people* who would gladly change careers if given the opportunity. Are you one of those? Welcome to the club.

There are two popular sayings when you ask people the question, "Hey, how are you doing?" The first answer is "Just livin' the dream, man. Livin' the dream." The other response I have been hearing lately is "Living my best life, brother. I'm living my best life." Well, if we study the above survey, not many of us are "livin' the dream" *or* living our best lives. If you are not enjoying your work life, it is hard to enjoy your life.

Change of Environment

When I got my first job as a newly trained physician, it was a very trying and difficult work environment. Going to work was a struggle. Most of my free time was spent reading books about retiring and investing so I could escape that job. I used to think to myself, *Is this how it's going to be for thirty or forty years?* I'll be honest—that place could only be described as a hell hole.

Being single and immature, I had a ritual when a friend of mine and I were going out to enjoy the night life. As we drove past my work, I would stick my head out and scream obscenities at it. It was a silly and childish thing to do, but I sure felt better afterward. You may be working in a similar place right now.

The work environment in this facility was challenging to deal with because the culture was one of indifference. From top to bottom, I worked with the most apathetic people I had ever been around, from registration clerks to nurses to techs to security and even to physicians. The only ones who were happy or greeted you with a smile were the ladies who volunteered in the gift shop. And something was a bit different about the people we treated. Maybe it was just me, but they seemed to have little appreciation for what we were doing for them. An air of rudeness, maybe even entitlement, penetrated the environment. I could never figure it out.

We all need some type of affirmation or acknowledgment of our efforts. When there is very little of that, a stressful work environment is made even more stressful. I've worked in seven or eight medical facilities before that one and seven or eight places since, and there was an obvious difference in that facility. Luckily, I found part-time work in a hospital that was completely different. The employees cared about the patients. The patients were polite and genuinely appreciative of what we did for them. Talk about a difference!

The whole point is that you can find another job doing the exact same thing in another environment, and it can make a world of difference. In marketing and business books, frequent references are made to the "culture" of a business and how they treat customers and employees. Having established a few businesses of my own, I realize this is very true, and so I've focused on creating a positive working environment for my teams. If you are unhappy in your job, you may be in an environment where the culture of the workplace is not consistent with your personality or your passion, so consider seeking employment in the same profession but in a different environment.

Passion That Inspires

If we want to study passion and energy, the business world is a good place to start because the principles we learn can be incorporated into our own lives. People who have been successful in their careers or in business have specific characteristics that allowed for their success. In his book *Start with Why: How Great Leaders Inspire Everyone to Take Action*, Simon Sinek writes:

> At the beginning, ideas are fueled by passion—that very compelling emotion that causes us to do irrational things. That passion drives people to make sacrifices so that a cause bigger than themselves can be brought to life. Some

> drop out of school or quit a perfectly good job with a good salary and benefits to try to go it alone. Some work extraordinarily long hours without a second thought, sometimes sacrificing the stability of their relationships or even their personal health. This passion is so intoxicating and exciting that it can affect others as well.[5]

Now that's passion that inspires. Sinek uses the examples of Bill Gates, Steve Jobs, and Martin Luther King in his book. He argues that there is a difference between this select group of leaders because they have an ability to do something that other leaders can't do—inspire others. He writes:

> Great leaders are able to inspire people to act. Those who are able to inspire give people a sense of purpose or belonging that has little to do with any external incentive or benefit to be gained. Those who truly lead are able to create a following of people who act not because they were swayed, but because they were inspired. Those who are able to inspire will create a following of people—supporters, voters, customers, workers—who act for the good of the whole, not because they have to but because they want to.[6]

Are you inspired at this very moment? Are you inspired to act by anything? Do you have a passion that is inspiring others? Do you yearn to be inspired?

Let's examine a few words and phrases from the above passages so that we can look at our own lives for evidence of these characteristics. We can look at these ideas and ask ourselves these questions. We'll start with one of the most important:

Passion. That is a biggie. Do I have any ideas fueled by passion?

Compelling emotion. Am I driven or inspired by an idea or passion that involves some type of emotion?

Intoxicating and exciting. Is there anything in my life that I am engaged in that is intoxicating? What about exciting?

Inspiration to act. Is there anything that I am engaged in that drives me to get up early or learn as much as I can about or that I yearn to spend time on?

A sense of purpose. Do I have a sense of purpose in anything I am doing in my life? This is crucial because purpose can protect and guide.

A sense of belonging. This is also critical. If you don't feel a sense of belonging in whatever you are endeavoring to accomplish, something will be lacking.

Lack of external incentive or benefit to be gained. This is an essential aspect of passion because there are really two types of passion: obsessive or harmonious. Obsessive passions can be harmful and detrimental to our spiritual lives and our families. We will get to these a little later.

Most of the successful people we can view as examples of having real passion were not concerned about themselves. Their vision was greater. Is there anything in my life I am pursuing for its own sake, a dream that is bigger than me? Do I have a purpose I can identify that I *know* is bigger than my circumstances, fears, trials, or troubles?

Bill Gates was not interested in being the richest person in the world. His vision was that every household in America would have a computer in it, an outlandish and unheard-of idea at the time he started to work on that vision. He believed that every person could be more efficient and reach their full potential with the help of a personal computer. Bill Gates wrote the Microsoft vision statement, “A computer on every desk and in every home,” around 1980 and first said it possibly as early as 1974.

Act because we are inspired, not because we are swayed. Is there anything in my life that I am inspired by?

Act for the good of the whole. This is another critical idea. It’s the idea of acting in support of others, not ourselves. We’re interested in the whole, not just us.

So, here is our checklist of attributes or characteristics of inspiration.

1. Passion
2. Compelling emotion
3. Intoxicating and exciting
4. Inspiration to act
5. A sense of purpose
6. A sense of belonging
7. Lack of external incentive or benefit to be gained
8. Act for the good of the whole.

Spend some time looking at this list. Can you identify with any of these characteristics of people who are passionate or who inspire others? How many of these attributes can you claim?

2

THE FINGERPRINT OF PASSION

The purposes of a person's heart are deep waters, but one who has insight draws them out.

Proverbs 20:5 NIV

BEFORE WE GET TO PASSION, I want to suggest that, as we are going along, you either jot down ideas or take notes in the margin of the book. When you get up and move or write down your thoughts, different areas of your brain are being activated because of motion and muscle control. It's a good idea to write down notes and ideas because they get ingrained into our psyche, as scientific studies have shown.

> Research on the forgetting curve shows that within one hour, people will have forgotten an average of 50 percent of the information you presented. Within 24 hours, they have forgotten an average of 70 percent of new information, and within a week, forgetting claims an average of 90 percent of it.[7]

It's important to remember that this is an adaptive mechanism. How many passwords are you required to remember to access email, online banking, Netflix, Amazon, and so on? Are you always forgetting them? We are bombarded with an onslaught of information in this world, so our brains try to help us survive this overload by acting as a filter. Consequently, we tend to discard things that don't have at least one of three characteristics:

1. Something new or unique
2. Something that is a threat or is dangerous
3. Something of value

Write It Down

When you're reading a book like this one, there will be ideas that are either new to you or that you are familiar with. The ideas that have the most impact are the "sticky" ideas—the pebble or boulder in the shoe, so to speak. But an idea won't have an effect until there is some kind of action, some type of implementation or behavior adjustment.

Many people will read the above ideas regarding information and taking notes, but they will say something like, "Yeah, yeah, I know that already. It doesn't work for me." Action or movement has the most influence when it comes to changing your life or releasing power. There is no negative associated with stopping to write down an idea that strikes you deep or stirs some emotion in you. It brings value to the table because it becomes the basis for change. Plus, you'll be taking a history of your own growth.

The difficulty is overcoming the resistance to movement. Fear, complacency, and the comfort of the status quo create resistance to movement. But when we can overcome those obstacles, we are moving toward action and change.

Life is more exciting when we get up and act. We also have more access to energy. I just heard something recently that got my attention. "If you look around and see someone more successful than you, it's because they listened sooner and took action quicker." One of the first questions I ask people when they complain that they have no energy is "How many days a week do you exercise?" I know immediately by the look on their faces that they don't exercise at all. It is consistent with the principle of reaping and sowing. Jesus talked about it two thousand years ago:

> Give, and it will be given to you. A good measure, pressed down, shaken together and running over, will be poured into your lap. For with the measure you use, it will be measured to you. – Luke 6:38

Want more energy? Invest more energy and time in exercise. You will get a return on that investment. Want more money? Give more away. Begin to see money as a tool, not as a god. Want more love? Give more away, and it will come back to you many times over. Want more happiness? Give happiness and joy to those around you.

Usually when I'm reading a nonfiction book, I take notes on my phone or write or type something down in a digital journal. Some powerful ideas that grab your attention can have real and useful value and can impact your life now and in the future. But the choice is yours. You can choose to read over a unique idea and just say to yourself, "Hmmm, that's interesting." But remember the stats—it's gone within a week. That's reality. If the idea is gone in a week, how helpful, powerful, or practical was it?

Unique ideas don't yield power until you implement them in your own life. If you stop, write it down, then think about how you can apply the idea in your own life, you can turn it into something practical. This is where there is true power. Energy comes through the application.

My recommendation is to start a journal either on paper (my preference) or make a new entry in your notes on your tablet or smartphone. This is my habit with almost every book that I read or listen to. The best books have many, many entries because of the number of compelling or interesting ideas.

Remember that list of the attributes of inspiration?

1. Passion
2. Compelling emotion
3. Intoxicating and exciting
4. Inspiration to act
5. A sense of purpose
6. A sense of belonging
7. Lack of external incentive or benefit to be gained
8. Act for the good of the whole

You may be saying to yourself, "You just went over this!" Right. Exactly. Repetition is an important idea that we will investigate further when we talk about spiritual ideas. Spend some time on the above list and write down your thoughts. Put some check marks or question marks down. We will go over many of these ideas, so it may be a good exercise for you to scribble down notes and see if any of these attributes apply to you. This activity makes things personal.

As you go along, you can figure out where you may need to act. That's when things turn from personal to practical. Write down your ideas. The person benefitting the most will be you, but hopefully, those around you will benefit as well.

Now let's look at passion.

Discovering Your Passion

Your passion is as unique as your eye color, your fingerprints, your DNA, or your facial features. It's unique to you. Our passion can be influenced by our beliefs, our experiences, or our family life. It can be colored or shaped and molded by any or all of these, and that's one reason it's unique.

Sometimes our passion is just in our DNA—we were born with it. One example is legendary baseball player Ted Williams. He was in the group of hitters that could see the spin of the ball as it was coming out of the pitcher's hand. They say that about one-third of major league hitters can see the spin of the ball as it's coming, a huge advantage when trying to decide if the next pitch is a cutter or a fastball.

> One of the greatest left-handed hitters in baseball history, Teddy Ballgame's physical skills were apparent from his first game in 1939. His vision took a little longer to gain the appropriate recognition. A 1996 article from USA Today's Baseball Weekly explained that it wasn't until 1942 when Williams joined the Navy to fight in World War II that a routine medical examination found his eyesight to be 20/10.[8]

If we had an early experience in childhood that really got our attention or made an impact on us, it could have a profound effect on our passion as an adult. We will get into the characteristics of our passion later in the book, but when it comes to our unique passion, it's as distinct as our fingerprint.

Sometimes a unique event occurs when we recognize an ability we have that others don't or we recognize something that really grabbed our attention. Remember "compelling emotion"? If there is passion, there should be some emotion involved, some stirring of the heart or excitement somewhere. A good clue is that you talk about it. And not only do you talk about it, you have no choice *but* to talk about it. Is there anything in your life that dominates your conversations? Here is an example where writing down some notes would be helpful. It clarifies your thinking.

One important rule of thumb is *no emotion, no passion.* If you look back at your own childhood, clues or events may stick out regarding your unique passion. Events in our childhood have a profound impact on our adult lives. Ask any psychiatrist. Many accomplished artists, athletes, or musicians discovered their unique passions very early in life. Here are some examples of accomplished people in a variety of areas:

1. Mozart wrote his first symphony at age eight.
2. Tiger Woods started winning tournaments at age five.
3. Pablo Picasso's father started his art education at seven, and Pablo was a better artist than his father by age thirteen.
4. The musician Prince started piano by six and wrote his first song by the age of seven.
5. At age fourteen, Howard Hughes took apart a seven-thousand-dollar Stutz Bearcat sports car and put it back together to see how it worked.
6. Serena Williams started her tennis career at the age of four.

The one consistent component in this list is that they became involved in their respective passions at an early age. I can remember the time of day and exactly where I was when I realized that one of my passions was music. As a seven-year-old boy, I had saved up some money and was having trouble trying to figure out what to spend it on. For some reason, I bought a record album. It was Jimi Hendrix, and the song was "Purple Haze." I remember when I heard that song, something happened. Something inside me grabbed my attention, and with compelling emotion, it stirred me. It still does, decades later.

Music has been a central part of my life since then. When you examine your own life, there may be clues to your own unique passion. Perhaps there is some event or activity that you realized you enjoyed or you were gifted to do—athletics, art, music, writing poetry, or creative writing. You may have had a profound interest in certain subjects like history, science, or math. One of the reasons I became a doctor was because of a fascination with how the human body works. It was easy for me to learn and study the human body because it was never boring to me.

We may feel sluggish and lackadaisical because we have abandoned our passions. They aren't as important as other concerns in our lives. We're too busy working and running errands to pay attention to the things that are there for a reason. Looking back is a good way to find clues to your own passion.

But there are also passions in your life that are totally hidden or undiscovered. You may have unique passions that lie dormant, undiscovered gifts and untouched treasures that have been totally ignored. Perhaps there is some desire in the back of your mind that you never got around to or you haven't spent any time developing or working on. Maybe it's an ability to draw or paint. How about learning to play an instrument? I began taking guitar lessons when I graduated from college, and it was one of the best decisions I've ever made. It brings tremendous joy in my own life. What about learning how to surf? I've always wanted to learn how to sail.

Have you ever thought about starting your own business? I've been involved in several. Many people have this dream to be your own boss. That sounds good, doesn't it? I've always told my own children, "You can either work for 'the man,' or you can *be* 'the man.' It's always better to *be* 'the man' (or woman)."

Wherever you are currently in your life, passion is both behind you and in front of you. Looking back to your past, you may have a passion you've just ignored for a long time. Looking forward, there are things you've always wanted to do or try, but you just haven't gotten around to them. They're right in front of you. Many times, the *process* of finding our passion and purpose is just as valuable as the purpose itself. We will come to that.

There is a prerequisite to having access to new power and energy—we must be willing to try new things. Inspiration isn't going to just walk up to our front door and ring the bell; we need to seek it out.

What will we use to discover and develop our passion? We need standards of truth that we can rely on to help us. Some of us may be pursuing passions that are outside of who we were created to be. That is why we need authenticity. The authentic self is a source of our passion. How do we find this authentic self? We need guidance.

Human Standards or God's?

I use two standards for guidance—the Bible and the near-death experience. The Bible is without question the most important standard we should rely on. If we are believers, we value the Word of God. God's Word has supernatural power. Remember, God spoke the entire world into existence (Genesis 1:1–2:3). We must accept the authority of the Bible, and if we don't accept the validity or authority of it, then we are left to choose something else to guide us when we are trying to find our passion and purpose.

We know that 25 to 30 percent of the population that considers themselves Christian reads the Bible regularly.[9] That means that about 70 percent of this group ignores it. If you aren't a part of the minority, you may want to consider starting the habit of daily Bible reading because of the supernatural power available to us in the Word. Sure, we're going to look at studies and statistics to help us as we go along, but there are standards that we need to use to help us that we can rely on. If we ignore the Bible and rely on our own judgment to find our passion, this could lead to bad choices and bad decisions.

Many people rely on culture and other people's opinions to guide them. When we place our faith in people and value their opinions over the word and guidance of God, that's when the trouble begins. See, there's one huge problem with that. Passion, power, and purpose are all supernatural principles, not fleshly, worldly, or human ideas.

Human opinions are valuable when it comes to human or fleshly pursuits. Recommendations for a good restaurant? Ask a friend or your boss. Recommendations for a nice hotel that has great activities for the kids? Ask your co-worker. Recommendations for a good movie? Ask a friend or sibling.

We can depend on other people and their opinions to tell us what our goals should be. But, honestly, they have no clue. We can value what other people think about us, but that leads to slavery to the opinion of others. We can rely on the world or society, but those are run by humans. We know that humans are human. We can even put our faith, like many people do, in science, but science is run by humans also. They make mistakes all the time. And some people with a naturalistic or atheistic worldview put their faith and trust in science.

In a documentary on mega-tsunamis, scientist Chris Goldfinger tries to explain the tsunami that hit Japan in 2011: "It turned out that we were all wrong. I think we need to have a big dose of humility and say we really just don't know, and in a way start over with a clean sheet of paper." Scientists make mistakes all the time because they are human. Chris Goldfinger has no problem admitting he was wrong. He knows he's human.

We can trust science to tell us about our passion and guide us to our authentic selves, but we know science makes mistakes. In addition, scientists admit to falsifying data and engaging in questionable research practices.[10] In other words, they lie. Are we really surprised by this? This is not to disparage science as a discipline full of liars and cheaters. Many good scientists value integrity and have devoted their lives to helping others through their research. What I am saying is that science is run by humans, so we must consider this when we seek guidance regarding our own unique passion or purpose.

The common denominator in the standards outlined above is people. We can rely on ourselves, other people, the world, science, or culture to guide us, but we could be going down a path that will lead us over a cliff.

Humans can't help us with access to the supernatural either. The power and passion we need are in the realm of the supernatural, or spiritual world, where true authenticity and true power lie.

There is only one person we can have confidence in who doesn't make mistakes: Jesus. That's the standard I highly recommend. We will be using his standard and guidance often. Why? Because it's the wisest thing to do. If you stop to think about it, Jesus was the smartest person who ever lived, plus he doesn't lie or make mistakes. The huge bonus that we can be sure of is that he loves us and wants what is best for us.

The second thing we will use to help guide us is near-death experiences, or NDEs. Are these experiences a supreme authority or standard to follow? No. But, I use them for two reasons. One is selfish. They are fascinating to me personally, and I love studying them. Two, I believe they are divine gifts from God to help guide us in this life. NDEs bestow nuggets of valuable truth to reveal what is important in this life and what isn't. They're also supernatural—pure spiritual experiences—and are valuable when you are looking at spiritual or supernatural ideas like passion, purpose, and the authentic self. We need spiritual guidance and truth when we are seeking our own unique passion and purpose because these are *spiritual pursuits*. Our unique passion and purpose existed in the mind of God before he created us:

> For we are God's handiwork, created in Christ Jesus to do good works, which God prepared in advance for us to do.
>
> – Ephesians 2:10

When it comes to our purpose and our passion, we can ask our best friend or a family member or our spouse, but we really should be honest with ourselves. They have *no idea* what our unique passion and purpose is. It's not their fault—they didn't create us. These people love us, but they still could be dead wrong when it comes to our passion or purpose.

What about the world or culture? All you need to do is look at social media, internet trolls, entertainment, and everything else that our culture represents. Just yesterday I heard a brilliant statement from Lady Gaga. It's brilliant because it's unique. She said, "Frankly, social media is the toilet of the internet." That statement has power because it has truth. We will get to social media in a second.

We know that the world and society and culture fill our minds with ideas and pursuits that are intimately associated with the false or inauthentic self. Jesus talked about this two thousand years ago:

> If the world hates you, remember that it hated me first. The world would love you as one of its own if you belonged to it, but you are no longer part of the world. I chose you to come out of the world, so it hates you. Do you remember what I told you? "A slave is not greater than it's master." Since they persecuted me, naturally they will persecute you. And if they had listened to me, they would listen to you.
>
> – John 15:18–20 (NLT)

Look at what Jesus is saying. "I chose you to *come out of the world*." That's a crystal-clear idea. We know what we need to do.

What about near-death experiences? NDEs can bring value to the table because they are supernatural experiences, and many pertain to power, purpose, passion, and energy. We should look at these with a critical eye just like we do with the opinions of others, but there is value in what the NDErs are saying. One crucial reason I'm not hesitant to use them in this book is that I believe there is a near-death experience described in the Bible, and we never fail when we use the Bible as an authority:

> I must go on boasting. Although there is nothing to be gained, I will go on to visions and revelations from the Lord. I know a man in Christ who fourteen years ago was caught up to the third heaven. Whether it was in the body or out of the body I do not know—God knows. And I know that this man--whether in the body or apart from the body I do not know, but God knows—was caught up to paradise and heard inexpressible things, things that no one is permitted to tell. I will boast about a man like that, but I will not boast about myself, except about my weaknesses. Even if I should choose to boast, I would not be a fool,

> because I would be speaking the truth. But I refrain, so no one will think more of me than is warranted by what I do or say, or because of these surpassingly great revelations. Therefore, in order to keep me from becoming conceited, I was given a thorn in my flesh, a messenger of Satan, to torment me.
>
> – 2 Corinthians 12:1–7

One important idea to recognize in this passage is that the experience was out of body. That is one of the most common components of the NDE. It's spiritual vision. If you've read my book *Brave the Wave*, you will know that these experiences are valuable and useful because they are purely spiritual. They are not colored or influenced by our physical senses and occur purely in the spiritual realm—they're supernatural experiences.

There is substantial value in remembering that we are spirits who happen to have a body, not bodies that happen to have a spirit. We are spiritual beings. Our bodies only last a short period of time and are slowly dying and weakening every day. But our spirits live forever and have the potential to grow and get stronger every day. (If we take our spiritual growth seriously.) When we seek our passion, it is a spiritual pursuit. Our passion lies within our spirit. You can't find a physical organ in the body, open it up, and see your passion. Our unique spirit reveals our unique passion.

NDEs are pure spiritual experiences that yield nuggets of wisdom and truth you can't find anywhere else. They are valuable insights and revelations. How do I know this? Look at what Paul says: "because of these surpassingly great revelations." Hey, don't believe me—believe the apostle Paul. These experiences bring important revelations that are divine gifts. They give us clues as to how we should live our lives and where we should focus our time and energy.

Critics, skeptics, and cynics will abound regarding the validity of both the Bible and the NDE. My response? Do your own research. Spend the time researching all the evidence available regarding the veracity of the Bible and the evidence regarding NDEs. If done properly, it will take years. It has taken me twelve years so far, and I'm just getting started.

Look at the research and veridicality studies that give credence to what people who have had NDEs are telling us. Veridicality studies involve looking at details of what the person experiencing the NDE saw and corroborating it with eyewitnesses. For example, one person gave a detailed account of what was going on in the operating room when her heart stopped before her NDE:

She had 'amazed the... surgery team' by reporting a clear, detailed memory of... the operating room layout; the scribbles on the surgery schedule board in the hall outside; the color of the sheets covering the operating table; the hairstyle of the head scrubnurse;... and even the trivial fact that her anesthesiologist that day was wearing unmatched socks. All this she knew even though she had been fully anesthetized and unconscious during the surgery and the cardiac arrest. But what made Sarah's vision even more remarkable was the fact that, since birth, Sarah had been blind.[11]

Studying the historicity of the life of Jesus is also fascinating to me. But we need to be clear. The Bible is primary and is the Word of God. The life and teachings of Jesus are powerful truths that we can anchor our lives to and try to emulate. The NDE is an adjunct that can help us when we are looking at these supernatural pursuits. Supernatural pursuits by their very nature require supernatural guidance. But we start with Jesus. His guidance and opinion are flawless.

Cynics, skeptics, or critics have already made up their minds. In a deep place in their own hearts, they don't want to believe. Many times, if you listen to debates on YouTube between believers and nonbelievers or atheists, it's easy to discern anger or bitterness. Something intense and personal is going on deep in their hearts. The very thought of the existence of God is abhorrent, a concept so terrible that they don't want to be convinced. "God doesn't exist, and I hate him" is the best way I've heard the atheist mindset described.

I remember watching a debate on YouTube about atheism and Christianity, and one woman stood up in the audience and said, "Well, you know, we really don't have any evidence that Jesus even existed. This could have all just been made up." Even the staunchest, most science-minded nonbelieving scholars categorically admit that Jesus existed.

If you picked up this book, most likely you are looking for answers to a problem. Maybe you don't have energy, or you feel unfulfilled. Perhaps there is no excitement, joy, or peace in your life. You could be seeking passion and are interested in discovering your purpose. It boils down to the "idea about ideas." Doing research and studying for over twelve years has exposed me to unique, powerful, and practical ideas that have been helpful to me. My hope and prayer is that you will find some nuggets in this book that will help you find your own answers. My objectives are to help provide guidance that will bring you closer to your passion and your purpose, to help you gain access to supernatural power that will open the eyes of your heart and bring clarity and vision into your life. I'm confident that there are things in this book you will discover that you've never seen or heard before and which have the potential to change your life for the better. Why am I so sure? Because it happened to me.

3

TRUTH & AUTHENTICITY

"Christianity isn't taking a leap of faith into the dark, it is taking a step of faith into the light."
John Lennox

About ten years ago, I bought an antique watch. When I started studying the unique identifying characteristics of this brand of watch from the early 1900s, I realized to my horror that it was a fake. So, I spent hours learning all I could about antique watches: the different brands and their intricate details, mechanical movements, and unique properties. I never got scammed again.

Humans are human. We all make mistakes. There needs to be a distinction made when it comes to people and guidance. Jesus said we are to love and serve people, but when it comes to guidance and wisdom, we start with God. Even Jesus got frustrated with people:

> He replied, "Every plant that my heavenly Father has not planted will be pulled up by the roots. Leave them; they are blind guides. If the blind lead the blind, both will fall into a pit."
> Peter said, "Explain the parable to us."

> "Are you still so dull?" Jesus asked them. "Don't you see that whatever enters the mouth goes into the stomach and then out of the body? But the things that come out of a person's mouth come from the heart, and these defile them. For out of the heart come evil thoughts—murder, adultery, sexual immorality, theft, false testimony, slander. These are what defile a person; but eating with unwashed hands does not defile them."
>
> – Matthew 15:13–20

When we are in search of our unique passion, we should begin with authenticity. We should seek to unearth the truth within our spiritual selves. We've looked at our own childhood to see if we can find clues to our passion or our interests based on our early experiences, but is the passion we are pursuing inauthentic? Is it who we were created to be, or have we created a false self? This is an important question because when you are being driven by a passion that is not a part of your authentic self, it can lead to misery, depression, anxiety, and feeling unfulfilled. It is following a path influenced by society or by the opinions of others. It is people-filtered rather than God-filtered and is separate from the supernatural.

Decades ago, writers Aldous Huxley and George Orwell each wrote a vision of what they feared the most about the future. I recently heard Christian apologist Ravi Zacharias describe the difference between their contrasting futures, concluding that Huxley's vision was more accurate in describing what our society has become today.

> Huxley feared that what we loved would ruin us,... that the pleasure syndrome would take over and create a kind of a darkness in the pursuit of exhilaration and ecstasy, we

> would actually become hollow and trivial and empty people till the most sacred things of life, sexuality and life itself, had been trivialized, and so the entertainment [that we seek] is a combination of killing and perversion, [a kind of] infinite appetite for distraction and amusement.[12]

You don't need to look very hard to see that our society has an "infinite appetite for distraction and amusement." If we consider our own lives, we may be spending most of our time focusing on survival or distraction. We are either working to make enough money to keep our families afloat, or we are seeking entertainment and distraction. How many times have you heard your own children say, "I'm bored"? How much time are we devoting to our cell phones? How about binge-watching Netflix?

Last spring, I was at Disneyland in the area around Space Mountain. Walking by a table, I couldn't help but notice a young couple with a toddler who was about two years old. He was laughing and giggling in his highchair and grabbing fries and throwing them around. On either side of him, both his parents had their heads down opposite each other buried in their cell phones. I stopped for a few minutes just to observe. That went on for at least five minutes straight. Isn't that an appetite or addiction to distraction? Let me be clear. I'm not saying something is inherently wrong with texting or social media. It's a good way to keep up with friends and family. It just seems obvious to me that this kind of distraction devalues and interferes with real-life, flesh-and-blood interaction with family and friends. We are conditioning ourselves to trade the authentic social interaction with others for the hollow interactions with a keyboard and our imaginations. What is more important than laughing and interacting with your child? What about your spouse? This kind of behavior is rampant in my own family, and it's distressing to me.

If we are being honest with ourselves, we are clueless as to the impact of spending inordinate amounts of time on social media. We have no idea what kind of effect limiting true social interaction and engagement will have on our relationships, especially with those closest to us, our families.

Unlike social media and our society's infatuation with itself, when we look at NDEs and study the Bible, we note that the emphasis is on other people: relationships and love. The New Testament mentions "each other" at least fifty-nine times. NDEs tell us that the whole reason for life is "learning how to love," and that God is love. In his book, *God and the Afterlife*, Jeffrey Long MD, writes:

> In the narrative accounts of people's encounters with God during an NDE, the most overwhelming feeling and the description of this being is one of love. God in near-death experiences is often described as profoundly loving. God's love may be described as enormous, unconditional and totally accepting. Some examples:
>
> "I felt the presence of pure love. This is very hard to describe. Everything made sense: God exists, God is love, we are love, and love creates all that is. Everything is pure love, God is love."...
>
> "I know that love is all there is and that God loves all of His children deeply and equally."
>
> "God loves us all infinitely."
>
> "I came to realize that God is more loving and caring than I could ever imagine."[13]

In the Bible, John, the apostle of love, tells us,

> Dear friends, let us love one another, for love comes from God. Everyone who loves has been born of God and knows God. Whoever does not love does not know God, because God is love. This is how God showed his love among us: He sent his one and only Son into the world that we might live through him. This is love: not that we loved God, but that he loved us and sent his Son as an atoning sacrifice for our sins. Dear friends, since God so loved us, we also ought to love one another. No one has ever seen God; but if we love one another, God lives in us and his love is made complete in us.
>
> – 1 John 4:7–12

Authenticity begins in truth, and as you just saw in John's message, the Word of God is ultimate truth. Our authenticity begins in our loving relationship with God through his Son, Jesus. From there, that love extends to our family and friends.

Think about your biggest worries, your greatest concerns, right now. As I am writing this, I've been dealing with what seems like a tidal wave of problems. I got hit with something that turned my finances and my work upside down. I've been dealing with stress, anxiety, and worry about work, along with a business to run and bills—you name it. It was consuming me and having an impact on my relationships with my wife and children. Then I saw a tragic news report about a boat that capsized due to weather. Most of the people on the boat drowned, and I started to think about being one of the people on that boat. If I had died and was standing before Jesus, how important would all these financial anxieties and worries about work and business be? I saw myself telling Jesus, "Hey, wow, thank

God you're here. Sorry, I mean, I'm glad you're here. Let me tell you about all these financial difficulties and work stresses I've been having." Suddenly, what had seemed to be a towering wall of worries became less than a series of ripples, so small that you couldn't even see them.

It is a matter of perspective. Sometimes when we pull back and look at the big picture, we can see what is most important. If we want to find our authentic selves and explore our passion, it all starts with our relationship with Jesus. That is the whole ballgame, the first through the ninth inning. Our search for passion, energy, purpose, vision, clarity, and wisdom begins and ends there. If you can believe and accept that, we can keep moving.

We need to take a hard look at our own lives when it comes to distraction and amusement. That isn't to say that we don't need some downtime to watch a sporting event or a movie or some time to relax, but we need to honestly assess how much time we are spending on these activities. Considering how many hours we are devoting to things like social media, television, or other distractions will be beneficial as we begin pursuing passion and purpose.

We need to be clear on one thing: While social media is a good way for family and friends to communicate and be aware of events in each other's lives, it becomes destructive and can keep you from finding your passion when it's taken to extremes.

There are some alarming trends in the phenomenon of social media, and if we care about our own relationships and the people we love most, then we need to look with open eyes at how this is affecting our society and our children. We know, for example, that the incidence of suicide has been rising over the past twenty years, and many people are speculating as to the cause.

> "Between 1999 and 2016, the suicide rate increased among all age groups younger than 75 years," said Anne Schuchat, MD, principal deputy director of the CDC, who led a media briefing on the topic Thursday. The rates have gone up more than 30% in half of all states since 1999, she says. More than half of those who died by suicide *did not* have a diagnosed mental health condition, the researchers found. But most did have life problems. "Those who died by suicide were somewhat more likely to struggle with relationship problems or loss, other life stresses, or deal with impending crises," Schuchat says. "But these issues were [found] in all, with or without a mental health condition."[14]

Looking at recent societal trends and the impact that social media has in today's society, it's easy to see how people can become anxious or depressed. If we are spending more and more time on social media, then we can infer that we are spending less and less time developing healthy and meaningful relationships in a tangible and personal way. These relationships require genuine conversation and active involvement with friends and family, sharing struggles, triumphs, tragedies, and trials. That is how Jesus intended for us to live.

Stagnant Spectating

It seems that more effort and energy are expended in seeking superficial or artificial interactions with people who we don't even know than is spent seeking real relationships with those who are physically present. If you spend a lot of time following celebrities or people who are "YouTube famous," you should ask yourself, *What is the value of knowing every detail of these people's lives? What is the value of knowing the details of anyone else's life other than the people closest to you?*

How many people do we follow on Instagram or Twitter or any other social media platform? Is there any give-and-take that involves any real and deep interaction? Are we able to share our deepest hurts or fears or concerns with a celebrity or a famous social media person? Is it a two-way street, or is it only one way?

Clarissa Silva, a scientist and relationship expert stated in an article:

> Social media has been linked to higher levels of loneliness, envy, anxiety, depression, narcissism and decreased social skills. As a Behavioral Scientist, I wonder what causes this paradox? The narratives we share and portray on social media are all positive and celebratory. It's a hybridized digital version of "Keeping up with the Joneses." Meaning for some, sometimes it appears everyone you know are in great relationships, taking 5-star vacations and living your dream life. However, what is shared across our social networks only broadcasts the positive aspects of our lives-the highlight reels. Since we're only getting people's highlight reels and comparing it to ourselves, it is natural to have reactions to what we're watching. How does this impact relationships, dating and our love lives? I conducted in-depth interviews with men and women, ranging from ages 28-73, that are active social media users and found that:

- 60% of people using social media reported that it has impacted their self-esteem in a negative way

- 50% reported social media having negative effects on their relationships
- 80% reported that is easier to be deceived by others through their sharing on social media

> Match reported 51% say social media has made them feel more self-conscious about their appearance. Flores further explains "research has also shown that Facebook users are becoming increasingly depressed from comparing themselves to their own profile. Meaning that if a person's reality does not match the digital illusion they post on their profiles, emotionally, one may feel they are not living up to the "best" form of themselves.[15]

What I would argue is that we should be spending time finding *our* "authentic self," not creating an artificial one. We should devote time to discovering exactly who *we* were created to be. We can't find our true or authentic selves by watching other people live out their lives. It is becoming a sport or form of entertainment—*life watching*. We know that the people whose lives are being watched or who have millions of followers are benefiting financially, receiving millions of dollars for posting pictures of themselves using products. What are we getting?

Authentic relationships consist of giving and receiving real love. If you look at the statistics above, it's clear that artificial relationships are harmful. Look at the loss of self-esteem and feelings of depression. If we stop and think about it, we also don't have any idea if the people whose lives we are watching are discovering *their* authentic selves. They may be spending time, energy, or effort on a life inconsistent with who they were created to be. That has the potential to cause damage if there are thousands of people trying to emulate that life or lifestyle, the "blind leading the blind" type of phenomenon. Jesus talked about this when he was describing the Pharisees: "Every plant that my heavenly Father has not planted will be pulled up by the roots. Leave them; they are blind guides. If the blind lead the blind, both will fall into a pit" (Matthew 15:13–14).

When we can be honest about how much time and effort we are spending on looking at the lives of others, this gives us an idea of where our passion lies. You can have passion that's based on a lie or based on things with limited value. When we focus on others' "highlight reels," the best and most exciting stuff, we forget that no one is posting pictures of themselves working in a cubicle or at a workstation. It's a false representation of what's really going on that tends to inspire envy in the people watching.

The Truth of Self-Examination

So, what is our first step? One of the most powerful tools at our disposal is the ability to self-examine and be self-aware. It's the critical precursor to a change for the better. If you can't look at your own behavior and see a problem or admit that there is something that needs to be changed in your life, *nothing will change.*

If you are spending inordinate amounts of time either posting or following people on social media, start by asking yourself a simple yet profound question: *Why?* "Why do I spend so much time watching what other people are posting? Why do I spend so much time and energy trying to get people to 'like' my posts? What is the payoff for me?" Only you can answer that question. Is it pride? Envy? Does it make you feel better about yourself? Is it boredom or, perhaps, simply habit?

These are important questions because you may be seeking validation from other people, which is all great when there is plenty of affirmation. But what about when the critics and the body-shamers come out of the woodwork. "Social media has been linked to higher levels of loneliness, envy, anxiety, depression, narcissism and decreased social skills." Are any of these characteristics the characteristics you are striving for? What about our children? Do we want them to be lonely, envious, anxious, depressed, narcissistic or have decreased social skills? Consider this comment by musician Ed Sheeran regarding Twitter:

> "I've actually come off Twitter completely. I can't read it," he told The Sun. "I go on it and there's nothing but people saying mean things. Twitter's a platform for that. One comment ruins your day. But that's why I've come off it. The head-f*** for me has been trying to work out why people dislike me so much."[16]

Ed Sheeran is just trying to write and perform his music. He's got some great songs, but he's attacked with mean and critical comments. How do we combat that? Twitter trolls post mean things because they're human. We as humans sometimes find it easier to criticize and tear down rather than praise and lift others up. We should be careful placing too much emphasis and value on the opinions of people. That is wisdom that should be shared with our children.

Social media can lead us on a see-saw ride of artificial highs and lows. On the one side, too much praise leads to pride and narcissism and can result in a sense of entitlement. On the other, too much criticism leads to feeling anxious or lonely and tends to knock self-esteem down a notch or two. We can see that both lead to a false sense of self.

We see a much more balanced approach illustrated in one of my favorite quotes about this concept from Pastor John Bunyan, "If my life is fruitless, it doesn't matter who praises me. If my life is fruitful, it doesn't matter who criticizes me."

There will never be a shortage of critics because it's easy to criticize others. It doesn't require much effort. It's much more difficult to look honestly at ourselves and make changes for the better. That takes maturity.

4

MISGUIDED PASSION

"The real enemy of truth is not ignorance, doubt, or even disbelief. It is false knowledge."

– Lee McIntryre

We are spending time on the idea of the "false self" because we may have passion or energy that is being directed in a way that is inauthentic or not consistent with who we were created to be. NDEs tell us the same thing. They shine a powerful light on the idea of the false self. Dr. Kenneth Ring writes in *Lessons from the Light*:

> "I have talked about this authentic or true self as something that is the Light's function to disclose to the individual. How does it do that? The answer is, often by first showing the NDEr his or her false or socially conditioned self." He continues, "In other instances, however, the NDEr is given a direct perception into the nature of the false self and is thereby allowed intuitively to understand that the person one has identified with and habitually thought of as one's essential self was nothing more than fiction."[17]

This is an example of the type of valuable insight these experiences can teach us. We know that NDErs make major life changes when they come back to their physical bodies. Everything they considered to be important is drastically altered. Life-changing impact comes from a radical encounter with truth. Fortunately, you don't have to die (or nearly die) to learn these valuable lessons. Studying the experiences of others can have a major impact on your life and change the way you spend your eternity.

If we look at what Dr. Ring is saying, it's clear that one of the functions of the Light or the being is to identify the "false or socially conditioned self." *Socially conditioned* is a good way to describe what is currently going on in our society. Look at the effect negative comments had on Ed Sheeran. They ruined his day. He talked about how those comments were messing with his thinking. He was wondering what it was about him that made people dislike him so much. What would I tell Ed Sheeran if he asked my advice? Well, when someone makes a derogatory comment or criticizes me, I give one standard response: "Honestly, your opinion of me is none of my business. Jesus loves me more than you can possibly imagine. He thinks I'm valuable, lovable, and forgivable. He thinks I'm unique. His opinion is what I value most."

I want to qualify these ideas by emphasizing that the opinion of those around us who love us and care for us has great value also, especially if they are concerned about a self-destructive behavior of ours. Often those close to us are better able to see things in our lives that are not good for us. Those opinions matter. We *all* have blind spots, and often, our loved ones are the best equipped to help us see them. But there is very little value in the comments of critics and cynics who don't know you or your family. There will never be a shortage of criticism from strangers because it's easy to sit back and judge others. Jesus talked about this:

> Judge not, that you be not judged. For with the judgment you pronounce you will be judged, and with the measure you use it will be measured to you. Why do you see the speck that is in your brother's eye, but do not notice the log that is in your own eye? Or how can you say to your brother, "Let me take the speck out of your eye," when there is the log in your own eye? You hypocrite, first take the log out of your own eye, and then you will see clearly to take the speck out of your brother's eye.
> – Matthew 7:1–5 (ESV)

This is a good passage to remind us of the importance of self-examination, or self-awareness. We focus first on how we can be better, putting our own behavior under the microscope. There is power in self-examination.

The Deception of Wealth

When we are scrutinizing misguided or inauthentic passion, all we need to do is look at our culture and what it values most. We're bombarded with images of wealth or material objects. Pastor Rick Warren sums it up most succinctly when he says the world is interested in three things, "looking good, feeling good, and having the goods."[18] It's everywhere—social media, reality television, movies, and magazines. The wisest thing we can do as believers is recognize that there is no eternal value in pursuing these activities.

What's most interesting to me is that the closer we get to Jesus, the clearer our vision of the circumstances and behavior around us becomes. It's enhanced spiritual vision. Hopefully, we gain insight into our own behavior and how we have allowed circumstances to impact our own lives. But, when we begin to see the behavior of other people more clearly, we must be careful to avoid judgment, which is the trap of pride. There is a vital difference between observing a behavior and reaching conclusions about someone else's actions versus judging or criticizing them.

For example, I was having a discussion with my friends about an article I read that described the $10 million mansion Pastor Joel Osteen owned. The article pointed out that this mansion was in the wealthiest neighborhood in Houston, Texas. One of my friends remarked that he paid for that mansion with the earnings from his books, not from the donations of his church members. It just made me stop and think about Rick Warren, the author of the ground-breaking book, *The Purpose Driven Life.* Rick made millions of dollars from his book. He has remarked many times that he gave away 90 percent of the profits to charity, a kind of reverse tithing—give away 90 percent and keep 10 percent. Both are pastors. Both made millions of dollars. We can make observations about how those pastors behaved with their financial rewards and have an idea about how they see those rewards.

Joel feels that God has blessed him and it's okay for a pastor to own a $10 million mansion. That isn't a judgment; it's an observation. If he didn't feel it was okay, he wouldn't have bought it. He was asked about it in an interview with Oprah Winfrey, and he responded, "We are givers, Oprah. God has blessed us, and we don't have a problem with owning a mansion." So, this is not making a judgment but outlining two approaches to material blessings by two different pastors.

In my own view and with my own vision, I have a problem seeing Jesus whipping up a smoothie in his huge kitchen and then going out to the backyard to lounge by his huge swimming pool. It's just hard for me to envision it. But that's just my layman opinion. With that opinion and five dollars, you can get a grande skinny vanilla latte at Starbucks. Jesus pointed these things out two thousand years ago: "The teachers of the law and the Pharisees sit in Moses' seat. So you must be careful to do everything they tell you. But do not do what they do, for they do not practice what they preach" (Matthew 23:2–3).

God blesses us, and he gives us financial blessings as a test. He's looking to see how we use that money. Are we going to use it all for ourselves, or will we try to help the less fortunate? Will we use our financial blessings to help further the kingdom of God? I've heard it said that it isn't a sin to be wealthy; the problem arises when we don't use that wealth to the benefit of others or if we don't use it for the kingdom of God. We are granted many gifts and talents and even material wealth. God is watching and fully expects us to use these gifts for something outside of ourselves. When we are talking about a "socially constructed false self," we can look at our lives and then look at our standard, Jesus. God sent Jesus to secure our salvation and as a path to the Father. Jesus said, "I am the way and the truth and the life. No one comes to the Father except through me" (John 14:6).

He is the way. He is the truth. But he is the life also. We are to emulate *his* life. He is a model for our behavior. It isn't easy, but our lives should model the life of Jesus. We can't get to that level of perfection, but that should never be an excuse for our lack of effort. We should make it the business of this life to get closer to Jesus in our thought life as well as in our actions.

> And Jesus said to him, "The foxes have holes and the birds of the air have nests, but the Son of Man has nowhere to lay His head."
>
> – Luke 9:58 (NASB)

One inspiring example for me was Christian songwriter Rich Mullins, whose story you may have seen in the movie *Ragamuffin*. Rich wrote the song "Awesome God," a big hit in the Christian music genre in the late '80s. He was a talented and successful songwriter who wrote numerous hits for Amy Grant. At the end of the movie, we are told that Rich told his accountant to give him a monthly allowance "that was equal to what the average working man in the country received." The rest he gave away to charity. He never really knew how much money he made. Tragically, he died in a car wreck in 1997. Rich wasn't a pastor or a preacher, but he sure as heck inspires me. Why? Because of his actions. We can make objective observations by his actions. He was more concerned with loving God and sharing the gospel. He walked the talk. In an interview posted on YouTube, he said, "Our calling is where the world's deepest need and our greatest joy meet."

This brings us to the idea of inspiration. Seek inspiration. Rich Mullins inspires me not only because he was a musician but also because of his selfless attitude. I connected with him because, while I play music too, our common source of inspiration is Jesus. Jesus is also *the* standard when it comes to our actions, values, and behavior. We never go wrong when we seek to emulate him. Just keep in mind that it is an ongoing, difficult journey that will take the rest of our lives.

When it comes to misguided passion, we should be careful to monitor and be wary of the influence and impact other people have on our lives. We should be cautious about spending time, effort, and energy on worldly goals that take us further away from our spiritual or authentic selves. We may be living and pursuing an artificial self that was created by society or influenced by those around us rather than relying on Christ as our inspiration. So while it can be of some value to observe what people say and how they act or behave and to reach conclusions about their values or how they see material blessings, the idea is not for us to spend too much time looking at other people's lives and trying to emulate them unless their behavior lines up with absolute truth—with Jesus.

Many unbelievers will point to the atrocities often associated with Christianity, such as the Inquisition, the Crusades, or the occasional scandals associated with the church. We can agree for the most part that these behaviors by leaders of the church are not consistent with the true standard that was laid down by Jesus and his teachings. The church is run by humans, so we can expect the church to be imperfect because people are imperfect. That's why we need a standard. We know that Jesus would have never led a movement like the Inquisition. One important point about "standards" is that when it comes to the Word and the teachings of Jesus, those don't change. They never have.

5

A STANDARD OF TRUTH

The process of becoming more like Jesus—sanctification—is one of the most difficult endeavors we can pursue in this life. But we can be certain that we will never go wrong when we devote time and energy to this undertaking. The idea is simple; the execution, difficult. When we look to Jesus as the standard for our behavior and habits, anything we do that is consistent with what he did or what he taught is loaded with true spiritual riches. Emulating Jesus only helps us; it never hurts us.

Get up early in the morning for a quiet time with God? It only helps us; never hurts us. Read the Word of God, know Jesus's words, and try to live them as best as we are able? Only helps; never hurts. Grow in love toward others and be as kind and gentle and as patient with others as we can be? Helps, not hurts.

We may realize that God loves us so much, he sent Jesus to die for our sins (John 3:16). But we also need to understand that Jesus is also a standard for our behavior. God knows exactly what is best for each individual person.

It would be difficult to argue that being like Jesus is a bad thing for the world. The world would be a better place if everyone on the planet suddenly acted as Jesus did. Boil it down to a personal level—if you, as a husband or a wife or a father or a mother, were to fully embrace the challenge of being more like Christ, would you not agree that there would be more love in your family? If you as a young adult behaved in a loving, kind, and patient way, as Jesus did, not only would your family benefit but also your workplace and your community.

Here is a nice experiment for you. Try to do the best that you can for a solid week trying to be as patient, kind, loving, peaceful, and gentle as Jesus, and see if there isn't a noticeable difference in your entire family. I've seen it happen. Attempt it in your own circle of friends. You will see a difference. It's vital to remember that as we grow and engage in our passion and as we move toward our purpose, this happens automatically, as we will see.

When we regard the lifestyles of others and spend inordinate amounts of time watching their lives, we begin to emulate them. It's unavoidable. That's why we should be careful to monitor how much social media intake we allow to enter our brains. We should also consider the types of television programs we watch. If we are consuming hours and hours of reality television, we will tend to behave like the people we are seeing.

In the 1990's a special type of nerve cell was discovered in the brain. These cells are known as *mirror neurons*. They are responsible for your feeling joy as you watch things like your team celebrating after winning the Super Bowl. You didn't play in the game, but you feel delight. If it's a team you have been following for years and years, you may even shed a tear or two. Or perhaps you feel sorrow watching a mother who lost her child being interviewed. You feel her pain and anguish as a mother, and you think about your own children, imagining yourself in her place.

In the same way, then, when we spend time studying the life and words of Jesus, we will begin to think the way he does and acquire his habits. Our focus on him will help us move closer to authenticity and to truth.

> Very early in the morning, while it was still dark, Jesus got up, left the house and went off to a solitary place, where he prayed.
>
> – Mark 1:35

Get up early in the morning? Good habit. Never hurts us.

> No branch can bear fruit by itself; it must remain in the vine. Neither can you bear fruit unless you remain in me. I am the vine; you are the branches. If you remain in me and I in you, you will bear much fruit; apart from me you can do nothing. If you do not remain in me, you are like a branch that is thrown away and withers; such branches are picked up, thrown into the fire and burned. If you remain in me and my words remain in you, ask whatever you wish, and it will be done for you. This is to my Father's glory, that you bear much fruit, showing yourselves to be my disciples."
>
> – John 15:4–8

Here Jesus is telling us how important his words are. Not only that, but he says we show ourselves to be his disciples when we bear much fruit. Studying the words of Jesus and bearing fruit are two spiritual habits that will never hurt you. They only bring spiritual power.

> Dear children, I will be with you only a little longer. And as I told the Jewish leaders, you will search for me, but you can't come where I am going. So now I am giving you

> a new commandment: Love each other. Just as I have loved you, you should love each other. Your love for one another will prove to the world that you are my disciples.
>
> – John 13:33–35 (NLT)

Here he is saying to us, "Be like me. I have loved you, now in the same way you should love each other." Learning to love those around us never hurts us.

> Jesus knew that the Father had put all things under his power, and that he had come from God and was returning to God; so he got up from the meal, took off his outer clothing, and wrapped a towel around his waist. After that, he poured water into a basin and began to wash his disciples' feet, drying them with the towel that was wrapped around him.
>
> He came to Simon Peter, who said to him, "Lord, are you going to wash my feet?"
>
> Jesus replied, "You do not realize now what I am doing, but later you will understand."
>
> "No," said Peter, "you shall never wash my feet."
>
> Jesus answered, "Unless I wash you, you have no part with me."
>
> "Then, Lord," Simon Peter replied, "not just my feet but my hands and my head as well!"
>
> Jesus answered, "Those who have had a bath need only to wash their feet; their whole body is clean. And you are clean, though not every one of you." For he knew who was going to betray him, and that was why he said not everyone was clean.
>
> When he had finished washing their feet, he put on his clothes and returned to his place. "Do you understand what I have done for you?" he asked them. "You call me 'Teacher' and 'Lord,' and rightly so, for that is what I am. Now that I, your Lord and

> Teacher, have washed your feet, you also should wash one another's feet. I have set you an example that you should do as I have done for you. Very truly I tell you, no servant is greater than his master, nor is a messenger greater than the one who sent him. Now that you know these things, you will be blessed if you do them."
>
> – John 13:3–17

This is one of the most powerful lessons in the Bible. It is an act of great humility. In those days, foot washing was the task of the lowest of the household slaves. It was something that hosts would offer to their guests when they would come into their homes because travelers would have been walking in streets full of animal refuse mixed with dirt and muck and who knows what else. Yet the King of Kings did this for his disciples as an example and model for us. After this display of servitude, we should look at no act of service as being beneath us. Following and emulating Jesus in humility and servitude? Never hurts us. Even more telling is the last line, "Now that you know these things, you will be blessed if you do them." He says that he has set an example for us so that we should do what he did. He even promises that we will be blessed.

So, we must be careful about who we spend time watching or following because we may be taking on their beliefs, values, or behavior, and we may not even be aware of it. Instead, we should be following the models of behavior of those who are following Christ so we can be inspired and encouraged. There are Christian "hall of famers" who have led powerful and impactful lives—the apostle Paul, Martin Luther, and Mother Teresa, to name a few. Whenever I am going through a tough time or when I start feeling sorry for myself, I try to think about all the trials and suffering that the apostle

Paul went through. It is very unlikely that most people living in our country will ever have to endure the kind of suffering that Paul did.

Why all this emphasis on imitating Jesus and mirror neurons and watching other people's lives? Because you may be engaging in a passion or expending energy on pursuits that are misguided and have limited value. Wrongly focused and inauthentic passion might be more dangerous than no passion at all.

If we don't identify the types of passion that are harmful to us, then we can't discern authentic and helpful passions. Let's look at what passion truly is in an article from *The Psychology of Well-Being*:

> Thus, Vallerand et al. (2003) define passion as a strong inclination toward a self-defining activity that one likes (or even loves), finds important, and in which one invests time and energy on a regular basis. The issue of identity is important. In fact, passionate activities come to be so self-defining that they represent central features of one's identity. For instance, those who have a passion for playing basketball or songwriting do not merely engage in these activities. They see themselves as "basketball players" or "songwriters." In sum, a passionate activity is not simply an activity that one loves dearly, values highly, and engages in on a regular basis. It is also something that comes to define oneself. The activity becomes an inherent part of who the person is.[19]

This is critical to defining or discovering our passion and is an important indicator to how you see yourself. Some people identify primarily with being a mother or father. Their children are their entire focus, and they spend most of their time and energy raising them. They feel deeply that they were created to be a mom or dad. The only problem is that when the kids go off to college and begin to lead their own lives, these parents experience a void, almost like a loss of identity. They must strive to discover other innate gifts or talents while seeking their authentic selves.

Some people see themselves as more than a parent and feel a sense of emptiness and lack of fulfillment in their own lives. They feel like something is missing, and they long for more than what they are experiencing. This is actually a good sign if you are thinking about your own passion. Something lacking or missing in your own life could be the spark you need to get the fire of your passion blazing. You just need to find it.

The focus of this book is on addressing the problem of a lack of energy, drive, or enthusiasm. But you must also consider your purpose or focus. You might have plenty of energy, but if you are lacking purpose, it's a lot like having a strong motor on your raft but no rudder—you are moving fast but not really going anywhere.

The key is complete honesty with yourself. From my own experience, a lack of drive, fulfillment, energy, or enthusiasm is a clue that you may need to discover your passion. God may be trying to lead you in a new direction, perhaps a more exciting, thrilling, and fulfilling path than the one you are on. It isn't always easy, but it's never boring. That is a clue you're on the right track.

Some people are afraid to pursue their passion because they believe it will take away from the image that *they* created for themselves—the loving, caring mom who is there for her kids, the strong dad who makes sure everybody has everything they need. The mistake we make is not spending time discovering the passions that define who we are. We can waste valuable time trying to discover or develop a passion or identity that we created for ourselves. The problem is that we didn't consult God in the process. It is a matter of faith and trust that he knows what is best for us because he created us and he has something in mind for us to pursue: our purpose.

God will not compare our lives to anyone else and will never say, "Why weren't you more like him or her?" We should realize and begin to truly believe that he will ask us, "Why weren't you more like *you*, the person I created *you* to be?" The genuine you. The authentic you. If you are living in fear or anxiety or feel unfulfilled or stressed, it may be because you are living a life inconsistent with who you were created to be. Real peace, love, and joy come from living within our harmonious, passionate, and authentic selves.

Accepting Our Assignments

Let's stop for a second and go back into the land of the near-death experience. As I have mentioned, the NDE can bring some valuable insight in the quest to discover our own unique passions. There are two extraordinary and powerful principles outlined in the following NDE account that can really help us to home in on our own unique passion. In *Lessons from the Light*, a person who had an NDE describes what they learned:

> One thing I (learned) was that we are ALL here to do an "assignment of love." We don't have to do it at all, or we can do as many as we like. It's up to us. Our "assignment" is programmed in at birth, and it is the very thing or things we love most.[20]

There is a double boom on this one. Boom. Boom. We are going to get into the supernatural power of love in a second, but this is a huge clue to our purpose and our passion. We have access to power when we are acting within the framework of doing what we love to do (our passion). Another point to mention is that free will comes into play. This is a critical concept because we are always given a choice. Without freewill, there is no love. Love is a choice.

We can choose to ignore our "assignment of love," or we can do as many as we like. Do you think there is zero difference between choosing to do nothing or choosing to do "as many as you like"? Go back and read what Jesus said about being "blessed if you do them." Have you ever noticed that when you are doing what you enjoy doing, time seems to speed up? That is one of the strongest clues that you have found your passion. Let me finish the above quote:

> I was such a bozo. I always thought doing what you loved most was selfish. I can remember how amazed and happy I was when this information "came into my mind." This other source of energy, using my voice said, "That is the most unselfish and constructive thing you can do for the world because that is your *assigned energy* and you will be happiest doing it, you will be the best at it, and most respected for it![21]

Assigned energy? Do you have an *assigned energy*? Did you even know that you have an assigned energy? Coming back to ideas that "stick," this was a unique idea to me. It's a unique idea for many people. Could it be possible that most people who are walking around with no energy and feel tired are not living or working toward their goal in the power of their assigned energy? Could it be that most people who are dissatisfied with their jobs and feel unfulfilled are not engaging in their passion at all?

Notice here that the term *assigned* is used again. We are given an "assignment of love," and when we do what we love most, we are participating in our assigned energy, the energy allotted or allocated at birth. We are to complete our assignment of love in the power of our assigned energy. Remember what we discussed about the supernatural? What if we are totally ignoring our assignments? If we ignore our assignments, we don't have access to energy. We are working under our own limited human power. Again, these are supernatural principles.

Another key idea to embrace is that our passion and our purpose are intertwined. That is one of the biggest clues you can have regarding your purpose. Our unique passion is linked to our unique purpose. If you are pursuing a purpose outside of your assigned energy, how easy or enjoyable or invigorating is that pursuit going to be? Here is a powerful study that drives home the point that most of us are not engaged or participating in our assignments.

> CareerBuilder.com today announced the results of a national consumer employment survey conducted by Harris Interactive that reveals nearly four out of five U.S. workers (84 percent) are not currently in their dream job. More than 6,000 respondents were polled, weighing in with their thoughts and insights regarding top dream job choices for different professions and regions.[22]

This study is telling us that many of us are not in our "dream job." We can put two and two together to figure out why a minority of people in this country are able to tap into their assigned energy or their assignment of love. It's no surprise that everyone is tired.

Here is where we are to be brutally honest with ourselves—brutally, painfully, and uncomfortably honest. The person we lie to the most is ourselves. We get comfortable in our own way of thinking, and we see ourselves a certain way, but if something is inside of you that is kind of grating or gnawing at you, one place I would look is your own view of passion. If we can identify with the majority of people who are unsatisfied or unfulfilled in our jobs, then we are in business. We need to feel uncomfortable about this; we are in the majority. The good news is that there is help available to us.

If you have no energy or feel anxious, unfulfilled, or depressed, it may be because you aren't spending *any time* engaging in *any activity* that involves your unique passion and propels you toward your purpose— your real and true purpose, not something that you created but that *God* created.

In my own experience, there can be no change in our behavior or in our way of thinking until we can look in the mirror and see reality—warts and all. The good news is that when we can be honest with ourselves and make some changes, our confidence begins to grow. We can start to become more optimistic. We can see the light because we are discovering our passion. Life becomes more interesting and exciting, and we begin to move closer to our authentic self, the person we were created to be. Everything doesn't get easy—in fact, it may get much harder—but our confidence and sense of fulfillment increase. Our peace and joy tend to increase despite the struggle. We become resilient to setbacks and mistakes. When things don't go our way, we just keep moving. Anxiety and fear decrease because we know that we are on the right path.

Obsessive or Harmonious

Before we go further, it's critical that we make a distinction between harmonious and obsessive passions. If we stop to look around, it's easy to see that plenty of people are focused on obsessive passions. Obsessive passions do not contribute to joy or a sense of well-being. One example would be playing video games. There is some lofty language in the description below, but you get the point.

> Because harmonious passion leads the person to experience positive emotions during activity engagement that, in turn, facilitate increases in psychological well-being, and because harmonious passion leads to activity engagement and thus to the experience of positive emotions on a regular basis (roughly 8 hours per week), it is posited that harmonious passion leads to increases in psychological well-being that are sustainable. Thus, passion for the activity is important because it is the motivational force that leads the person to engage in the activity on a regular basis. Further, the type of effects that will be experienced on a regular basis depends on the type of passion one has for such an activity. It is proposed that to the extent that one's passion is harmonious, then this will set in motion two positive functions: promoting psychological well-being and preventing the occurrence of ill being. However, if one's passion is obsessive, then the positive effects may not be forthcoming on psychological well-being and an increase in ill-being may even take place.[23]

We need to carefully look at our own behavior as well as our own passion or purpose. These are some questions that we can ask ourselves:

1. Am I engaging in activities that reflect my authentic self or promote a false, socially constructed self?
2. Am I engaging in activities that reflect my unique passions or a passion that is socially constructed, created by people around me or by society (e.g., materialism)?
3. Am I engaging in a harmonious or an obsessive passion?
4. Have I embraced or ignored my assignment of love?

5. Have I embraced or ignored my assignment of energy?

This brings me to the idea of "can't not." This is the idea that it is impossible to ignore or not engage in this activity. Three examples come to mind. One of those is author Stephen King. He has written every day of his life for many, many years. Pablo Picasso painted and created constantly. Violinist Itzhak Perlman practices eight hours a day, every day. Perlman has said, "I am playing the violin. That's all I know, no education, no nothing. You just practice every day."

Here is another quote from Perlman that I hope you follow as you read this book:

> You must practice slowly. If you learn something slowly, you will forget it slowly.

6

PURPOSEFULLY PASSIONATE

Passion and purpose are inextricably bound together. Jesus modeled living a life of passion when he got down and washed the feet of the disciples. He told us that he came not to be served but to serve. His purpose and his passion were to fulfill the will of the Father.

Jesus exhibited humility and the heart of a servant, and our purpose must reflect the same things if it is to be genuine. When engaging in our purpose, someone is being served—not ourselves, but others. Jesus said:

> Whoever wants to be my disciple must deny themselves and take up their cross and follow me. For whoever wants to save their life will lose it, but whoever loses their life for me and for the gospel will save it.
>
> Mark 8:34–35

As we talked about earlier, NDEs tell us we have an assignment of energy and an assignment of love. Those assignments are not stamped on our foreheads at birth, so all we need to do is look in the mirror. If you feel a lack of energy or power, you may not be engaging in them.

Love is an action, and it involves giving. The focus of unconditional love is someone else. It involves denying the self. It takes real maturity to love in that way. We must first deny our *self* before we can pick up the cross and follow. Deny ourselves, pick up our cross, follow—that is the sequence. It is in the process of following Christ that we become authentic. The first step is the hardest.

For our purposes, I would make another cautionary distinction between obsessive and harmonious passions because of the parallels we can draw to our own individual authenticity. Obsessive passions most likely lie within the construct of our "false self." We should stop and examine our lives closely for evidence of these types of passions.

For example, if a dad loves playing golf and spends all weekend on the course and no time with his family, that is more like contributing to an increase in "ill-being," not well-being. Usually, well-being is associated with love, joy, and peace, all spiritual attributes. This is an excerpt on the contradistinction of obsessive versus harmonious passion that I think is important to spend some time on to avoid the former and embrace the latter:

> Those who have a passion for playing the guitar, for reading, or for jogging do not merely play the guitar, read, or jog. They are "guitar players," "readers," or "joggers."

Passionate activities are part of who they are. However, there is an important distinction in exactly how the activity is internalized in one's identity. Two distinct types of passion arise as a result of an internalization process that varies in how fully it is developed:

> Harmonious passion (HP) results from an autonomous internalization of the activity into the person's identity. An autonomous internalization occurs when individuals have freely accepted the activity as important for them without any contingencies attached to it.

This is a crucial concept. Contingencies are things like money or other tangible benefits to the individual. This helps us make a distinction between our obsessive passions and our harmonious passions.

> This type of internalization produces a motivational force to engage in the activity willingly and engenders a sense of volition and personal endorsement about pursuing the activity. Individuals are not compelled to do the activity, but rather, they freely choose to do so. With this type of passion, the activity occupies a significant but not overpowering space in the person's identity and is in harmony with other aspects of the person's life. [24]

This type of passion should be in harmony with the other aspects of the person's life.

Now, let's look at obsessive passions:

> Obsessive passion (OP), by contrast, results from a controlled internalization of the activity into one's identity. Such an internalization originates from intrapersonal and/or interpersonal pressure either because certain contingencies are attached to the activity such as feelings of social acceptance or self-esteem, or because the sense of excitement derived from activity engagement becomes uncontrollable. Thus, although individuals like the activity,

> they feel compelled to engage in it because of these internal contingencies that come to control them. They cannot help but to engage in the passionate activity. The passion must run its course as it controls the person. Because activity engagement is out of the person's control, it eventually takes disproportionate space in the person's identity and causes conflict with other activities in the person's life.[25]

If we look closely, it's clear this is describing the false, inauthentic, or "socially constructed" self. When I mentioned NDE experiences, the whole purpose was the revelation or identification of the false, socially constructed self. NDErs were shown aspects of their lives that were deemed to be meaningless or a waste of time. Look at all the phrases here that point out an obsessive or false, socially constructed passion.

Social Acceptance

How much time, effort or energy are being wasted on this one goal? How about feelings of self-esteem? There is nothing wrong with self-esteem or confidence. The problem begins when you rely on other people for your sense of worth, they can turn on you (see note on Ed Sheeran).

The best thing to do as we look at our own situations is to develop a sense of self-worth, self-confidence, and value based on the opinion of Jesus. His opinion never changes and brings the most value to the table. One of the best things I've ever heard from a sermon is "If you ever hear any voices in your head or outside of your head tell you that you are helpless, hopeless, or worthless, that is never Jesus, ever." This is a powerful concept that we need to instill into our children from birth.

Part of what drives these obsessive passions is the matter of control. People are compelled to engage in these passions because of the linkage to these internal contingencies and their own identity.

Let's try to expand on this for a second for the sake of clarity. When we are talking about obsessive passion, the focus is on pressure. This pressure is caused by the need for the *social acceptance, personal excitement, or entertainment* experienced from engaging in that activity. Obsessive passion is of no lasting benefit because it is purely selfish. We are focusing on our feelings and what we derive personally from the activity. We are either getting excitement or a rush, or we feel the pride of getting a big thumbs up from the people around us. Engaging or being involved in this kind of activity does not reflect or involve the actions of our authentic self. It is a socially constructed, inauthentic shell of our true self. Now is when we need to develop our skills of observation to be able to see this type of obsessive engagement in ourselves and in others. It's very easy to see all around us.

We can become aware of this **in**-authenticity if we can be honest and ask ourselves, "Who is the one benefiting from this activity? Is anyone being served, encouraged, inspired, or supported by this passion?" This is summed up very nicely in a quote from Dr. Kenneth Ring in *Lessons from the Light*:

> In examining the lives of the NDErs we have met in this chapter, do you not feel that all of them, to various degrees, have been aided to live more authentic lives, much more in keeping with their previously dormant gifts and propensities, and emboldened to throw off the social shackles, where necessary, that previously constrained them? The Light told Peggy, in effect, that she should "follow her love" and that yielding herself to it was, in

> fact, to do the most unselfish and constructive thing in the world. The Light seems to be telling us, each of us, that we have a unique gift, an offering to make to the world, and that our happiness and the world's happiness are both served when we live in such a way as to realize that gift, which is no less than our purpose in life.[26]

You may have seen this in my last book, *Brave the Wave.* When there is repetition, pay attention. Important things are worth repeating. If we can look at our passion in the context of our authentic selves, we are to make an offering to the world that will contribute to "our happiness and the world's happiness."

When we are involved with obsessive passions, the benefits are limited to how it makes *us* feel or how we think it impacts other people's perception of *us*. For instance, in being a great football or basketball player, we may focus our time and energy to become the best we can be in the sport but only in relation to how it makes us feel (pride) or how we enjoy the attention, accolades, or money that come with being engaged in that activity. But, like life, these are team sports, and the best individual athletes are the ones who focused on helping their teammates to excel—a focus on others rather than on self.

Now don't get me wrong. There are many athletes who use their status as athletes to do wonderful things in society and speak out about injustice. They also devote time and energy to serving others less fortunate than themselves. People like Jim Brown, Tony Dungy, Muhammad Ali, Lebron James, Peyton Manning, or Serena Williams, and many more, understand they are not here just for themselves.

The distinction when it comes to harmonious passion is that the internalization of that passion or engagement in that activity is autonomous. Nothing is attached to that internalization—no pride or social acceptance.

> This type of internalization produces a motivational force to engage in the activity willingly and engenders a sense of volition and personal endorsement about pursuing the activity.[27]

One powerful component to this idea is "can't not." It is the thought that "if I don't do this, I will stop breathing." It is something that is needed, or obligatory, to do. It's an overwhelming drive. It is the painter who must paint. It is the songwriter who works tirelessly on getting the song just right. And when they can see the benefit to others and understand that the world around us is a better place, the purity of that passion is sealed. When we can look at passion as our "unique gift" and an offering that is made to the world and not ourselves, that is the essence of engaging in an activity that is in the realm of our authentic selves.

There is nothing like a real-world example to illustrate these ideas. I remember reading an article about musician Tom Petty. He was feverishly working to complete a music project around the time of his death. It was something he had to do. It was almost like there was no choice. Look at this description of seventy-five-year-old David Crosby of Crosby, Stills, Nash, and Young:

> At a time when many artists would be happy to rest on their laurels and live off their classic hits, Crosby has made three albums in the last four years (Well, it's actually four albums, but we'll get to that in a bit), writing a plethora of new songs and working with Snarky Puppy's Michael League, and with his son, James Raymond, who doubles as keyboardist and producer.[28]

Can you see the harmonious passion? Three albums in four years. That is something you "can't not" do. In contrast, I was reading an article about Gene Simmons from the rock band KISS. He said that there was no incentive for him to go into the studio and work on an album because people were going to just download the album for free anyway, so why bother. Can you see the difference in their attitudes and passion? Do you think David Crosby cared about people downloading his album for free? In his mind, that means more people are listening to and appreciating something that he created. There is a benefit that is outside of himself. In Gene Simmons's defense, he may look at music as a vocation. Simply a job he does to support himself and his family. There is nothing wrong with that. He may also have a harmonious passion in some other area that we know nothing about.

A painter paints because he must, but he wants other people to enjoy his work. It's not only for himself. When you think about your passion, is it something that you can't *not* do? Is it an integral part of who you are? Your authentic self is a passionate self. A harmonious passion is part of your identity. It is how you see yourself, and it is who you were created to be. It is linked to your contribution to the world, but it is also unique and very personal to you. We can't expect other people to get excited about the things we get excited about. What we should expect is that each of us should be getting excited about *something*. If we can't put our finger on any activity that we can get excited about, we are living in dormancy, a dormant life.

> Dormancy is a period in an organism's life cycle when growth, development, and physical activity are temporarily stopped. This minimizes metabolic activity and therefore helps an organism to conserve energy.[29]

This is how some plants survive in harsh climates. It is an extreme survival mechanism that the plant needs to continue to grow under better conditions. It is like hibernation, a mechanism used by bears and many other mammals to reduce energy expenditure and survive the decreased food availability during winter. Brumation is an example of dormancy in reptiles that is similar to hibernation where the reptile often wakes up just to drink water and then returns to "sleep" and can go for months without food.

Growth, development, physical activity—all stopped.

Remember that this is a survival mechanism to conserve energy. Could *that* be the reason why we have so little energy? That's something to think about. Your assignment of energy may be bound and locked up, "hibernating" in the center of your undiscovered passion and waiting for you to release that power and energy.

We can't acquire someone else's passion nor can we make other people passionate about our interests since they are unique to us. Let me give you another example. In a New York office building during the 1950s, a group of record company executives were sitting around a table listening to albums. They were trying to decide which singles to release for the radio. As the executives were arguing about which single to release, one of the custodians sweeping in the hallway stuck his head into the office and said, "I would go with the one you are playing now. The other one isn't very good." Then he kept on sweeping in the hallway. These record company executives were shocked, but they listened to this man and, in fact, continued to ask his opinion. He was able to pick a number of hits for them, and he ended up leaving his job as a custodian and got involved with talent evaluation. When they asked him how he was able to pick the hits, he said, "I just know it's good when I feel the hair on the back of my neck stand up."

That was fascinating to me, because I discovered very early in my childhood that I had this same type of reaction to certain songs. Musicians talk about "chill bumps" they get when they are in the studio coming up with a good song. They know it because they can feel it.

When Sonny Bono wrote "I Got You, Babe," he woke Cher up at two in the morning and said, "I got a hit." When Pete Wentz of the band Fall Out Boy wrote "Sugar, We're Goin‘ Down," he turned to his bandmates and said, "Boys, we just made enough money to pay for our children's education." They knew it. They had insight. They had a unique experience. It doesn't happen all the time, but sometimes there is magic in the air, and they can feel it.

I believe those are spiritual experiences. They allow for insight and vision and are totally connected to our authenticity. We now know this response is unique to certain individuals, and the evidence tells us that people who have this physiologic response have brains that react differently to music:

> If listening to music gives you goosebumps, you're not just in touch with your emotions, you might actually have a unique brain, research has found. Scientists at the University of Southern California examined the brain scans of 20 students, half of whom had intense reactions to music and half didn't. After each participant listened to a piece of self-selected music, researchers compared the scans and found that those who reacted to songs in this heightened manner had a distinctive neurological structure. People who experienced chills had a higher volume of neurological fibres which link their auditory cortex to the part of the brain that processes emotions. "More fibres and increased efficiency between two regions means that you

> have more efficient processing between them," explained Matthew Sachs, a co-author of the study. As a result of these enhanced neurological communications, Sachs also concluded that people who get goosebumps upon listening to music may experience emotions at a more intense level than those who don't, regardless of whether they're listening to a song or not.[30]

What is most interesting to me is that last part—that people who get goosebumps when listening to music may experience emotions at a more intense level than those who don't, even if they are not listening to a song.

Some people may protest this data and say, "You just said that we can't trust science!" Let me be clear. What I am arguing is that when it comes to passion and purpose, we need supernatural guidance. When it comes to physical attributes and objective data like unique brain-fiber architecture, we need science. We absolutely need research and studies when it comes to medicine. We need data to help guide us in taking care of patients.

From the information above, we can conclude that there is a very real possibility that there are passions that may be unique to us, and we don't even know about them. They could be undiscovered, dormant. You may be a lizard in brumation. Just kidding. I became aware of this "chill bump" thing around the age of eight. For years, I just assumed everybody had it. Just last year I stumbled onto this research about music, emotions, and unique brain-fiber architecture. It was an "a-ha moment" for me.

The whole point is that our physical brain structure is unique. It's different. We may not even be aware of it. Think about smell. There are certain things I can smell that help me with my job as a physician. Sometimes when I ask other doctors about it, they look at me like I'm crazy.

What about hearing? Can you pick out a tambourine in a song or a shaker that is driving the rhythm. I once pointed out to a friend how one band likes to use a particular shaker during the chorus of most of their most famous songs. He said, "I can't hear all the details of each instrument. I only hear the song as a whole." That is interesting to me. It's similar to how dogs smell. When someone is cooking a stew on a stove, all we can smell is stew. Dogs smell carrots, onions, meat, and potatoes. Each individual scent is picked up by the dog. It is in finding those unique elements that we will discover clues to our passion.

7

I WAS BORN TO BE A...

Knowing yourself is the beginning of wisdom...

-Aristotle

Look around you the next time you are at work or a store or getting your car washed. How many people do you see who look like they are living a life of passion and purpose? Those people may have found the secret to living within their authentic selves. They aren't fighting the next wave; they're riding it. They're living a life inside of their own unique interests and gifts. The key is to work to discover your passion and then work toward finding your purpose.

> Far and away the best prize that life has to offer is the chance to work hard at work worth doing.
>
> – Theodore Roosevelt

When we discover our true passion, it usually happens at a young age, but it can happen when we are older. Record producer Clive Davis said when he heard Janis Joplin sing for the first time, "It changed my life." Here is a young lawyer who liked music, but he had a life-changing experience in his thirties. Another interesting point about Janis Joplin herself is that she didn't realize that she had a talent for singing until she was nineteen years old. That should motivate us and keep our minds open to the idea of discovering our unique passion.

Sometimes, when we discover our passion, it is a ground-breaking event. It is noteworthy because you remember exactly where you were, what you were doing, and what time of the day it was. It also had on impact on your life in some way, like when I heard "Purple Haze" for the first time. It was a weekday afternoon, and I was listening to it in our living room on an old stereo. It was an event that I remember clearly even though it was decades ago. It had an impact on me and on my life because, since that day, music has been a big part of my life.

When I was a senior in high school, I went to visit a family friend to ask about the music industry. He played in a band and had a recording studio in an old wooden shack in his backyard. I clearly remember being amazed at all the things on the walls he used to keep the sound from reverberating when he was recording. It was fascinating watching him work all the knobs on the studio console as he was helping someone record vocal tracks for a song. After about an hour of just silently watching and getting up enough courage, I asked my million-dollar question: "Hey Jerry, uh, you know that I really like biology and science and stuff like that, right? We've talked about it."

He responded, "Yeah, sure."

I continued, "I know that my dad told you that I am thinking about being a doctor." (I knew this because my dad told everyone within earshot that I wanted to be a doctor.)

He said, "Yeah, I think that's a great idea."

I kind of stammered a little, "Well, I was also kind of thinking about maybe being a record producer. You know, I really love music, and I think I would enjoy doing stuff like what you are doing right now."

He didn't hesitate for a single second. "Be a doctor. It's very hard to earn a living in the music business. Just be a doctor first so that you can support yourself and then do music as a hobby."

So, that is what I've been doing. I often wonder where I would be if I had ignored his advice.

When you think about the statement, "I was born to be a ____," what comes to your mind? Some people have no hesitation at all and can fill in the blank without thinking much about it: Mother. Father. Salesperson. Teacher. Lawyer. Accountant. Musician. Artist. Doctor. Athlete.

What if, in the job you are in right now, you have been in that career for decades and it's just not cutting it anymore? There's no excitement. It's not interesting or inspiring. We have already gone over the fact that most of us in the working population are not satisfied in our jobs. What now? Well, the answer lies in passion—discovering our unique passion and how passion and purpose are inexorably linked.

The Power of Discovery

You may be looking for power or energy because you feel tired, like you are just existing and there's no fulfillment in the things you spend your time on. Or you have so many things going on that nothing ever gets completed, so life is just a plethora of unfinished tasks swirling around you. I'm going to suggest to you that your power comes from and is intimately enmeshed in purpose. But the search for purpose should begin with passion.

When you find your passion, it propels you toward your purpose. When you find and pursue your passion, it yields power and energy, an assignment of energy that powers your engine to complete your purpose.

Just looking at the example of music and unique brain structure should pique an interest in finding our unique hardwired gifts. We all have them, and we should devote time to their discovery, as this leads to finding our passion. I'm going to suggest that when we are seeking our authentic selves, reaching and fulfilling our purpose is one of the keys to reaching that authentic state of well-being.

> And we know that in all things God works for the good of those who love him, who have been called according to his purpose.
>
> – Romans 8:28

The mistake we make is coming up with *our* idea for *our* purpose. There are a couple of prerequisites in order to claim this promise. We want God working for our good in all things, but that is reserved for "those who love him." Love is the central tenet and the critical linchpin, and we will cover the critical role that love plays concerning power and energy in the coming chapters. But we must start with love before we get to God working for *our good.*

The other part of this is that "we have been called according to his purpose." Everyone is called. You are called. I am called. Rich Mullins said, "Our calling is where the world's deepest need and our greatest joy meet." This is contingent on our willingness to accept that call and pursue it as part of our lives. Part of accepting that call is finding our greatest joy. That really is our assignment of love. We don't have to worry too much about being worthy—we just need to be willing.

When it comes to the idea of being "worthy," we know that God uses imperfect people to carry out his plan. If you spend any time in the Bible, it's easy to see this truth played out again and again. Once we get over the incorrect notion that being called is just for pastors or priests, then we can acknowledge that we, too, have a calling. When we accept this truth, things will begin to change.

One very important caveat is that God's plan for your life is without a doubt the best possible scenario. In addition, when we follow God's plan, we have access to his power, grace, and guidance. Who wouldn't want that? If we want God working in our lives, we should know and love him and accept and embrace what we were called to do. We can't get to purpose without a relationship with Jesus.

> Jesus answered, "I am the way and the truth and the life. No one comes to the Father except through me."
>
> – John 14:6

One critical point is that we don't have access to supernatural power without Jesus. Pursuing our passion and our purpose is firmly rooted in the realm of the supernatural.

> I am the vine; you are the branches. If you remain in me and I in you, you will bear much fruit; apart from me you can do nothing.
>
> – John 15:5

If you read my last book, you know I quoted this verse multiple times, and lo and behold, here it is again. If you notice, Jesus doesn't say, "Apart from me, life is just a little harder," although I believe life is hard whether you have Jesus in your life or not. He doesn't say, "Apart from me, you may have to work a little longer to get to your goals and complete your purpose." He says, "Apart from me you can do nothing." *No Thing. No Goal. No Purpose.*

Our relationship with Jesus brings triple the value regarding passion because it helps us with *plan*, *power*, and *purpose*. We can't get to God working for our good until we get to love. Loving Jesus and loving God is where we must start. This is the source—the root of wisdom, power, love, and energy, and the wellspring of his perfect plan.

When we think of ourselves as an instrument, a tool, or a machine, we can see that we have a unique purpose that God had in mind when he created us. Tools are crafted for a specific purpose and designed to accomplish that purpose effectively. If we can accept that he is our all-knowing, all-powerful Father, then we can accept that he created us with the power to fulfill exactly what he had in mind for us to do.

Occasionally when I am on vacation with my family, my kids will ask, "What are we going to do this afternoon, Dad?" To be honest, sometimes I don't know because I haven't formulated a plan. That is when my wife throws in the ol' "let's play it by ear" response. That takes some of the pressure off me. Now and then I enjoy *not* having a plan when I'm on vacation, and I like the adventure of playing it by ear. It's funny to me that the most memorable and fun times, the ones that come to mind when we think about our trip, are when everything *doesn't* go as planned, and the plan falls apart. That's when we improvise and come up with our response on the fly. That's fine when you are on vacation, but that doesn't work very well in real life.

In medicine, we like to have safety parachutes all the time. If this doesn't work, we go to plan B. If that doesn't work, then we go to plan C. Contingency plans are critical, especially when someone is starting to become unstable or when things crop up that you weren't expecting. It happens all the time. The problem with living our lives "playing it by ear" or "flying by the seat of our pants" is we are just responding to the circumstances life is throwing at us. We are reacting. We aren't striving or trying to reach our primary goal. Our actions end up having little to do with discovering or realizing our authentic selves, and instead, we find ourselves striving after a purpose or plan that is of our own design. Why is this important? Because we don't know what is best for us. We have never known and will never know. If you stop to think about the biggest mistakes you have ever made in your life, most likely they were part of "my plan for my life." Most likely, it was a bad plan.

The Perfect Plan

I remember reading something that Green Bay quarterback Aaron Rodgers said once in a magazine article. He was talking about how he had just won the Super Bowl and was sitting on the bus outside the stadium. He was surprised at how he was feeling. He was experiencing feelings of satisfaction and accomplishment, but he just kept thinking to himself, "Is this all there is?" To me, if you are asking yourself that question, then God is gently knocking on the door of your spirit trying to get your attention.

God has a plan. God not only has a plan, he has dreams for your life. He had those dreams for you even before he created the world. Those dreams are older than the planet. The dreams for your unique life and those for your distinctive purpose and passion are older than the world itself.

> Even as he chose us in him before the foundation of the world, that we should be holy and blameless before him. In love, he predestined us for adoption as sons through Jesus Christ, according to the purpose of his will.
>
> Ephesians 1:4–5 (ESV)

We are chosen. He wants us to be holy and blameless, and he wants us to become sons and daughters through Jesus. It is through Jesus that we get to our authenticity. That is a big part of his plan for us. Passion. Power. Purpose.

The majority of people are following their own plan for their lives. How do I know this? Well, if we believe that God has a plan for us, and his plan is perfect, then we should be consulting God. One of the primary ways to consult God is by reading the Bible. We know that 70 percent of the people who identify as believers ignore the Bible.[31]

We should spend time with Jesus and learn his plan for our lives. His plan is always best.

In an interview, former Texas Longhorns quarterback Colt McCoy mentions God's plan. Colt tells a story about being in a locker room with trainers and his dad in the middle of the national championship game with Alabama. He had been injured in the first half. He said that trainers were giving him treatment on his shoulder injury to get him back into the game. He tried to throw a football to his dad who was in the locker room with him, but it was physically impossible. He threw the ball to his dad, and he knew immediately that he would not be able to finish the game. He broke down crying. The thing I remember the most was the smile he had on his face and the statement he made about that whole set of circumstances as he was retelling the story sometime later. To this very day, I still quote that powerful line to my kids: "I knew I wouldn't be able to go back in the game, but I was okay with it because I know that God's plan is always perfect."

Is that your mindset when it comes to God's plan for your life? I will tell you this. If you can believe that statement down to your very bones, it will empower you in countless ways in this life. When the wave hits you, it gets easier to ride. Believing God is sovereign and that he loves you and wants what is best for you can be a great source of peace and power. God is causing or allowing events to take place in your life for your good. Whatever they are, they are to your benefit. This attitude builds confidence and diminishes anxiety. That's why it's so important to learn and discover God's plan for our lives. If we are following his plan, we can know that we have access to his power, wisdom, grace, and guidance. This is his promise.

> The eyes of the Lord search the whole earth in order to strengthen those whose hearts are fully committed to him.
>
> 2 Chronicles 16:9 (NLT)

When our hearts are fully committed to him, we spend time with him. We spend time in the Word and in prayer. We learn and know the words of Jesus. We spend time meditating on the Word. When we spend time seeking guidance for our lives, God notices. His eyes are searching the entire earth looking for those who seek him. He promises that he will strengthen our hearts. He will also guide you toward your passion.

If you don't spend any time in the Word or in prayer and meditation, you are leaving a lot of power on the table. It's right there, right inside the Bible. All we need to do is open it.

8

WHOSE PLAN IS THIS ANYWAY?

Think about how many times you have come up with a plan that totally bombed. I am assuming I am not the only one this has ever happened to. Remember that we talked about our DNA, brain structure, and mirror neurons and how we can emulate other people's behavior. We still understand very little about the complexity of the brain. We used music as one example because that is a new discovery, but there will undoubtedly be many discoveries to come in the decades ahead. Each new discovery gives us a clearer picture as to the nature of God and how he operates.

One way we can gain some insight into how God works is by looking at the number of miracles in the Bible. Pastor and professor David Stancil came up with eighty-six, though he admits that it is not an exhaustive list. It's interesting to think about miracles and how God reveals himself throughout history and in the present day.

> As I continued to look at the data, though, I noticed that miraculous events don't seem to be equally spaced across the two thousand years of biblical history. Though there are outliers here and there, miracles actually seem to cluster around four periods of time: (1) the period of creation through the destruction of Sodom and Gomorrah,

an unspecified length of time; (2) the period of Moses and Joshua, about seventy years; (3) the period of Elijah and Elisha, about seventy years; and (4) the period of the New Testament, about seventy years.[32]

Does it seem strange to you that seventy years is repeated three times? It seems a little unusual to me. Why seventy years? What is the significance of that? We know that forty years or forty days is a common number in the Bible. These kinds of patterns are fascinating to me.

> This means that, *out of two thousand years of biblical history, miracles seemed to occur in a span of about two hundred years.* Further, these four seasons of miracles were all pivotal periods in biblical history. In the first period, the period of creation, God was planting human life on this planet. In the second period, the period of Moses and Joshua, God was establishing the nation of Israel as a chosen people. In the third period, the period of Elijah and Elisha, God was calling the ten northern tribes of Israel to repentance in an attempt to avoid their destruction. And in the fourth period, the period of the New Testament, God was establishing a spiritual nation composed of those who follow Jesus as God's one and only Son, who was crucified and resurrected to bring us healing and eternal life.[33]

The thing that is interesting is when those miracles occurred. They usually occur around times of revelation, when God reveals himself to his people. Two important periods are the times of Moses and Jesus, but huge lapses of time occur between Moses and Jesus when there really aren't many miracles going on. Revelations are important in the grand scheme, and they are important individually. Here is another verse you may have seen before.

> Those who accept my commandments and obey them are the ones who love me. And because they love me, my Father will love them. And I will love them and reveal myself to each of them.
>
> –John 14:21 (NLT)

I will love them and reveal myself to each of them. This is a personal revelation. Our relationship with Jesus is personal. He will reveal his plan for your life to you as an individual. The best starting point to figuring out God's plan for our lives is the Word. We start there because it's the primary way that God speaks to us. The Word reveals God's will. Jesus repeatedly tells us we are his brothers and sisters if we know and do the *will of the Father.* If we want to get closer to Jesus, we need to value God's Word and his will. He has a will for all of us and a will for each of us as individuals.

That doesn't mean we ignore the other myriad means of revelation. They occur in surprising ways. Circumstances or impressions can be revelations. A movie or a song or something one of your children says can strike a chord. A book, magazine article, or documentary, something that happens in nature, or a dream can all contain revelations. Impressions and revelations are all around you. As we become more aware and we begin to pay attention to these revelations, we should check them against the perfect truth of Scripture.

Let me share an unusual experience, an example of "something that happens in nature." About ten years ago I was just beginning to take my spiritual journey more seriously and was starting to acquire new spiritual habits. Daily Bible reading and taking notes in my journal were becoming part of my routine. Late one night, as I was arriving home from work, I saw an enormous owl perched at the entrance of my driveway. I stopped suddenly and was taken aback because, for one, I had never seen an owl up close before, other than maybe at a zoo, and two, it seemed like this owl was at least two feet tall. It just stayed there for at least ten seconds staring at me. It didn't move or flinch or even turn its head. It just stared. Just as I was reaching for my phone to snag a picture of it, it flew off. The wingspan was amazing to behold as it flew away. That was just one little event on my own journey that I wanted to mention. To me, it was meant to show me that I was on the right track.

God communicates with us in many, many ways. I just shared one minute event, and there have been many more far more compelling and powerful. Sure, there will be people who say, "Yeah? An owl? So what? That has happened to me at least ten times." Exactly my point. In my mind, this was a personal revelation that happened to me *once*. I am including this because when I have read books on NDEs, some people have mentioned unusual experiences regarding nature and other phenomena after they came back to this life. Affirmations and revelations make our lives exciting, interesting, challenging, and fulfilling.

One critical idea to point out is that there is no power or purpose if we totally ignore God's will. We can't express our passion in true authenticity if we are totally focusing on our plan. Stop and think about your plan. Do you know what it is? We get into trouble when we come up with our own plan for our lives, especially if we are focused on worldly goals and values or are far removed and not engaged in our passion while seeking purpose. This is when we lose energy and become discouraged. Many times, we pursue passions or a purpose that we think will make us happy or we operate within an inauthentic self.

We must remember one cold, sobering fact. *God is far more interested in our being holy than in our being happy.* We should keep in mind that God knows what he has planned for us. We don't. We know that whatever is awaiting us will be beyond our wildest imaginations, though, which is why we need to focus on the unseen, not the seen.

Sometimes the Plan Is Uncomfortable

I was listening to a lecture the other day about tragedies in this world and how God allows pain and suffering. The speaker made an interesting point about God taking a child in a tragic way. He said that it's not murder, it's merely *translocation.* He is changing their location from a dark, sinful, imperfect world to a wonderful, peaceful, heavenly existence full of love. In the same way, when we are going through some difficulty, trial, or painful experience, God knows the exact benefit to us as individuals. He is also looking to see how we respond and if we can focus on what is ahead. If we have faith, it's a little easier to handle discomfort because we know that whatever he has in mind is what's best for us.

God isn't interested in our living comfortable, squishy, easy lives. He doesn't want us comfortable here on earth because he wants us looking forward to heaven. Earth is not our home. We are supposed to be uncomfortable here. We sometimes get caught up in pursuing maximum comfort. We dream about retiring and lying on a beach or swinging in a hammock with a coconut cocktail in our hand while watching a sunset. The word *retirement* isn't in the Bible.

Let's look at the origin of that word.

Retire: "Mid-16th century (in the sense 'withdraw to a place of safety or seclusion')"[34]

First look at the date of the origin of the word. It's only been around for four or five hundred years. Then look at the meaning. "Withdraw to a place of safety or seclusion." Safety? Seclusion? Does the Bible tell us to seek safety and seclusion?

We have talked about wisdom and how the best definition of it is thinking the way God thinks. When we are focused on safety, we will be afraid to venture out and pursue purpose. Jesus spent some time in seclusion at the start of the day, but for most of his waking hours he was around other people. Prolonged isolation or seclusion is a bad idea for anyone. It harms our mental health and sense of well-being. We need to be around other people. As always, Jesus is our role model.

Think about the great characters in the Bible. Did anyone have an easy, safe, squishy, comfortable life? Most of the apostles were beheaded or crucified. Any safety or seclusion in that? In fact, most of the time when seclusion is mentioned in the Bible, it is a bad thing, a punishment even. Consider the time of seclusion for the apostle John in his exile to the island of Patmos. Not exactly the kind of retirement that we see on the AARP commercials, is it?

If we want to life watch, we should try Jesus and the apostle Paul. Their lives are the ones we should be watching. No comfort, ease, or safety, just faith, obedience, love, and total focus on the will of the Father. We don't want to shift to being too draconian because God does allow blessings and joy while on this earth. He loves us and wants to bless us, just like we love our children and want them to be happy. But sometimes, when our children are being challenged or are going through a tough situation, we are comforted in the fact that hard circumstances will make them stronger and more resilient. It gives us some measure of comfort knowing they will be better prepared for the challenges and troubles they will be facing in the future. One of our principal jobs as parents is to prepare our children for the challenges and trials that come with living in a fallen, broken, difficult world.

That's how God thinks. He wants us to be like Jesus, so he will allow difficulties, pain, and trials to toughen us up, develop our resilience, and grow our faith. That is our family motto, and my kids know it by heart, "Don't give up. Toughen up." Resilience and perseverance are two chief components of passion.

Holiness is Part of the Plan

We talked about how God would prefer that we be holy rather than happy. Why is holiness such a big deal? When we act in unholy ways and willfully engage in activity that is in direct conflict with who we were created to be, it interferes with our spiritual communion with Jesus. It affects our communication. It creates static or bad reception on our spiritual cell phones.

> Therefore, with minds that are alert and fully sober, set your hope on the grace to be brought to you when Jesus Christ is revealed at his coming. As obedient children do not conform to the evil desires you had when you lived in ignorance. But just as he who called you is holy, so be holy in all you do; for it is written: "Be holy, because I am holy."
>
> –1 Peter 1:13–16

I'll admit that sometimes when listening to a sermon by one of my favorite pastors, I notice a recurring focus on sin. *God hates sin. Sin is bad. We are all sinners. Sin this and sin that.* Sometimes they will scowl and clench their teeth and get angry. They want to squeeze the sin out of us because they know it's what best for us. It comes from a place of love, but there is a kind of negativity associated with those types of sermons.

We already understand that we are sinners. It's obvious. If we can focus on our relationship with Jesus and on love, we behave in a way the moves us away from sin. Sin is something we want to avoid, of course, because it disrupts our communication and spiritual communion with him. It's not like Jesus has a weakness; it's just that he is absolutely holy and pure. When we are willfully defiant and engaging in sinful behavior that we know is not consistent with God's will, it interferes with our communication. That's just the nature of sin. Communication is a two-way street and is essential to any relationship. That's why starting the day in the Word is the best way to begin.

What I have come to understand is that holiness is not about being a saint or being perfect or doing spiritual activities. It is based on our relationship with Jesus. When we allow Jesus into our hearts and have formed a relationship with him, we are holy. The apostle Paul says, "I have been crucified with Christ and I no longer live, but Christ lives in me" (Galatians 2:20).

When Christ lives in us, it doesn't mean perfection. No one is perfect. No one but Jesus has ever been perfect or will ever be perfect. It means that we keep a clear mind, a pure heart, and focus on humility and service.

> Who may ascend the mountain of the Lord? Who may stand in his holy place? The one who has clean hands and a pure heart, who does not trust in an idol or swear by a false god. They will receive blessing from the Lord and vindication from God their Savior.
>
> – Psalm 24:3–5

When we have "clean hands," that means we confess our sin. When we sin and stumble, we are uncomfortable with that sin and confess it quickly. We want to clear our conscience of that sin. We know it was wrong, and because of our love and our relationship with Jesus, we know it hurts him. We don't want to hurt him because of our love, just like when we do something that hurts our spouse or our children. We hate it. We apologize and ask for forgiveness. We feel their pain, and we experience pain too. We don't laugh and enjoy their pain and seek to repeat it. If we love with real love, we have empathy. We feel the pain *we* caused them. That is holiness, and holiness is love. We are all capable of love, and we are all capable of loving Jesus. So, we are all capable of holiness.

Because God loves us, when we confess our sin, he forgives us. Therefore, we have "clean hands." When we are pursuing our purpose and have purity of intent, we have a "pure heart." We are not seeking our purpose in selfish ambition; we are looking to fulfill God's will for our lives. When we are moving toward authenticity, love, joy, kindness, and peace, we won't "trust in an idol or swear by a false god." We seek truth. We lift our souls to Jesus alone. So, we are holy, and we stand before him ready to receive our "blessing from the Lord and vindication from God [our] savior."

No one knows the plan God has for your life or knows the neurochemical or brain structure he gave you that make your passions unique to you. But God does speak through people. Yes, he speaks through the Bible, but he also uses people. The habit of filtering what others are telling you through the truth of the Word is the best approach, especially the words of Jesus. Listen to the advice and see if it matches up with the Word. There are people out there I listen to, and sometimes, I think God is speaking to me directly through them. But I always line it up with what the Bible teaches. We must test the idea or message.

Pride Is Not Part of the Plan

When it comes to our plan for our lives, if we realize the whole goal of that purpose or plan is to impress other people, then it is time to abandon that plan! If there is any inkling, whiff, or sliver of selfish ambition, it needs to go. We just talked about our hearts being pure and purity of intent. If we are motivated or moved by selfish ambition, we are on our own.

> But if you have bitter jealousy and selfish ambition in your heart, do not be arrogant and so lie against the truth. This wisdom is not that which comes down from above, but is earthly, natural, demonic. For where jealousy and selfish ambition exist, there is disorder and every evil thing.
>
> – James 3:14–16 (ESV)

We need to look at these verses very carefully. This is where we need brutal honesty because we may be pursuing a plan or purpose that is rooted in envy or selfish ambition, and James tells us plainly that the ultimate origin of that purpose is earthly, natural, and demonic. We could be convincing ourselves that what we are doing is for the benefit of others or to serve God, but the whole time, we are the only ones benefitting. God is the one who should be getting the glory.

Self-awareness and mature self-examination are absolutely required on this road to discovery of passion and purpose. Jealousy, envy, and selfish ambition are linked to disorder and *every evil thing*. I've heard it said that a pastor can serve in the church for thirty years and be serving his or her own pride or be seeking financial gain by this service. The only way that you can see this type of behavior *within yourself* is to approach authenticity. If we move toward the Word and spend time with Jesus, growing in intimacy with him, our vision and insight will sharpen. We will be able to tell if we're lying to ourselves.

The biggest lies we tell are the ones we tell ourselves.

Oh, my excessive drinking and pornography addiction aren't hurting anyone.

Yeah, I may have excessive pride or anger, but it's no big deal. It's not hurting my wife or my family.

Oh, my pride and my hypercritical attitude with my husband and children doesn't hurt anyone. It is for their own good. If I wasn't here to point out their flaws, they would never be able to learn from them.

All lies. Not only that, they are disruptive lies that interfere with our true purpose and with the growth of love in the family.

Jealousy, pride, envy, or selfish ambition all interfere with true purpose and true passion. If those are the most significant motivators for our actions, we are living within a socially constructed or inauthentic self. We may impress people, but we are wasting valuable time, effort, and energy on activities with no eternal value. We are rowing in circles.

Imagine standing before Jesus after you die and showing him a video clip of the task or activity you are currently spending time and energy on. How would you feel playing that clip? One of the most valuable aspects of studying NDEs is that they can have a real impact on our own behavior. We should look carefully at the painful descriptions NDErs use when discussing their own behavior as it was being shown to them in their life review. Remember that learning how to love is part of God's perfect plan for every one of us. Reading some of these statements below from *Lessons from the Light* makes me think twice when I start to get angry or prideful around my own family.

- "Often, of course, what one sees in the life review is painful to witness."
- "One woman, for example, told me that when she got emotionally caught up in a scene that was distressing to her, 'I stopped and I said, "I don't want to be here anymore; I don't like that situation."
- "Like, if you were going to have a life review, and we were going to have a play of it, I would be in the play, but I'd also be watching the play from the audience. And I would feel all the emotions, pain and suffering of all of the characters around me in the play. And I'd feel it as an actor in the play, and I'd also experience it as the viewer of the play."
- "Multitudinous actions or thoughts, derived from my own meanness, unkindness, or anger, caused me to feel the consequent pains of the other people. I experienced this even if at the time I had hurt someone, I had chosen to ignore how that would affect them. And I felt their pain for the full length of time they were affected by what I had done."
- "What my life had done so far to affect other people's lives, using the feeling of pure love that was surrounding me as the point of comparison. And I had done a terrible job. God, I mean it!... Looking at yourself from the point of how much love you have spread to other people is devastating."
- "I remember one particular incident... when, as a child, I yanked my little sister's Easter basket away from her, because there was a toy in it that I wanted. Yet in the review, I felt her

> feelings of disappointment and loss and rejection. What we do to other people when we act unlovingly! Everything you have done is there in the review for you to evaluate (and) when I was there in that review there was no covering up. I was the very people that I hurt and I was the very people I helped to feel good.... It is a real challenge, every day of my life, to know that when I die I am going to have to witness every single action of mine again, only this time actually feeling the effects I've had on others. It sure makes me stop and think."[35]

As we read over those statements, the words of Jesus should be echoing in our heads, "Do to others as you would have them do to you" (Luke 6:31).

These are examples of the power and spiritual insight we gain from studying NDEs. When it comes to passion, power, and purpose, love is the common element. We need to be so conscious and aware of this fact that we don't even have to think about it. It should be ingrained into our very nature.

One other powerful concept to grasp is that anything that leads us to feeling prideful about whatever purpose we are working on is a bad idea. Pride kills love, interferes with relationships, and will lead to pain. Pride is the invention of Satan. It is how he broke his relationship with God.

Jesus wants a relationship with us based on love, trust, reliance, and commitment, and most importantly, humility. Pride interferes with all of that. When we focus on humility, we are being most like Jesus.

We need to look at an underlying concept here because it's an idea that has been twisted and bastardized to suit the needs of the people trying to sell you something. That is, it is a means to manipulate you into buying something. This is the idea of *belonging*. Everyone wants to belong, right? Everyone wants to fit in and be a part of the group.

I recently watched a documentary about the Fyre Music Festival. The festival was to be held in the Bahamas, and the tickets were very expensive. The reason it got so much attention and buzz in the beginning was because of the postings of super models and celebrities and "influencers" (social media celebrities with many followers). The whole idea is related to "belonging"—*if you come to this festival, you can be around celebrities and supermodels and experience something unique and special that no one else has access to*. It's an exclusive group, but it is still a group. Many people spent thousands of dollars and were all scammed out of their money. The desire to "belong" to a group of celebrities and musicians and supermodels is what drove them to attend the festival. The idea of belonging is a powerful motivator.

Belonging to a group was a good thing in the early Christian church. They shared everything. They prayed together, ate their meals together, and supported each other. That type of belonging is exactly what Jesus has in mind for us and for the church at this very moment in time. We now have, by some estimates, thirty thousand Christian denominations. Jesus said,

> "My prayer is not for them alone. I pray also for those who will believe in me through their message, that all of them may be one, Father, just as you are in me and I am in you. May they also be in us so that the world may believe that you have sent me. I have given them the glory that you gave me, that they may be one as we are one—I in them and you in me—so that they may be brought to complete

> unity. Then the world will know that you sent me and have loved them even as you have loved me."
>
> – John 17:20–23

The point here is that going along with the crowd will get you lost in the crowd. We want to be around others when we can serve and meet their needs. We should be careful just blindly following what society and the world values because, most of the time, those "values" have very little value.

9

THE ALLURE OF BELONGING

Belonging is a good thing, especially in the church, where we are bound in love. The problem is that we are hit with messages of being happy or important or special if we go to this festival, buy this thing, eat at this place, drive this car, or live in this neighborhood. Identity becomes intertwined with things that are material and outside of ourselves.

I've seen pictures of celebrities posing with stacks of one-hundred-dollar bills. What are these people trying to tell us by posing with large bundles of money? Are they attempting to inspire envy in us? Are they seeking to get likes?

Just recently, I read about an interview with Kim Kardashian where she was describing the repercussions of her harrowing experience of being robbed at gunpoint. She said, "There was a lot of me that measured who I was by how much I had. I thought, 'Oh, I'm worth so much.' So that changed in me. And, that needed to change in me. So I'm grateful for the experience."[36] As we can clearly see, the frightening and painful experience was necessary for her to see things in the way they truly are. She changed her view as to how she measured or saw who she was. She has recently been spending her time working on using her influence to help release prisoners who have been unjustly imprisoned for prolonged periods of time. She has also decided to become a lawyer and to focus on helping others. She has found her passion. But she needed clarity, vision, and self-awareness.

How you look at yourself plays a major role when it comes to passion and purpose. We all have value because we are loved. The love that Jesus has for us can't be measured. That is the wisest way for us to measure our own value. Painful or frightening experiences can change us and help us to see ourselves in a clear light. It's a step toward maturity.

We need to look at ourselves and see if we have feelings of envy when we see a picture with a bunch of money or see pictures of celebrities at huge music festivals like Coachella. Do you get envious and yearn for these types of things? Why do you think that is? Maybe there is a void in your life. Maybe you just want to belong or feel like you are a part of a group.

When we are envious of somebody posing for a picture with a stack of money or a big house or an expensive sports car, we lose. We lose because we are telling God he made a mistake with what he gave us. We waste valuable time comparing instead of cooperating. It's more helpful to cooperate with the Holy Spirit in formulating a plan tied to your purpose. Also, we are coveting. Envy is the only sin of the seven deadly sins that is no fun.

The people who post these images of themselves with money or objects lose too. They become prideful because their own sense of value is validated in a way that is false or inauthentic. They become closer to their *inauthentic* selves. No one wins. We lose, and they lose.

Let's contrast that with a viral video taken by an onlooker and posted this past winter. It showed a homeless man in the cold standing by a sidewalk without a jacket. Then from the side you can see a gentleman walk up to the homeless man. This man takes off his jacket and puts it on the homeless man, who is so excited to receive a warm coat that he gives the kind stranger a hug. This video was posted unbeknown to the kind, giving person.[37] The point is that everyone wins in this scenario—the homeless man who received the jacket, the man who gave the jacket, even the person who took the video and posted it. Most of all, you and I win. We win because we are inspired to go and do the same. We are inspired to do something totally selfless. We are driven to get closer to our authentic selves. We all win. And if we look at this one act of kindness, we can see it is consistent with the "standard" Jesus outlined for us by his life and his words:

> Give, and it will be given to you. A good measure, pressed down, shaken together and running over, will be poured into your lap. For with the measure you use, it will be measured to you.
>
> – Luke 6:38

The idea here is vision. When we have Jesus as our standard, we are more in tune with the needs of others. Our hearts are more open to suffering. As we grow closer to our authentic selves, when we see a need we automatically do what we can to fill it. We act. We love. Vision is needed for our passion and our purpose. We need clarity of vision.

When we focus on having or belonging, the focus is on our own needs and satisfaction. The message of having or belonging is being blasted at the young and the old, males and females. It is not dependent on your job or your race or how much money you make. The message is everywhere, and we are being inundated with it on the internet, television, books, and magazines. It is everywhere we look. *We, too, can belong if we buy this. We, too, can be important if we have stacks of money.* The idea of belonging is especially powerful because it is part of being human. We evolved as humans and survived because of belonging to a group.

Everyone has an innate desire to belong. It's in our DNA. To survive, we have to belong. We must be a part of a group. We need water, food, and shelter, and we need to belong to a group. Think about all the groups you are involved in. You have a group of friends. You may have a group of co-workers you spend time with and go to lunch or happy hour on Fridays with. You have your immediate and extended family. Belonging is important.

How is this related to passion? If we stop and look around, we can see that belonging and societal ideas can interfere with the purpose of the individual. People get caught up in "groupthink." We just go along with the crowd. Everyone in the group is pursuing the same goals: larger house, nicer car, pleasurable vacations, big bank accounts, kids' college savings, flashy jewelry, fashionable clothing, retirement.

When it comes to belonging, spending time with co-workers, friends, and family—especially church family—is significant. Jesus wants us to be around other believers. His purpose and plan for our lives usually involves other believers, in cooperating with or serving them. This is part of the process.

Sometimes, especially when we are younger, we are not allowed in the group. We want to be a part of some unit, but we aren't allowed in. Psychologists tell us that one of the most difficult things to deal with as we are moving through our formative years is rejection. It impacts everything in our lives when we are in our teenage years.

Being a Rebel Can Have Value

Do you remember all the various cliques in high school? The jocks, the nerds, the cheerleaders, or the guys who wore the rock-concert T-shirts. Personally, breaking it down by *The Breakfast Club* categories, I wasn't the Emilio Estevez jock guy or the Anthony Michael Hall nerd guy. I was more the Judd Nelson criminal guy, maybe a combo of the nerd guy crossed with the criminal guy, who was dating the popular Molly Ringwald princess girl while secretly having a crush on the Ally Sheedy "basket case" girl. Whew. That was weird.

I liked the character played by Ally Sheedy because she was a rebel. I've always identified with rebels. The ones who do things not for the sake of the opinions of others but because they don't care what others think. I'm probably a little too much of a rebel. My wife and kids will attest to this. In my opinion, to escape "groupthink," we have to be rebels in one way or another. You know who was one of the biggest rebels ever? Jesus.

When we understand we have a unique purpose and that we have access to power, then we can stop rowing in circles. The problem with thinking about our unique purpose and being somewhat of a rebel is you tend to catch a lot of criticism. People in the group may disparage you if you begin to take your faith and your purpose seriously. Whenever you act in a way that is outside of the "norm" or the group, expect people to criticize you or challenge you on your beliefs.

Marketing guru Seth Godin says, "Courage is the willingness to speak the truth about what you see and to own what you say." If we can look around and really see what is going on in our own families or in the workplace, we have a chance to make the changes that have an impact. We need to be observers. But remember, this starts with looking closely at ourselves. It's easy to just sit around and look at everybody else and take shots or fling critiques at everyone.

If you've been to any museums or historical sites, you'll notice that most of the statues are of people who were doers, people who have done something of value that benefited others besides themselves. Most were not unduly influenced by the opinion of others. In fact, no paintings or marble statues have been made of the people who criticized the doers as they were going about their business getting things done. Critiquing the doers is of zero value.

When we criticize the doers, we sabotage our own journey because we ignore our individual growth and maturity. We need to move from the group of critics into the group of doers. That takes effort and sacrifice. Also, when we are in the doers group, we are too busy getting things done to sit and critique others. Being in the group of doers and going about fulfilling our purpose protects us from wasting our time and becoming critical sitters. One valuable idea that is supported by research is that *purpose protects*. We will get to that in the coming chapters.

> For God has not given us a spirit of fear and timidity, but of power, love, and self-discipline.
>
> – 2 Timothy 1:7 (NLT)

That doesn't mean we shouldn't be prepared to be criticized when we are trying to fulfill our purpose. We should not only be prepared, we should expect it. We need to have the right attitude because it is going to come.

The opinions of critics are irrelevant. The opinion of Jesus has value. The things other people think about us are none of our business. Not only that, we have a good idea from the verse in 2 Timothy above that those opinions come from a place of fear and timidity. When we choose to demean others, we are afraid to look honestly at ourselves and we are unwilling to make the changes needed to pursue passion and purpose. It's an escape hatch, an easy way out.

If God wanted us to know what everyone was thinking about us, he would have given us the ability to read minds. Think about how uncomfortable or insecure you would be if you could read everyone's mind whom you came across. You would probably be totally obsessed with every little blemish, flaw, hair out of place, or small bit of lettuce in your teeth, and you'd probably be afraid to leave your house.

> You probably wouldn't worry about what people think of you if you could know how seldom they do.
>
> – Olin Miller

Most people are too busy thinking about what other people think about *them* to spend time thinking about you and what you are wearing. So, don't worry too much about what others think about you.

Again, that isn't to say that we shouldn't listen to the people around us who know and love us. These are the people who can point out when we are getting a little out of line. We need the hall monitors in the family. We need checks and balances on our behavior because sometimes we can't see clearly. We may go overboard with anger, for example, when we parent our children. When moms and dads can police each other and they are willing to listen to each other, that makes for a stronger and happier household. We all screw up sometimes. If you are like me, you screw up all the time. Especially when it comes to parenting. My wife is very good at just looking at me in the eyes with a look that is conveying, "Ok, Einstein, you are going a little overboard. Tone it down a notch." I know that look like the back of my hand.

Strong Faith Has Been Tested

When we move toward implementing the plan God has for us and we begin to be attacked or criticized, we must rely on our faith. When it comes to passion and purpose and fulfilling God's plan for us, faith is absolutely required. Faith doesn't come easy, and we will be constantly tested with trials, troubles, and roadblocks. We are going to fail on occasion, and we are going to stumble and fall. Count on it. We should remember that whatever comes our way is either coming directly from God or he is allowing it. Blessings or trials. They are part of his plan for us. Having a good attitude and being thankful for both is our goal. It's hard to be thankful when we are going through a trial, but it is not impossible.

Sometimes it is very difficult to endure some of these trials because we may be working toward a goal that we believe is helping to bring others closer to Jesus. This is when the real trouble starts. When we focus on tasks that are for the kingdom, that is when Satan notices and that is when he gets involved. Satan takes spiritual warfare very seriously and he recognizes us as his enemy. We need to be prepared for those challenges. We need faith to carry us through.

The one truth that is hard to escape is that real growth and intimacy in our relationship with Jesus requires pain. Pain is hard to accept and fully understand, but it's absolutely required. It's true, even if we don't want it to be. Suffering, hardship, sacrifice, and pain are part of the process. We shouldn't be surprised by it. God allowed Jesus to go through pain and suffering, so we shouldn't be shocked when God allows *us* to go through pain and suffering. It's actually an honor and a privilege. Look at what Jesus says:

> God blesses you when people mock you and persecute you and lie about you and say all sorts of evil things against you because you are my followers. Be happy about it! Be very glad! For a great reward awaits you in heaven. And remember, the ancient prophets were persecuted in the same way.
>
> – Matthew 5:11–12 (NLT)

The trials, arrows, and critiques are coming. Sometimes you can see them coming, sometimes you can't, but just know that they are coming. They are required because our faith and devotion to Jesus is going to be tested. Strong faith is built persevering through the storms, trials, and troubles. Strong trees have deep roots that developed due to many storms with lots of wind. God wants our faith to be strong in the same way, deeply rooted in Him. The good news is that storms, trials, and testing allow for greater vision, clarity, and special revelations. They also allow for a richer relationship with Jesus. When it comes to love, sacrifice is part of the highest form of love. *Agape* is the word used, and it is the Greek word for sacrificial, unconditional love. Sacrifice and suffering prove our love. There is no downside to that. Jesus tells us,

> Yes, a person is a fool to store up earthly wealth but not have a rich relationship with God.
>
> – Luke 12:21 (NLT)

If we are to trust in what Jesus is telling us, we will typically need to go in the opposite direction of the crowd. We should be a little on the rebel side and not too enamored with what the groups around us value. When we get criticized or ridiculed, we can look to Jesus for inspiration. He didn't care about what other people thought. He focused on his passion (God's will) and his purpose. He came to bring people to the knowledge of the truth. He even called himself "the truth."

> Jesus answered, "I am the way and the truth and the life. No one comes to the Father except through me."
>
> – John 14:6

A Relationship That Inspires

Our sense of passion, purpose and belonging is intimately related to our relationship with Jesus and what he offers us—a deal we can't get anywhere else no matter how hard we try. When we accept his offer of salvation, sealed for us by his work on the cross, our sins are forgiven, we have a *purpose* for living, and we have a home in heaven. Notice that when it comes to purpose, that is *our* responsibility. We should be fully aware that we will be held accountable to discover and fulfill our purpose. That is why finding our passion is critical. But there is more to it than that. When we are looking for inspiration that has real value, he is the leader we want to look to. Let's go back to the quote in the first chapter:

> Great leaders are able to inspire people to act. Those who are able to inspire, give people a sense of purpose or belonging that has little to do with any external incentive or benefit to be gained. Those who truly lead are able to create a following of people who act not because they were swayed, but because they were inspired. Those who are able to inspire will create a following of people—supporters, voters, customer, workers—who act for the

good of the whole not because they have to, but because they want to.[38]

If we read that again within the context of following Jesus, we are inspired to act. When we grow in intimacy with him, it impacts everything about our very nature. It's a relationship based on love, and the closer we get to Jesus, the more love we have at our disposal. Love is a huge source of power. Love is an action, and it involves movement and energy. But that is not all. We also belong. We belong to a family of believers, and that belonging, or membership, never ends and is never revoked. It lasts for eternity. The benefits of that membership are beyond our wildest dreams or even the most vivid imaginations.

You can recognize the people who belong to the family of believers and have the love of Jesus in them just by their demeanor. You can also see people who are slaves to anger and bitterness by their attitude. When we are inspired to acquire, there is no love being gained. There is no energy. How much love can you get from a stack of hundreds? Remember the movie *It's All about the Benjamins*? You have to ask yourself a question: *Is that really true? Is it really all about the Benjamins?* The answer to that question has the potential to change your life and, more importantly, your eternity.

The more your relationship with Jesus grows, the easier it is to see people who are joyful and full of love. We get vision and clarity, purpose and power. Think about someone who values himself or herself so little that they have to show you or tell you about the "things" they have acquired to validate themselves. They pose with money or objects to signify their worth. All these things rust and fade. Objects or money lead us to our false selves.

When we begin to understand that our real value is in knowing and loving Jesus, then objects and stacks of money mean absolutely nothing. Plus, with our renewed vision and clarity, it is easier to see anger, bitterness, or insecurity in ourselves and in others. We need this vision. We need this clarity. It helps us find our passion and our purpose.

Once we can accept Jesus and we recognize and appreciate the breadth and depth of his love, that is when we understand that not only does he belong to us, more importantly, we belong to Him. It's a two-way street. That relationship brings love and power. We begin to see our value, our passion, and our authentic purpose. When you pursue your passion and purpose in the power of the Holy Spirit, you have access to supernatural power and energy. In addition, you have the hope of the Bible—eager expectation. You know you have a home in heaven waiting for you no matter what happens while pursuing your purpose. That should bring everyone great joy and confidence. It's what got the apostle Paul through all his trials, waves, and troubles.

> For our light and momentary troubles are achieving for us an eternal glory that far outweighs them all.
>
> – 2 Corinthians 4:17

I don't know about you, but my troubles don't seem to be very light or momentary but heavy, hard, and unbearable, and they last way too long. We will have tribulations and trials, but what matters is that we stick to the plan and keep trusting God.

> In all my prayers for all of you, I always pray with joy because of your partnership in the gospel from the first day until now, being confident of this, that he who began a good work in you will carry it on to completion until the day of Christ Jesus.
>
> – Philippians 1:4–6 (NLT)

This is a promise. God will carry the good work in you to completion. We must believe and trust. One of my favorite sayings is "perfection is a road, it's not a destination." That is a good line to remember when we seek authenticity. We may not get there during this life. The journey to true authenticity is what makes life exciting, fun, mesmerizing, challenging, fascinating, joyful, fulfilling, and totally worthwhile. There are no promises in the Bible that suggest the task is easy. That is why we need passion and power. Those will help get us through the tough times while focusing on our purpose.

10

THE ELEMENTS OF PASSION

As we dive into the elements of passion, we can start to identify some clearly associated characteristics. Is it evident in our behavior that we are living a life driven by passion? How are we spending our time? How about our money? What are the markers of a life driven by passion and purpose? Let's start by looking at a list of the most common characteristics of passion:

Excitement (this tends to bring energy)	Determination
Positive attitude	Perseverance
Focus	Resilience
Infectious enthusiasm	Servant's heart
Self-motivation	Goal-directed behavior

Let's look at some of these characteristics of passion one at a time. Let's start with a biggie: excitement. Are you excited about anything you are doing in your life? Is there any excitement in the activities you are pursuing? Most people are living the "Wednesday is hump day, working for the weekend" type of lifestyle. They are trying to escape work so they can do the things they enjoy on the weekend. I see it every day in people with minor ailments who are just looking for a week-long excuse to miss work. I'm not faulting or blaming them; they are just looking for a reason to avoid a job that they hate and have no excitement in. It makes perfect sense. That's why I give day-off slips like I am throwing confetti from a parade float. Of course, the days off are within reason. We don't give a month off for a sore throat. But if my patients don't work for me, I'm generous with days off.

When are you excited or motivated? Do those emotions only come around when you are leaving on vacation? Ask yourself, *What activities make me the most excited?* Pay attention to what you are talking about— this is an important clue. Are there things you talk about with a tone of excitement or buzz? *That* is where passion lies.

We all have been given a heart for something, a passion or interest in something. It is God-given, and it is there. If you have no excitement in your life, you may have a dormant gift or passion that is buried deep in your heart. Have you discovered it?

You can find many clues to your own innate passion. If you know what your unique passion is, have you spent any time, effort, or energy cultivating it? Are you determined to develop your passion? It won't grow and develop by itself. Effort is required.

How about a positive attitude? Do you feel good about the passion you are pursuing? What about focus? Determination and focus are strong indicators you are heading in the right direction. Positive attitude, determination, and focus are a powerful trifecta that bring energy and power and will make you more effective when pursuing passion and purpose.

The good news is that putting time and effort into growing and developing your passion is enjoyable. That by itself is a valuable clue. Passion is important. It's the essence of the authentic you. Start paying attention to your conversations. Take note of what you are thinking and talking about most. When it comes to passion, you can't avoid talking about it. This is also helpful in figuring out if you are thinking and talking about passions that are obsessive, self-serving, or merely entertainment.

This is the time for tough questions. Some examples include, *Am I the only one benefiting from this?* or the ever-popular *Am I doing this so I can impress other people or inspire envy in others?* Then there is the sneaky and subconscious, *Am I doing this to acquire things or a lifestyle that other people have?* Passion driven by envy that gratifies the flesh or the inauthentic self has little value. That is why comparing ourselves to other people never leads to anything truly worthwhile.

Envy is an insult to God. We're telling him that he made a mistake with what he gave us. God doesn't make mistakes; we do. Ignoring our passion and purpose is a prime example.

We should also remember that our passion is an important facet of who we were created to be. When linked to purpose, we are engaging in an activity closest to what God had in mind when he created us. God is our loving Father, and the plan and picture he has in mind for our lives and for our purpose is, without a doubt, the best plan.

Living with passion and energy is what God has in mind for each of us. It leads to joy, peace, and a sense of fulfillment. When you are doing what you love to do and what you were created to do, this brings peace and joy. Those are two critical components of the spiritual fruit:

> So I say, walk by the Spirit, and you will not gratify the desires of the flesh. For the flesh desires what is contrary to the Spirit, and the Spirit what is contrary to the flesh. They are in conflict with each other, so that you are not to do whatever you want. But if you are led by the Spirit, you are not under the law. The acts of the flesh are obvious: sexual immorality, impurity and debauchery; idolatry and witchcraft; hatred, discord, jealousy, fits of rage, selfish ambition, dissensions, factions and envy; drunkenness, orgies, and the like. I warn you, as I did before, that those who live like this will not inherit the kingdom of God. But the fruit of the Spirit is, joy, peace, forbearance, kindness, goodness, faithfulness, gentleness and self-control. Against such things there is no law. Those who belong to Christ Jesus have crucified the flesh with its passions and desires. Since we live by the Spirit, let us keep in step with the Spirit. Let us not become conceited, provoking and envying each other.
>
> – Galatians 5:16–26

Notice how envy is of the flesh. It is of no value, and like we said earlier, envy is the one deadly sin that is no fun at all. It gnaws on your soul and steals your joy. The happiest people on the planet are those who are developing careers or are working in a job that reflects their passion. They have mastered the principle of being content with what they have been given. They are overwhelmingly grateful for their gifts, passion, and purpose. They have true joy. They don't *have to* go to work, they *get to* go to work.

Our passion resides in the spirit. People who have joy at work are using all the skills and gifts they were given in a way that benefits not only themselves but others as well. Near-death experiences point out the value of these dormant gifts:

> In examining the lives of the NDErs we have met in this chapter, do you not feel that all of them, to various degrees, have been aided to live more authentic lives, much more in keeping with their previously dormant gifts and propensities, and emboldened to throw off the social shackles, where necessary, that previously constrained them?39

Authenticity in the context of NDEs and in the context of what God had in mind means finding and developing your "gifts and propensities."

Look for the Buzz

Let's look at another element of passion, *infectious enthusiasm*. Do people around you become energized when you are talking about your passion? Is there energy or buzz or electricity around when you are discussing or engaging in your passion? This is a huge clue.

It is our responsibility to discover our passion. It is on us. We can choose to find excitement, focus, and determination, or we can ignore it. Infectious enthusiasm in our lives is an indicator that we are engaging in activities clearly driven by passion. We should find these attributes because it's our responsibility. If you are not spending any time on this effort, don't be surprised if you are lethargic, unfulfilled, or you feel weak. We shouldn't be surprised, because passion is empowering. When we ignore it, we ignore power.

We will be held accountable for our willingness to discover our gifts and talents. We'll be asked about how we used these gifts to implement and fulfill our purpose. We are to use these gifts in service to others. That's why a servant's heart is one of the elements. These gifts are not meant to be kept for ourselves or to be used simply for our own benefit.

There are many people who are living their lives in a rubber raft in the middle of the ocean. Some have a motor but are puttering around in circles. Others have a direction or a compass but have no motor and no energy or passion to propel them toward their destination.

I just read an article about a politician who has no rudder; he simply reacts. He says things that he thinks people want to hear. He does things, waits for a reaction, and then adjusts his plan according to what he thinks people want him to do. That isn't leadership or effective governance.

There is an old saying among NFL coaches: "If you listen too much to what the fans say, you will soon be sitting in the bleachers with them." And if you are a mother or a father, you are the coach of your team. You are responsible for preparing the team for this life and teaching them important life principles to help them survive.

The Source of Our Positive Attitude

Getting back to our list, can we see a positive attitude within ourselves? Most people can look at themselves and know instantly if they're a positive or negative person. It's the glass-half-empty or the glass-half-full image we are all aware of. If you ever have a negative thought about your value, or if you feel worthless or hopeless, those thoughts or ideas are *never* from God. God is always positive, and Jesus is continuously picking people up and making them feel good about themselves.

> I tell you, my friends, do not be afraid of those who kill the body and after that can do no more. But I will show you whom you should fear: Fear him who, after your body has been killed, has authority to throw you into hell. Yes, I tell you, fear him. Are not five sparrows sold for two pennies? Yet not one of them is forgotten by God. Indeed, the very hairs of your head are all numbered. Don't be afraid; you are worth more than many sparrows.
>
> – Luke 12:4–7

Here Jesus is telling us we have value and worth. Plus, we know we are valuable because he gave his life for us. If we have value and worth, then we should be approaching life with a positive attitude. We know we have value, and we know our destiny. Why be miserable or negative?

Just the other day, I was discussing anxiety, stress and troubles with a friend and I asked, "If I gave you a million dollars right now, would that solve your problems?" He said, "Yes, yes, it would." I responded, "Then your problems are not very big."

If we think about it, all of us—every single one of us—have one big problem: eternity. If we believe we are all spirits and that our spirits are immortal, where we spend eternity is a big issue because eternity lasts forever. Salvation and a relationship with Jesus are the only way to solve our biggest problem. Every other problem we have compared to this one is tiny.

We know that people with depression feel worthless, hopeless, or helpless. All those feelings are not consistent with true authenticity. This doesn't apply to people with a diagnosis of true clinical depression. I have been around plenty of people with true chemical imbalance depression, and those people are suffering. I am speaking about people with low self-esteem who feel like they are worthless or helpless, the ones who tell themselves or have been told their whole lives that they are no good or have no value. This type of background noise is of no benefit and undermines the effort to discover our passion.

The wisest, most eye-opening, brightest epiphany you can incorporate into your life is that the most valuable opinion is that of Jesus. His opinion is the most valid, and he says we have value. When it comes to our view of ourselves, choose to listen to Jesus. He has already solved our biggest problem. The wisest decision you will ever make in your life is to put your relationship with him at the center of your life. The second wisest thing to do is value his opinion. He's never said anything stupid, and he is still guiding us if we will allow him to. We know for a fact that we aren't worthless. The cross and the love of Jesus prove that. He just said it in the above verse too. We know that we have hope. We have the hope of the Bible. In the Greek, the hope of the Bible is *eager expectation*. He tells us,

> My father's house has many rooms; if that were not so, would I have told you that I am going there to prepare a place for you? And if I go and prepare a place for you, I will come back and take you to be with me that you also may be where I am.
>
> – John 14:2–3

Let me give you an illustration.

Let's say it's Friday afternoon, and you have gone to happy hour with some co-workers to celebrate Cinco de Mayo because, in the United States, this historic date was critical to our history. We know this because we see many people packing Mexican restaurants all over the country on this day. You have a couple of margaritas, and you and your co-workers are enjoying yourselves. You notice it is getting a little late and your significant other is at home with the kids. You had promised to pick up take-out for the family, and you get some texts mentioning something about "We're hungry. Where are you?" Uh oh. You get the bags of food you ordered and get into your car. (Now, looking back, you should have used Uber.) You are rushing to get home, and as you are crossing an intersection, you accidentally clip the back tire of a purple bike with yellow streamers coming from the handlebars being ridden by an eighty-year-old man. (I have no idea why there are yellow streamers. It's my vision, so I choose the streamer color.)

Now we cut to the scene where you are in the county lock up. Never mind that you stopped to render aid and helped the paramedics stabilize this man's broken leg. The things that this man said about your mother while you were trying to help him are still echoing in your head. "How could he possibly know anything about my mom?" you keep asking yourself.

You are in an orange or yellow prison jumpsuit, whichever you prefer. This part is all you. You have your ankles shackled, and you are shuffling into the courtroom. God is sitting behind the bench. You recognize him, and he recognizes you. You look over, and you see Jesus. He is defending you. He smiles with a loving smile because he recognizes you. He motions for you to come over and sit next to him. If you can put yourself into this situation, you know that if you walked into that courtroom in this scenario, you would be scared to death. No one should feel comfortable in this type of scenario.

How much better would you feel if your best friend, who you have known for years, who loves you and you love him too, were defending you? Would you feel more comfortable and less afraid? Of course you would! Not only that, based on your long-term close relationship and friendship, you know that he would do everything he could to get you a pardon. The good news is that he already has. That's why the gospel is called the *good news*.

I have some friends who are attorneys. I know that if I walked into a courtroom, I would feel much better if one of them was defending me and the other was the judge in the case.

Our relationship with God and Jesus is on us. It is totally dependent on how much time and effort we are willing to put into it. Jesus wants to be your defense attorney more than you do. God wants you in his court more than you do.

We know that we have worth, we have hope, and we aren't helpless. We have access to power. There are multiple sources of power, and we will get to those in the coming chapters. We have the full knowledge of our worth because Jesus told us we have worth. We have courage because Jesus told us not to be afraid. So with all this, why be negative? Why not be positive and have confidence? A positive attitude is infectious. If we want to be leaders in our own families, there is nothing more helpful than keeping a positive outlook, especially when things don't go our way. We should look at tough circumstances as an opportunity—an opportunity for adventure, growth, wisdom, clarity, and knowledge. It's a big wave, but it is also an opportunity for a fun ride.

This brings me to another story. This one involves Thomas Edison. I read my first biography about him when I was ten.

> At around 5:30 in the evening on Dec. 10, 1914, a massive explosion erupted in West Orange, New Jersey. Ten buildings in legendary inventor Thomas Edison's plant, which made up more than half of the site, were engulfed in

flames. Between six and eight fire departments rushed to the scene, but the chemical-fueled inferno was too powerful to put out quickly. According to a 1961 *Reader's Digest* article by Edison's son Charles, Edison calmly walked over to him as he watched the fire destroy his dad's work. In a childlike voice, Edison told his 24-year-old son, "Go get your mother and all her friends. They'll never see a fire like this again." When Charles objected, Edison said, "It's all right. We've just got rid of a lot of rubbish."

Later, at the scene of the blaze, Edison was quoted in *The New York Times* as saying, "Although I am over 67 years old, I'll start all over again tomorrow." He told the reporter that he was exhausted from remaining at the scene until the chaos was under control, but he stuck to his word and immediately began rebuilding the next morning without firing any of his employees. Was there any other viable response? In the new book, *The Obstacle Is the Way: The Timeless Art of Turning Trials into Triumph*, author Ryan Holiday says there wasn't. Sure, Edison could have wept, yelled in anger, or locked himself in his house in a state of depression. But instead, he put on a smile and told his son to enjoy the spectacle.[40]

This whole story is about perspective and perseverance. How do you see circumstances and challenges when they arise? Can you see them as opportunities? Edison lost reams and reams of notes and data on his experiments. He just accepted the fact that he would be starting over—at age sixty-seven. He did a lot of productive work into his eighties.

Nothing takes the air out of a room quicker than negativity and pessimism. One thing that is clear is that when we are pursuing our purpose or a goal, if we don't strongly believe in what we are doing, we might as well not spend time or energy. We should believe that what we are engaging in is exactly what we were created to do.

One powerful and useful idea to keep coming back to is that *our purpose is bigger than our fears, circumstances, trials, and failures.* This purpose is built on the framework of our authentic selves. It is bigger than our own selfish pursuits. We were created to do things that are to benefit the world.

Sometimes we get caught up in scale. What can I do? I am just one person. Think about the one act of kindness that gentleman in the viral video displayed by giving someone his coat. Thousands and thousands of people saw that video. It's a beautiful, selfless act made more beautiful because the Good Samaritan had no idea anyone was watching. Think about how he inspired others to act in kindness. Every single one of us is capable of an act of kindness like that one. In the movie *The Shack*, there is a line: "One act of kindness can change the world."

As I am writing this, Senator John McCain has just died. There are memorial services and ceremonies being planned and news shows talking about his life. He had a quote when he was close to the end of his life: "It was a good ride." It reminded me of what Paul Newman told a close friend at the end of his life: "It was one helluva ride." Both these men did great things for others, Paul Newman with all his charity work, and John McCain with all his service to our country, especially for veterans. Both men spent their lives living in the power of their passion and fulfilling their purpose. The focus of that power, passion, and concern was *service*—serving others. At the end of their lives, they had a sense of satisfaction, peace, and comfort knowing that though they had ups and downs, they each accomplished big things more important than themselves. Those are two examples of people who inspire.

Every Path Has Obstacles

When we have perseverance and a positive attitude, this gives us perspective. We can't have a positive attitude unless we have access to our passion. We know that whatever we are engaged in, it is who we were created to be. We have infectious enthusiasm, and we don't get discouraged by setbacks, roadblocks, or obstacles.

One useful indicator of your pursuit of your unique purpose is the ease with which you are getting to your goal. If it's easy, be careful. Terry Goodkind says, "If the road is easy, you're likely going the wrong way." Or here is another one: "If the path you are on has no obstacles, it probably doesn't go anywhere."

I am not a big fan of cheesy little quotes or cute little euphemisms. These are straight-up warnings, and one important distinction needs to be made. When I mentioned looking for your unique passion and gifts, I did say it was something that is easy for you. What I mean is that it is something you do that comes naturally, like art, singing, or playing a musical instrument. When I am talking about purpose, it is in the framework of using these gifts for an overall goal. Using that God-given skill is the easy part. Completing a purpose or goal in the service of others or one that includes bringing others to Jesus is when things become difficult. Jesus said,

> I have told you these things, so that in me you may have peace. In this world you will have trouble. But take heart! I have overcome the world.
>
> – John 16:33

Peace isn't free, and it isn't cheap. Peace is hard to come by because of the endurance and perseverance required for overcoming stressful or trying circumstances. Notice that Jesus says, "Take heart." When we are doing something that has value and is for the kingdom, we are going to have to take our hearts with us. It must come from passion.

When we can fully understand that God is more interested in our character and maturity, this gives us confidence, perseverance, and a positive attitude. We know that whatever we are going through, it is in our best interest, even if it is painful or difficult. The bottom line is that we know that he loves us and wants what's best for us. That is how we learn to trust and depend on him. It is the attitude of being "poor in spirit." It is the opposite of pride and is the type of attitude that he blesses most.

When we pursue wealth or material things, we move away from a dependence on God. Jesus tells us in the parable of the sower that wealth can be a deceiver:

> The seed falling among the thorns refers to someone who hears the word, but the worries of this life and the deceitfulness of wealth choke the word, making it unfruitful.
>
> – Matthew 13:22

Notice what is happening. When we focus on the worries of this life, it "chokes the word." When we fall for the "deceitfulness of wealth," that also chokes the word. We know there is plenty of "word choking" going on in this country because statistics tell us that many people are ignoring the Word. What do we do? We can start good habits like reading and studying the Bible. Start a routine.

We all have certain routines when we go about our jobs, like parking in a certain space or arranging things on our desks exactly the same way or even putting our lunch and snacks in a certain place in the breakroom. Why go through the trouble of these routines? Isn't it really about control? If you consider your morning routines or habits, they are things you have control over.

We live in a world where you feel you must provide for your family, perform at work, pay your bills, make sure the kid in college has everything they need, and so on. Plates are spinning on poles, and you are holding all of them up. If you are a mom with young kids, you have a different set of plates spinning—dirty diapers, feeding and clothing small children who can't do anything for themselves, play dates, and the list goes on. Even if you are single and employed, there are still many things you are responsible for at work and at home. The best advice for establishing some measure of order, control, and sanity is to start with a quiet time with God every morning. Give some time to him and spend time growing in your relationship with Jesus. Seek intimacy with Jesus. It's a source of power, love, and energy available to us that sets the tone for the day and gives you the focus you need to keep those plates from crashing down around you.

When we learn to depend on God for guidance and we are confident that he will look out for us in our most trying circumstances, this brings order, reduced stress, comfort, and in the end, peace. He yearns for us to spend time with him. He wants the first and best part of our day. In view of our blessings and the grace bestowed on us, he deserves it.

When we can accept that God wants us to grow in maturity and that sometimes this requires trouble, trials, pain, and suffering, then we have power. We can see things more clearly.

Stop and take some time to examine your own life. Where can you see the biggest strides toward growing in maturity, clarity and wisdom? Look for times when you overcame obstacles or endured trials. It's the ol' "what doesn't kill me makes me stronger" idea. Bet you ten bucks that most of the times you grew in your spiritual life and grew in maturity were after a painful experience, some trying circumstance. Personally, I have never had any leaps of growth in my spiritual life and in maturity while lying on a beach sipping a margarita. I know this because I keep trying and it doesn't work.

11

THE DRIVE TO THRIVE

We have looked at excitement and determination, a positive attitude, perseverance, focus, resilience, and infectious enthusiasm. Here is our list again for another quick review.

Excitement (this tends to bring energy)	Determination
Positive attitude	Perseverance
Focus	Resilience
Infectious enthusiasm	Servant's heart
Self-motivation	Goal-directed behavior

The next ideas that I want to touch on involve self-motivation and goal-directed behavior, two critical components of passion. I can confidently say that if these elements are missing, it is likely that passion is missing also. Goal-directed behavior is one key to the drive and perseverance you need to fulfill your purpose, but another necessary step is a clear definition of the goal itself. If you have no goals, there is evidence to suggest that you are less satisfied. There aren't large groups of studies available on goal setting, so we are at a bit of a disadvantage, however, one study looking at Harvard graduates found that 84 percent of students who were set for graduation had not set any goals prior to graduation.[41] We also know that 80 percent of New Year's resolutions (goals) are abandoned by mid-February:

> Making a New Year's resolution is a great way to make a positive change in your life, whether it's going to the gym, waking up earlier, or saving your money. But, it's very rare to keep your resolutions for the whole year. According to U.S. News, approximately 80% of resolutions fail by the second week of February, so the odds are against you.[42]

Wow. This tells us that a huge majority of people are giving up in only *six weeks*. That means no perseverance, determination, focus, or resilience. Critics will say, "Yeah, but those New Year's resolutions have to do mostly with losing weight. Everyone knows how hard that can be." I'll leave the weight-loss idea alone for right now because that is something I have studied and have experience with. But let's look a little closer and focus on passion, purpose, and energy.

Let's consider what the most common New Year's resolutions are and see if we can decipher an explanation as to why there is so much failure.

One simple suggestion would be to try to break down a larger goal into simple, attainable targets. For example, when it comes to exercise, we can set goals that are realistic and attainable within the framework of our current fitness level.

This is from an NBC news report.43 These numbers are derived from Google searches, so there is power in this data. These are the most common things people are looking to do to improve their lives.

According to the data pulled from Google by iQuanti, these are the most popular New Year's resolutions. My comments follow each one:

1. Get Healthy: 62,776,640 searches.

This is too broad and too general. A better idea would be to choose a goal like "lose 10 pounds." Then give yourself a deadline—that goes along with being specific. "Lose ten pounds by April 15." With this goal, you pay your taxes, and you feel good about losing the weight, so you give yourself a nice celebratory dinner. Remember, with any new goal, write it down, write it down, write it down. You are 50 percent more likely to achieve a written goal. That's another big reason to start a spiritual journal.

2. Get Organized: 33,230,420 searches.

Again, we should be specific. We can say "clean out and organize my office desk by January 31." This is something that is attainable and has a deadline. If we can choose attainable and reasonable goals, we can get in the habit of setting goals and reaching them.

3. Live Life to the Fullest: 18,970,210 searches.

The problem with this one is that my "full life" may be way different than yours. Again, this one is too broad and not specific enough. Maybe we should say, "Find my passion." Look at your life and how you spend your time and money. That will give you a clearer picture of what is important to you at this moment in time. It is an accurate snapshot of where you are on the "living life to the fullest" goal.

4. Learn New Hobbies: 17,438,670 searches.

This goal is helpful for exploring your passions. These are things you have thought about but never really got around to doing, like learning how to play an instrument or taking a cooking class. You can learn how to prepare food that is healthier. There are so many things you can do. The whole idea is to dive in and try something new.

5. Spend Less/Save More: 15,905,290 searches.

Everyone should be looking at their spending habits and try to improve their finances. This should involve picking a specific goal like "pay off the Visa card by next January." This is not a finance book, but I know from experience you can never go wrong paying off debt.

6. Travel: 5,964,130 searches.

There have been studies to show that you get more satisfaction and happiness from exploring a new location or having a new experience than from buying something that is material, like a new car. When you buy something new, the excitement you get wears off quickly, so you start looking for the next thing to buy to give you the same kind of adrenaline rush. When you invest in new experiences, you don't need to spend large amounts of money. You can take short trips close to home. As I have mentioned, the stories my family and I like to share about our trips usually involve something that went wrong on the trip, some misadventure.

7. Read More: 4,746,560 searches.

This goal has real value. You either can be entertained by a fictional adventure, or with nonfiction, you can learn something new or valuable to help you see the world a little differently. Knowledge is power.

Grand Total: 159,031,920

If we look at the above numbers, we know there is plenty of evidence showing that people either do not reach their goals or do not take any action.

NFL running back Emmitt Smith said in his Hall of Fame induction speech, "It's only a dream until you write it down, and then it becomes a goal."

We know from the Harvard Study on goal setting that most successful people who accomplished something of significance wrote down their goals. They also had an idea of how to execute the plan and complete the mission. Do you see the correlation between the pervasive lack of energy we see and the absence of clearly identifiable and definable goals? Specifically, goals that are written down and attached to a plan? What it comes down to is not the pursuit of happiness but the happiness of pursuit.

Passions or Wishes?

Why do you think there is such a high rate of failure when it comes to choosing a goal and successfully carrying it out to completion? Why do so many people give up on their resolutions within six weeks? These statistics can be depressing if you just look at them at face value, but what if we dig a little deeper? Let's look at this list of the common searches people are seeking to do as far as New Year's resolutions.

1. Get Healthy
2. Get Organized
3. Live Life to the Fullest
4. Learn New Hobbies

5. Spend Less, Save More
6. Travel
7. Read More

Now, if we look at any of these goals, where is the passion? Let's review the elements of passion: excitement, infectious enthusiasm, determination, resilience, focus, self-motivation, positive attitude, and goal-directed behavior. And don't forget servant's heart. If we look at these goals, they can all be helpful when we discover our passion and pursue purpose. But when it comes to these most common New Year's resolutions, they are focused on the self. These aren't bad ideas. They are good ideas when we see ourselves as instruments. When we seek passion and purpose, these goals can be helpful in getting us there. *Get Healthy* (exercise) can help. *Read more* helps with discovering and developing passion. Knowledge is useful. *Learn new hobbies* can help with exploring our unique passions. *Travel.* Traveling offers new experiences. All these goals help with passion. *Get organized.* This can help with reaching goals associated with our passion. *Spend less, save more.* That can help if we are going to need money for learning about our purpose and developing our passion.

The reason people give up and have no resilience, focus, or determination when pursuing these goals is that there is no passion, no linkage with our identity. There is no "can't not" in any of these goals. If we look at the above list, we see that these are more like wishes. "I wish I could travel more or get healthy or get organized." They leave themselves a way out, a built-in excuse that gives them a path to giving up. Passion is different. There is no escape hatch. It's a "can't not" activity. It is also an "only I" activity. We will get to that a little later. These "wishes" may not be passions, but they can be tools to use in discovering our passion and our purpose.

When it comes to passion and purpose, we should remember our assignment of energy and our assignment of love. In true and authentic passion, our concern is the benefit or service to others. We are going through these ideas so that we can begin to see the unique identifying characteristics that differentiate resolutions, passion, and purpose.

As we are starting to see the differences between resolutions, goals, and passion, what do we do? Start with passion. Find that first. Passion will energize and drive our lives toward our purpose. Passion has power—innate, supernatural power.

Goal setting is just one part of passion and the pursuit of our purpose. When we have a better understanding of our passion, we will see the goal-directed behavior and self-motivation in our lives. When we can see those two characteristics combined with the other elements of passion, we know that we can set the goals we need to help us pursue and implement our purpose.

We shouldn't ignore excitement, infectious enthusiasm, positive attitude, focus, and resilience. These should all be there before we can label a pursuit as an authentic passion. We need these because they are critically important when we set goals related to purpose.

Most self-help books talk about goal setting first. Therein lies the problem. Just like New Year's resolutions, starting with goal setting is a setup for failure. Look at the raw data. We can see that it's true.

Passion Brings Goal Management

Goal setting is a tool. But we need the self-motivation and goal-directed behavior first. We need the excitement, emotion, and the infectious enthusiasm also. We need focus and resilience as well. If not, we don't have the power or the energy to drive us through the inevitable setbacks and obstacles, which are actually a sign that we are headed in the right direction. Is that a strange concept or what?

Be honest. How many times have you seen excitement, positive attitude, energy, focus, determination, and infectious enthusiasm in anyone making a New Year's resolution list? What about when *you* have made a New Year's resolution? Most of the time we have a certain amount of dread or listlessness about it. No emotion, excitement, or energy. Not only that, we want to get it over with, like losing weight fast. If it involves passion, then *quick*, *fast*, and *in a hurry* are not part of the plan. If there is genuine passion involved linked to purpose, we enjoy the process. We want it to last.

When we are closer to discovering our passion and we can see the characteristics of that passion in our lives, we can use goal setting as a tool to help us on our way. Here are some of the benefits of goal setting (*after* we have discovered our passion):

1. Provides direction—remember the rubber dinghy and rowing in circles?
2. Clarity of focus—clarity of focus helps to maintain that direction.
3. Sense of control or power—remember that if there is no sense of control, you feel powerless at work and powerless in life. When you set a goal, you are in control. You decide how you are going to go about reaching that goal, including the plan for implementation.
4. Gives energy and motivation—you know exactly where you are headed, so you are motivated.
5. Gives you a sense of purpose—you know you aren't wasting time. You feel confident and assured.
6. Brings a sense of satisfaction and fulfillment when you achieve a goal. Your self-confidence soars because you

> focused on the goal and you reached that goal. You feel confident and powerful, able to reach just about anything you truly want to achieve.

There are no studies that I could find that show that most Americans have goals of any kind, much less one that is written down, with a plan to implement and realize that vision. That's not surprising. Just ask your own individual tribes. Ask your family and friends. Take an informal survey. This book was written because of one simple question, "What is your passion?" Try that experiment.

Keep in mind the distinction between harmonious and obsessive passions. There are plenty of obsessive passions around. Those are ubiquitous. Ever hear of *Fortnite*? A recent survey showed that eighty million people are playing that game.[44] Now let's be clear. I'm not saying that video games are evil; I even play them on occasion. What I am saying is that if they become obsessive and addictive, that is when the problems begin. There is a distinction to be made between obsessive and harmonious passions.

Once we have discovered and nurtured our passion, the resultant behavior involves setting goals as we go about pursuing our purpose. Look at this excerpt from an article about optimism and quality of life:

> In particular, both optimism and goal adjustment can be expected to relate to an adaptive management of critical life circumstances and personal goals. Such goals might involve, for instance, recovery from a serious disease or attainment of broader life goals, such as establishing a successful career and building a family. Why are goals important for understanding differences in quality of life? First, it is noteworthy that some researchers have almost

> equated successful goal management with quality of life. For example, Emerson has described quality of life as the satisfaction of individuals' values, goals, and needs through the *actualization of their abilities or lifestyle.* In addition, goals are seen as central building blocks of human development because they *structure and direct behavior into particular pathways.*[45]

Notice the action that is involved in those last lines. There is an actualization or realization of our abilities and then a direction of behavior onto particular pathways. Also be aware that we are discussing principles of goal management, not goal setting. In other words, goal setting is being taken for granted because passion provides the goals. They come automatically and therefore need to be managed.

From this article, we can see that *goal management* brings

1. Quality of life
2. Actualization of our abilities
3. Building of our character
4. Direction of our behavior onto a clear path

We can see that passion is associated with the actualization of our abilities. It enhances our quality of life and delineates our direction, all of which are hugely beneficial to our sense of well-being and happiness.

There is a clear distinction between happiness and joy. We should be focused on joy because that is part of our authenticity, our spiritual selves. Happiness involves circumstances, and those are constantly changing. Joy is different. It is intimately associated with our spiritual selves and our relationship to Jesus. Jesus said,

> As the Father has loved me, so have I loved you. Now remain in my love. If you keep my commands, you will remain in my love, just as I have kept my Father's commands and remain in his love. I have told you this so that my joy may be in you and that your joy may be complete. My command is this: Love each other as I have loved you. Greater love has no one than this: to lay down one's life for one's friends. You are my friends if you do what I command.
>
> – John 15:9–14

We never go wrong when we follow the advice of Jesus. True wisdom is living our lives in a way that mirrors him. We need to activate our mirror neurons. When we remain in his love and keep his commands, this leads to joy. Not only joy but joy that is complete. When we love one another and serve each other, we remain in his love. We remain in the Father's love.

When he talks about laying down our lives, he is talking about what he did for us, but it is also a challenge for every one of us. When we lay down our lives and devote ourselves to him and the gospel, we are acting in a way that is pleasing to him. "There is no greater love than this." This brings power, love, energy, and joy.

Some people may ask, "Look, this is all great, but what does this have to do with energy and goal setting and me being happy. Dude, get to the point."

The whole point and essence of who we are is wrapped up in John 15:9–14. When you discover your passion first and then set goals that are intimately tied to and uniquely driven by what that verse reveals, there is no downside, no negatives, no loss. You will always come out on the positive side of the balance sheet.

If you can set goals within the framework of your passion while looking for direction from Jesus, you know that you are heading in the right direction. Ask yourself, *Does this goal help me with any of the ideas listed below?*

1. Remain in the love of Jesus
2. Keep Jesus's commands
3. Have the joy of Jesus in me
4. Make my joy complete
5. Love other people the way Jesus has loved me
6. Serve other people the way Jesus served others
7. Lay my life down for Jesus
8. Be a true friend of Jesus

If you can answer yes to any *one* of these principles, you know you are headed in the right direction. These are just guidelines. Your goal doesn't have to fulfill all or even most of these ideas. If there is even one being fulfilled, there is true value in pursuing that goal, especially if passion is involved.

This is critically important when we begin to find and develop our passion and seek the purpose God has in mind for us. Remember that our passion is God given, and so is our purpose. We know that everything on the list above pleases God and is within his plan for every single one of us.

When pursuing our unique passion and purpose, we need to figure out the *why*. Simply ask yourself the question *Why am I doing this?* The answer to this one question will answer a lot of others. When you have passion and authenticity, you know your why and you have a conviction as to the value and worth of your purpose. You know exactly why you are pursuing a goal. This helps with resilience, direction, and determination.

It doesn't necessarily equate with easy. From scientific studies we know that:

> Goals are the way we can turn our values and dreams into reality. Happiness doesn't just happen - it comes from thinking, planning and pursuing things that are important to us. Scientific research shows that setting and working towards goals can contribute to happiness in various ways, including:

- Being a source of interest, engagement, or pleasure.
- Giving us a sense of meaning and purpose.
- Bringing a sense of accomplishment when we achieve what we set out to (or milestones along the way) - this also builds our confidence and belief in what we can do in the future.

> Goals help focus our attention. Actively working towards them appears to be as important for our well-being as achieving the end results we are aiming for.
> Goals are most successful when they're something we really want to achieve and when we set them for ourselves.[46]

Look at the line, "Actively working towards them (goals) appears to be as important for our well-being as achieving the end results we are aiming for." Your level of peace and well-being are being bolstered while you are working toward the goal, not solely because you achieve it. If you are not enjoying the process, you should rethink that goal. It most likely is devoid of passion. Remember, the value lies in the happiness of pursuit, not the pursuit of happiness.

So, we had a "goal management list," and now we have a "goals and happiness list." Goals bring happiness because:

1. They are a source of interest, engagement, or pleasure.

2. They give us a sense of meaning or purpose.
3. They bring a sense of accomplishment when we complete them.
4. They help us with the confidence to set new goals and believe we can achieve them.
5. They give us a sense of focus (remember focus is part of passion).
6. Actively working toward a goal seems to be as important to a sense of well-being as achieving that very goal.

As we are going along, some may be saying with a slightly sarcastic tone, “Wow, set some goals, what a novel idea. Tell me something I don’t know.”

We must mention several things, but the most important idea is that passion comes first, not goals. That within itself is not unique, but it is helpful when it comes to getting power. Next, making a distinction between harmonious and obsessive passions will put you at a major advantage. Then there is the idea of identity. The novel idea is the concept of identity and how it is linked to our unique passion, our unique alpha identity and its relationship to passion.

Then we look at the harmony that comes from our unique and authentic self. You have heard about a “better version of yourself,” or “your best self,” or “your best life.” The most authentic, harmonious, unique, powerful self is within your spirit. It’s really the *only* self that is real and true. There is only one version. It resides in the mind of God and within us. “Better versions” or “best versions” are our own *human* approximation of what we *think* is a better version. It’s our idea and our judgment, and many times it is unduly influenced by people around us and our culture.

Our real, authentic self is accessible only as you grow in your relationship to Jesus. It's a three-step process that comes from following Jesus.

> Then Jesus said to his disciples, "Whoever wants to be my disciple must deny themselves and take up their cross and follow me."
>
> – Matthew 16:24

- Deny the self (inauthentic self or fleshly self)
- Take up our cross (we all have one)
- Follow me (we grow into our authentic self)

The irony is that we must deny the self to get to the authentic self, the organic self God had in mind when he created us, the self that has all the gifts, talents, and passions we possess.

Looking at all the above ideas and then tying them together is what is unique, novel, and powerful—it is far more than just goal setting.

When it comes to happiness, it would be preferable to seek joy because that is one of the spiritual fruits. Spiritual fruit is intimately linked with authenticity, while happiness is associated with circumstances. If we recall, the statistics say that 84 percent of the population is not setting goals. I've seen numbers as high as 97 percent. Let's look and see what we may be missing if we choose to ignore goal setting:

1. No source of interest or engagement
2. No sense of meaning or purpose (purpose protects, we will get into this)
3. No pursuit of passion
4. No sense of accomplishment

5. No confidence or belief in ourselves
6. No focus for our attention (easily distracted)
7. No sense of well-being (this could be related to the high levels of anxiety and increasing suicide rates we are currently seeing)

This may be a good time to stop, look at this list, and take notes. These ideas don't become powerful or practical until they become personal. Do you have a sense of interest or engagement in anything? Do you have a sense of meaning or purpose? Do you have a sense of accomplishment? How about confidence or a belief in yourself? What about feelings of peace or well-being?

It makes perfect sense that there is a paucity of energy, excitement, drive, determination, infectious enthusiasm, or self-motivation. No passion? No goal? This leads to no energy. It also leads to no interest, engagement, meaning, or purpose. The result will be no confidence or sense of well-being.

One of my favorite movie scenes is from *Gladiator*. Russell Crowe, as Maximus, leads his men into battle and tells them, "Brothers, what we do in life echoes in eternity." This ties together all the things we have just gone over. Remember that nothing will grab your attention until it's perceived to be unique, valuable, or a threat. Look at all the components we have outlined:

1. Find passion first.
2. Make a distinction between harmonious and obsessive passion.
3. Seek direction and guidance along the continuum of authenticity (I'll go over this in chapter 14; this is called a tease) by growing in our relationship with Jesus.
4. Tap into the power within us and surrounding us (chapters 15 and 16, another tease).

Passion helps us to achieve our goals, and goals help us to develop and fulfill our purpose while further developing our passion. They also bring a sense of joy and well-being as we are working toward our goal.

The Opposite of Passion Is Apathy

None of this will get your attention until you begin to realize that ignoring your passion leads to apathy. One important thing to realize is that apathy is the opposite of love. When we think of opposites, we usually think of love and hate, but when we begin to look more closely, when there is no love, we tend to find apathy. Synonyms for *apathy* are *indifference* or *lack of concern*. When a marriage crumbles, it's because of indifference or lack of concern. When you have no concern for others, that is the opposite of love. It is *a-pathos*, a lack of feeling. No emotion. No enthusiasm. No passion. No love.

If we want to develop our skills of observation, all we need do is look around. Most people are engaged in one of two activities—survival or distraction—which leads to ignoring goals. It leads to listlessness and no energy. So what should we do? Find your passion and seek enthusiasm. We all have passion.

The benefits of passion, goal setting, and how you can have meaning, energy, purpose, confidence, interest, or engagement have all been outlined above. These ideas are supported by research, but if you don't believe or don't realize the value of passion and goal setting, there will be no action, no change, and no source to tap into for energy, peace, or a sense of well-being.

From my own experience, the most important precursor to action and a positive change in behavior is self-awareness and self-examination. There is a point of vision or a moment of clarity when you realize, "Hey, I'm literally just sitting here wasting my time. I'm wasting my entire life."

For me, that epiphany came through studying the Bible and near-death experiences. It's the idea that stuck. Ideas that stick are the ones that make the most difference, the ones you can't get out of your head no matter how hard you try. It's kind of like getting a song "stuck" in your head, and it just stays there. It repeats on a loop over and over. Hit songwriters call that a "hook," where something in the song gets your attention and brings out some type of emotion. It could be joy, sadness, or anger, but whatever it is, it sticks with you. Ideas behave in a similar way. The ideas that "stick" are the ones most likely to have the impact we are after, the kind of impact that results in change.

One of the ideas that "stuck" for me was the notion of getting to the end of my life surrounded by regrets. That's a big fear for me. Regretaphobia. That reminds me of what someone told me in college when I wanted him to watch one of the *Nightmare on Elm Street* movies with me. He said, "I can't watch that with you. I'm a phobophobe. I'm afraid of being afraid."

In a recurring dream I have had for years, I'm back in college running through the campus to get to my class. I get there in the nick of time. Sitting down in my seat and arranging my notebook, I see the professor passing out exams! I am totally unprepared for this exam. The anxiety of trying to answer the test questions with no clue as to what the material is about is overwhelming. I've been having that dream for decades. Why? Who knows? Maybe that is why the study of NDEs had such a powerful impact on me. I want to be ready for the test when I get the question, *What have you done with the life I gave you?* For me personally, the idea that I will be asked "Do you love me?" when I stand before Jesus changed everything. Then the idea that I will be asked, "What have you done with the gifts and talents that I gave you?" was just more gravy on the chicken-fried steak.

One important point for Christians when it comes to value and goal setting is intimately tied to your relationship with Jesus. No matter what the outcome on this planet, the pursuit of a godly goal "echoes in eternity"—even if you fail. That is the beauty and value that godly goals bring to the table.

Dr. Mary C. Neal, an orthopedic surgeon who wrote *To Heaven and Back*, said something interesting in an interview about her near-death experience. She said she was able to see the impact she had on someone's life reverberating through time, kind of like a pebble being thrown into a pond and the ripples moving outward. Mary relayed that being able to see those positive effects of what she had done for others gave her great comfort. They were "echoes in eternity."

One vital truth when it comes to my own purpose and passion is the fact that my biggest failures and disappointments I have suffered while pursuing godly goals are the ones that yielded the largest strides in my spiritual growth. They provided the most vision and clarity, bringing me closer to Jesus.

When it comes to a godly goal, I am still waiting for what the world would consider to be a positive outcome. Nothing that I have done to help with the kingdom has worked out for me, as far as what the world considers to be success. However, in terms of spiritual rewards, I've received clarity, revelations, vision, impressions, glimpses of the "peace that passes all understanding," and love. I've always wanted a taste of that type of peace. I can tell you that the only way to get even a glimmer is through Jesus, the Prince of Peace. There is no other way.

I've received those blessings and the reward of significant strides in my relationship with Jesus. Nothing is more valuable. These are true spiritual riches.

Whatever happens when it comes to the spread of these ideas, any success will be confined to "God's bubble of grace." Everything related to God's favor is found within the confines of his grace. This may be a small bubble, but it is the bubble that God created. Whatever happens, it's consistent with his will. I'm good with that because I know that his plan is perfect. He knows what is best for me. He knows exactly what I can handle. He will not give me so many trials or troubles that I get discouraged and give up. He's also wise enough to not give me so much success that I get prideful or maybe move into the ever-dangerous land of entitlement.

If there is a selfless component to any godly goal and it has "purity of intent," then we are on the right track. That is why self-awareness and self-examination coupled with honesty is so important. There is zero value and, in fact, great danger in deceiving ourselves.

One thing evident in our culture is the pervasiveness of bitterness, anger, and a sense of entitlement. Bitterness and anger need to be jettisoned before we start to pursue these ideas. They are huge weights in the dinghy, creating drag and holding us back as we paddle toward our destination. Throw bitterness and anger overboard, and you will lighten your load considerably.

While you are tossing things out of the boat, give entitlement the ol' heave-ho as well. The two most dangerous words in the English language are "I deserve." If we stop and think about it, everything we own is a gift from God. We don't *deserve* anything. So get rid of bitterness and anger. They leave less room for the love of Jesus, the love that we are to share while we are pursuing our passion and our purpose. Use the paddle of gratitude. A large dose of gratitude eliminates anger, fear, bitterness and entitlement as you paddle forward towards your goal. Being grateful eliminates anger. Being grateful eliminates fear and a sense of entitlement.

When we formulate goals that are within the framework of our passion and our authentic selves, we reap the benefits of goal setting and goal management. We also acquire meaning, purpose, energy, engagement, a sense of accomplishment, confidence, and well-being. These are all helpful when we are living our lives on a broken, fallen, imperfect world. When we are setting our goals within the construct of serving others out of love and with an eye toward greater intimacy with Jesus, we reap the benefits of spiritual fruit: peace, joy, love, kindness, gentleness, patience, and self-discipline. You win, the people you serve win, everyone you love and care about wins. These benefits continue to echo throughout eternity.

> But the fruit of the Spirit is love, joy, peace, forbearance, kindness, goodness, faithfulness, gentleness and self-control.
>
> – Galatians 5:22–23

12

MOTIVATE THINE SELF

All of God's people are ordinary people who have been made extraordinary by the purpose He has given them.

– Oswald Chambers

A vast amount of power is contained in our capacity to self-motivate. Why is this so important? Because most people who are successful within their respective fields have had to push themselves beyond their own limits. No one else is likely to push you every step of the way when you are trying to find your purpose and fully realize your goals. It's not easy to find someone in this life who is willing to sacrifice all their time effort and energy and their whole being to push *you* to succeed. *Fuhggedaboutit.* It's going to have to come from within you. If you just look at people around you and look at your own children, you know who you need to push and who you need to be careful with pushing too hard because they already have their own built-in self-motivation. There's a spectrum.

If we don't take responsibility for our own growth and development, nothing will happen. It's on us; we can blame no one else. That's not to say that we're alone. There will be family and friends who can support and encourage us as we are moving toward a goal. We can also draw power and strength from our spiritual lives and spiritual habits. Bible study, prayer, meditation, our small group and church family—God's plan always includes other people. We are focused on helping others, and we have the support and encouragement of one another. We can also take comfort in the fact that there is always power, guidance, and strength available to us when we move toward intimacy with Jesus.

Self-motivation is one powerful indicator that we are pursuing our unique passion. No one needs to push us to get up early or to work on our goals. *We want to.* We don't have to set an alarm to wake us up in the morning. The desire is already there right when we open our eyes. It's in our heart. As we go about trying to reach our written goals, we aren't always going to feel so energetic.

Consider Olympic swimmer Michael Phelps. I'm sure he didn't feel like getting up every morning at four o'clock to start his training regimen. He works out in the pool and with weights five to six hours a day, six days a week. That takes significant self-motivation.

Who Determines Value?

There is an idea that floats around among the self-help, motivational-speaker crowd that makes a distinction between *high-value* and *low-value* tasks or activities. If you want to do a fun experiment, do an internet search for "high-value" tasks and success. You will find this catchphrase everywhere. When it's linked with success, there is a point constantly made that successful people spend most of their time on high-value tasks.

But there is a problem with this way of thinking. Who is measuring the value? What if these life coaches and self-help gurus think that success means retiring at fifty with $30 million in the bank and living in a mansion on a beach in the Bahamas? If that's how you think, and you consider that success, this isn't the book for you.

God blesses our finances on this earth, but the love or pursuit of money is not a high-value item when we stand before the Creator of the universe and give an account of what we have done with our lives. I've never heard or read an NDE account that mentions money or possessions. If you look at just one of the many things that change in the lives of NDErs, it is the realization that the pursuit of money and other worldly things is pointless. When we begin to pursue high-value goals, we're going to have to change the way we think about what constitutes value.

It's easy to see how much time, effort, and energy people are devoting to pursuing worldly goals. This is something that I have experience with. If you have the command "Show me what you have done with your life?" echoing in the back of your mind, you will think about what you consider to be high value.

Honestly, I wouldn't mind living in a mansion on a beach in the Bahamas for a week just to see how it feels. Knowing my history when it comes to lounging and relaxing, after about five days, there would definitely be some discomfort or a powerful unsettled feeling. From my own experience, that's about how long it takes when I'm on vacation before I start feeling a little restless. Uneasiness begins to develop usually after about four or five days on vacation, then a voice comes into my head, saying, "Okay, playtime is over, bud, time to get back to business," or one of my favorites from that old Dunkin' Donuts commercial, "Time to make the donuts. Time to make the donuts."

If I lived on a beach and sipped those drinks with a little umbrella for over thirty years, an image of Ricky Ricardo pops into my mind, with him standing next to Jesus, and I'm standing before them right after I die. All I can hear is Ricky telling me, "You have some 'splaining to do."

One related NDE that I saw on YouTube really got my attention. It involved a young mother who had a heart ailment and died. She had an encounter with Jesus in her NDE, and Jesus told her directly, "Now that I have your attention, there are some things that we need to discuss." The way she said it was conveying a tone like when your dad sat you down to kind of straighten you out a bit when your grades were dropping.[47]

We can't be the ones who decide "value." Why? Because we screw things up too much. Our judgment and insight are not very good. You may be saying, "Well, my judgment is pretty good." Really? Let's look at the stats for a second.

1. The scientific evidence in support of the many benefits of regular exercise is overwhelming. It's just a fact. (We are going to talk about exercise in a bit.) Most people in the United States (70 percent) do not get the recommended amount of weekly exercise.[48]
2. Goal setting leads to multiple benefits of meaning, purpose, energy, and confidence. That's just a fact. Some studies show that 84 percent of people do not set goals. I've seen some estimates as high as 97 percent of the population do not have any goals written down.
3. God is omniscient and omnipotent, and the Bible is the primary way that he speaks to us. Most Christians believe this. We accept this on faith. But only 32 percent of believers in this country read the Bible regularly.[49]

I am not pointing this out to guilt you or shame you into action. It is merely a means to illustrate that we as humans don't have the best judgment. I didn't start reading the Bible regularly until about eight or nine years ago. Writing goals down has been a sporadic habit for me since high school.

I'm mentioning these activities or habits because we know from studies that they only help you as sources of energy. If you are looking for power, energy, and confidence, incorporating these habits into your life brings value.

Spending time with Jesus and reading the Word are the most reliable sources of power, energy, and guidance. Look at this verse closely:

> Those who are dominated by the sinful nature think about sinful things, but those who are controlled by the Holy Spirit think about things that please the Spirit. So letting your sinful nature control your mind leads to death. But letting the Spirit control your mind leads to life and peace. For the sinful nature is always hostile to God. It never did obey God's laws, and it never will. That's why those who are still under the control of their sinful nature can never please God. But you are not controlled by your sinful nature. You are controlled by the Spirit if you have the Spirit of God living in you. (And remember that those who do not have the Spirit of Christ living in them do not belong to him at all.) And Christ lives within you, so even though your body will die because of sin, the Spirit gives you life because you have been made right with God. The Spirit of God, who raised Jesus from the dead, lives in you. And just as God raised Christ Jesus from the dead, he will give life to your mortal bodies by this same Spirit living within you.
>
> – Romans 8:5–11 (NLT)

When we look at a verse like this, it's important to remember a few things. This was written by the apostle Paul, one of the most fascinating men in Scripture. He was a Pharisee and a murderer of Christians. He was granted a unique experience with Jesus on the Damascus road (Acts 9) and given special revelations in an event that sure sounds like a near-death experience to me (2 Corinthians 12:1-10).

We can agree that Paul was granted special revelation. It would be just plain silly to argue otherwise. If he was granted particular insight, wisdom, and spiritual clarity, we should look at this verse in Romans very closely. When we delve into our authentic selves, we go deeper into our spirit. We have access to the power of the Holy Spirit. We have life, and we have power. Those things come about because of spiritual practices and habits—reading the Word, prayer, quiet time, meditation, spiritual journaling, and fellowship with other believers. All these bring power, vision, and clarity.

As believers, we know we have value. We know we are lovable, forgivable, acceptable, and valuable. Our self-motivation comes from our relationship with Jesus and our passion. It emanates from love.

When we grow in intimacy with Jesus, we begin to understand high-value tasks. Loving others, high value. Serving others, high value. Growing our relationship with Jesus, high value. Getting closer to our authentic selves, high value. Discovering and developing our passions and gifts, high value. If we can see value in any of the above activities, we will act. That's another one of the characteristics of people who are successful. They spend most of their time on high-value activities, but they also act. They are self-motivated and possess self-discipline.

No one is going to wake you up early in the morning so that you focus on your high-value tasks or get you working toward your goals.

No one is going to stand over you while you carry out high-value tasks. If you are married or in a serious relationship, you can ask your spouse or significant other to help you reach your goals. We were meant to support each other. But remember, they have their own high-value tasks to work on, don't they? You will have to develop some measure of self-discipline or self-motivation to achieve your goals. If you are missing self-discipline and self-motivation in whatever you are trying to achieve, you should question whether you have genuine passion associated with that activity. It could very well be low value, or it could be a passion inconsistent with your authentic self. It could be obsessive in nature.

When you are struck by an idea that stirs inside of you, pay attention. Don't just think about it, get up, get some paper, and write it down. Ponder it. Why? It may be the spark you need to develop into a fire. It's like lighting a fire out in the woods when you are trying to survive. You may have a small flame flickering in some kindling. It needs oxygen. You have to fan the flame. Then you transfer that flame to a bigger pile of kindling or fuel. That fire needs work to get it going. But when it gets going, that is the start of real change. It is also a source of real power and energy.

When I worked on the flame generated by the spark of my passion, my life changed for the better—in every single area. Home life. Work life. Family life. Friend life. Faith life. Spiritual life. All life. But that early spark and flame had to be nurtured and grown with effort, time, learning, and research.

In an interview with *Forbes* magazine author Angela Duckworth argues that "A passion is developed more than it is discovered. In other words, it takes time and experience and encouragement to be able to say, one day, "I have a calling." My advice to young people is to get started right now."[50] What she is saying is that your passion is like a small fire that has to be stoked and developed and grown by time and effort. But that effort yields power and energy. It builds on itself. Without any effort, it will die.

This book wouldn't exist if I didn't listen to that stirring, calling, or prompting. That call was from the Holy Spirit. There is no question in my mind about that. We can read plenty of books, but real change only comes from the supernatural power of the Holy Spirit.

Real change also begins with self-awareness and self-examination. Brutal honesty is required. Remember, the biggest lies we tell are the ones we tell ourselves. But we should understand that the world, other people, and Satan are filling our heads with worthless lies also. There is zero value in a lie.

One crucial truth is that once we realize and fully grasp how much we are loved, it's much easier to look at ourselves in the mirror and see where we can improve. If you are being honest with yourself, you can ask yourself about the habits listed above. *Do I exercise regularly? Do I write down my goals? Do I spend any time reading the Bible and seeking God's guidance for my daily life?* Those are just three ideas that I wrote down off the top of my head in response to the statement, "Yeah, well, my perception and judgment are pretty good." If we are all being honest with ourselves, no one's perception and judgment are really that great. Why? Because God wants us to depend on him. He wants us to spend time with him so we can receive his wisdom, love, and guidance. He doesn't show us the whole path, only the next step.

We have plenty of history to support the notion that humans have poor judgment and perception. When you believe you have good judgment and perception, not only have you lost the battle, you have lost the war.

I am the wisest man alive, for I know one thing, and
that is that I know nothing.
– Socrates

There is value when we focus on and repeat these ideas because we all have our own past mistakes and failures. We have all stumbled and fallen using our own judgment. It would not take long to come up with some examples in my own life, and I suspect you could do the same. We all fail without guidance and wisdom. If you can couple this saying above with my favorite definition of wisdom (thinking the way God and Jesus think), then you are in business. When we start thinking that we have good vision, perception, judgment, and make good decisions on our own, that's when the trouble starts.

Habits Focus Behavior

This brings us to habits. We are the sum total of our habits. You are what you habitually do. If we incorporate habits into our goal setting, this helps with self-discipline and self-motivation. Habits also keep us focused on the plan and the path. Good habits are valuable. They keep us from veering off into low-value activities. If we incorporate high-value tasks into our habits, this helps to motivate us. The problem with starting any new habit is that it takes at least six weeks to get a habit fully ingrained into our lifestyle. That means discipline.

The important thing to remember is that you should take on a new activity or new habit *one at a time*. If you try to change too much at once, you will fail. That's what happens to people who make a New Year's resolution to lose weight. They drastically change their diet and begin to exercise until they are sore. They want to lose the weight as quickly as possible. It's a process that is painful and requires discipline, so they want to get it over with. If the process is painful, most likely passion isn't involved. Most people who want to lose weight want quick results. *Fuhgeddaboudit.* Get it out of your head. It's a sure way to fail.

Embrace slow and steady, like the tortoise and hare. That's also the best way to improve your finances and invest wisely. Everyone wants the get-rich-quick scheme. *Fuhgeddaboudit.* Get it out of your head.

There is no quick way to a new habit, just like there is no quick way to financial security or to weight loss and physical fitness. There is no quick way to discover your passion and purpose, and there is no quick way to spiritual growth. That is why we are given our whole lives to grow. It takes time. One important and valuable clue is that when you discover your passion and purpose, trying to develop passion and fulfill your purpose quickly to "get it over with" are never part of the equation. If you have those kind of inklings or thoughts about your passion, it is not an authentic passion or purpose. Genuine passion and purpose are savored. The process is enjoyable.

So where do we start? Wisdom. Power. Love. Guidance. The Word. The smartest thing you can do is spend time in regular Bible study. Think about the greatest commandment. The Bible says,

> "Teacher, which is the greatest commandment in the Law?" Jesus replied: "'Love the Lord your God with all your heart and with all your soul and with all your mind.' This is the first and greatest commandment. And the second is like it: 'Love your neighbor as yourself.' All the Law and the Prophets hang on these two commandments."
>
> – Matthew 22:36–40 (NLT)

Jesus is telling us this is the "first and greatest commandment." The best way to start any day is devoting it to loving God with all our heart, soul and mind. This is the wisest thing you can do. Spend time with Jesus in prayer and meditation and read the Word of God. Getting to know Him is the essence of power, love, and wisdom.

In my experience, one of the most life changing habits to acquire is starting a spiritual journal. Write down the things that God is telling you and write down your own prayers. Document the date and the time. Record spiritual ideas and principles that you have learned from books or from sermons or teaching series. But don't just write them down, ruminate, contemplate, and meditate on them. Write down Bible verses that stir up something inside you. Open your heart and your mind to the Word. God speaks to our hearts and our minds through his Word. We are to love with all our heart, all our spirit, and all *our mind.* We must engage our minds. Ask questions of the Bible. Look things up. All of these activities fan the flame that is burning inside of you.

One of my favorite go-to people to help me understand scripture is John Piper. But there are passages that we can discern for ourselves. The Bible has power. Supernatural power. There is no disadvantage to spending time in the Word. None. Here are some advantages to Bible reading:

- We learn the mind of God.
- Knowledge of the Bible helps us defend our faith
- We spend time getting to know Jesus
- We grow our faith by understanding God's promises
- Acquire wisdom
- Helps us see and understand true spiritual warfare
- Easily find guidance for every situation
- Gives us the weapons to fight in spiritual warfare

- Memorized Bible verses help us stay on track
- Helps us in our interactions with other people
- Memorized Bible verses help us defeat temptation
- Helps us in our own finances and business dealings
- Helps us to see worldly values as empty
- Helps us in our marriages
- Allows us to focus on eternal values
- Helps us in our role as parents
- We begin to see the spiritual world more clearly
- We can see more clearly the sacrifices that Jesus made for us
- Acquire discernment which opens up the Word even more
- The more we learn, the more we learn
- Inspires us to be more like our early church leaders like the apostle Paul
- Recognize the importance of Truth
- Gives us the best insight into the very nature and person of Jesus

Jesus wants us to spend time with him. He wants us to grow in our love for him. One of the most important ways is spending time in the Word and abiding in his love.

> As the Father has loved me, so have I loved you. Abide in my love. If you keep my commandments, you will abide in my love, just as I have kept my Father's commandments and abide in his love. These things I have spoken to you, that my joy may be in you, and that your joy may be full.
>
> – John 15:9–11 (ESV)

John Piper talks about abiding and has several important points to make:

> Believing is an attachment to — a coming to — Jesus, and a receiving from Jesus. It is trusting in Jesus, remaining in fellowship with Jesus, connecting to Jesus so that all that God is for us in him is flowing like a life-giving sap into our lives. That's number one: abiding is believing, trusting, savoring, resting, receiving.
>
> Second, Jesus gets very specific about what is flowing between the vine and the branch. He mentions words — his words — his love, and his joy. John 15:7 says, "If you abide in me, and my words abide in you, ask whatever you wish, and it will be done for you." And John 15:9 states, "As the Father has loved me, so have I loved you. Abide in my love." Also, John 15:11 says, "These things I have spoken to you, that my joy may be in you, and that your joy may be full."[51]

The way John Piper is describing it, if we wish to abide then we must cherish God's Word. There is no other way to do that than spend time, effort, and energy studying the Scriptures, and especially the Gospels and the New Testament. We should study the whole Book—New and Old Testament, as both are vitally important to our spiritual growth and both guide us on the path that God has in mind for our lives. Jesus said:

> Remain in me, and I will remain in you. For a branch cannot produce fruit if it is severed from the vine, and you cannot be fruitful unless you remain in me. Yes, I am the vine; you are the branches. Those who remain in me, and I in them, will produce much fruit. For apart from me you

> can do nothing. Anyone who does not remain in me is thrown away like a useless branch and withers. Such branches are gathered into a pile to be burned. But if you remain in me and my words remain in you, you may ask for anything you want, and it will be granted! When you produce much fruit, you are my true disciples.
>
> – John 15:4–8 (NLT)

Jesus isn't giving us a license to ask for a Lamborghini with that promise. We need to be clear on that. It is a promise, though. When we are one with him and we abide in him and his words, we can call on that promise. We don't have access or the privilege of calling on this promise if we are ignoring the Bible and his words. No Word, no power.

Keep in mind that the "whatever you wish" must still be within the framework of the will of our sovereign God. God knows what's best for us. That is probably why we won't ever win the lottery. He knows he can't trust us with that much money. We couldn't handle it. He probably knows that we couldn't handle the power of a Lamborghini and would kill ourselves on the highway because of inexperience. Or he knows that driving an expensive sports car would likely lead to pride and maybe a sense of entitlement—two of the biggest killers of spiritual growth and love.

It looks like if we abide in the words of Jesus and value them, we can ask for things that will really help us as we are going through trials, storms, and big waves hitting us in the face. Like what? Guidance and wisdom to choose the right path. That is power. Food feeds the body; the Word feeds and strengthens the spirit.

13

GOD'S MIND, OUR TREASURE

We have talked about the habit of daily Bible reading and the value that it brings to the table. It's a personal and practical guide to living our lives to their full potential. When it comes to setting a goal, that is one of the easier habits to start, especially if you are already writing in a spiritual journal.

As you go further in your Bible study and grow in your relationship with Jesus, you will start seeing a kind of spiritual vision or clarity. One of the things we begin to see is how much emphasis Jesus placed on money. It is interesting that Jesus talked about money more than he did about heaven or hell.

> Jesus talked much about money. Sixteen of the thirty-eight parables were concerned with how to handle money and possessions. In the Gospels, an amazing one out of ten verses (288 in all) deal directly with the subject of money. The Bible offers 500 verses on prayer, less than 500 verses on faith, but more than 2,000 verses on money and possessions.[52]

Why is there so much emphasis on money? Because money and possessions are the two candidates most likely to interfere with your spiritual growth and your relationship with Jesus. Remember in the parable of the sower of seeds, "the deception of wealth and the worries about this life" were the most likely to "choke the word." You may want to look at the role that money plays in your life. It may be one of the biggest "chokers of the Word" currently interfering with your power and energy.

Take out a piece of paper and review your bank statements over the last two months. Look at the purchases you have made with discretionary or disposable income. Write down the things you bought and the money you spent. Make a list. Now take the time machine test. Ask yourself, "If I put this thing that I bought in a time machine and go forward twenty years, how much value will it have?"

The point is that most things have very little to no lasting value. Some jewelry holds its value, but what about golf clubs, cars, televisions, iPads, or clothes? Someone may say, "Well, we need clothes." Yes, I get it. I'm not talking about necessities. But contrast that with giving your money to the poor or to food banks or to missionaries who spread the gospel. Here is a verse that has real power. It caught my attention because it is only mentioned one time in the Bible—*once*.

> If you help the poor, you are lending to the Lord—and he will repay you!
>
> – Proverbs 19:17 (NLT)

How can we possibly *lend* anything to the Lord? God owns everything. Everything we have is on loan to *us*. Whatever you own or think you own is just being borrowed, and yet the Lord will reward us for being generous with his belongings! The only things you can take with you are the things you give away to others.

> "He is no fool who gives what he cannot keep to gain what he cannot lose."

– Jim Elliott, martyred missionary

Love, peace, kindness, goodness. We store treasure in heaven when we help the poor. There is no disadvantage to that. We are lending to the Lord, and we are guaranteed to be repaid. We may receive spiritual blessings like wisdom or vision or spiritual strength, or we may receive blessings while we are here on earth. Regardless, we will be blessed. And there are acts of love that have value. We can do small acts of kindness out of love that have tremendous worth. They last forever, and those can be taken with you. We should keep in mind that the act comes from a place of selflessness. We are putting the needs of others before our own, not for reward but because of sacrificial love. Jesus said:

> "And if you give even a cup of cold water to one of the least of my followers, you will surely be rewarded."
>
> Matthew 10:42 (NLT)

It's a Wonderful Life is one of my favorite movies. On the wall of George Bailey's office is a small framed quote that says, "You can only take with you that which you give away." This doesn't necessarily mean money. It could mean love, support, encouragement, or knowledge. There are many things we can give away—our time, for example. Giving away your time for the benefit of others is a selfless act of love. One of the most valuable things you can give away is your time because you only have so much of it, and you can't buy one second more. That is why it is so important to be aware of how much time you are spending on low-value activities.

We can't do anything about wasted time in our past, but we sure as heck can do something about the time we have left. We can focus on our passion and purpose and we can spend time and energy on activities that create lasting or eternal value. When we look at "high value" activities, we should look to Jesus as our standard. He tells us what is "high value" when he talks about our lives. Jesus said,

> If you insist on saving your life, you will lose it. Only those who throw away their lives for my sake and for the sake of the Good News will ever know what it means to really live. And how does a man benefit if he gains the whole world and loses his soul in the process? For is anything worth more than his soul?
>
> – Mark 8:35–37 (TLB)

This is a very powerful verse. What things do you "throw away"? More than likely you throw away what you have determined has no value. That is not what Jesus is saying. He is saying that compared to the value of Jesus and the value of the good news, our lives are not important. Rick Warren summed it up best: "What matters is not the duration of your life, but the donation of your life." If we donate our lives—our time, energy, effort, and money— for the sake of Jesus and the good news (telling others), we will "know what it means to really live." No activities are more high value than that. Serving Jesus by serving others.

That brings us to the idea of having a servant's heart. Let's review the components of passion once again.

Excitement (this tends to bring energy)	Determination
Positive attitude	Perseverance
Focus	Resilience
Infectious enthusiasm	Servant's heart
Self-motivation	Goal-directed behavior

Thinking about the mind of God and how we get to know how God thinks reminded me of a debate I was watching on YouTube between Christian apologist Jay Smith and Islamic scholar Sabir Ally. I enjoy watching these debates because the participants are vast resources of knowledge. They know much more about all these subjects than I do, so there is no way to avoid learning something new.

The topic of this particular debate was the nature of heaven. Jay Smith was pointing out how the view of heaven from the Muslim perspective was filled with carnality—rivers of wine, sex with virgins, and many physical pleasures. Sabir Ally made the point that we're physical creatures and enjoy sex with our wives, why wouldn't we have sex in heaven with women?

This point of view is interesting because it all boils down to how we see God and if we have clues as to what he values and how he thinks. When you spend time with God in the Word, you begin to know the mind of God. You discover what he thinks is important and what he thinks is unimportant.

When you hear someone talking about what God values or what he emphasizes, you can, based on your own Bible study and prayer, say, "Yep, that sounds like God," or, "No, that doesn't sound like the God I know." This is why spending time in prayer, meditation, and Bible study is so important.

It also comes down to what Jesus emphasized in his teaching. In *Brave the Wave* I used the analogy of a ladder of love. At the bottom is *eros* which is totally focused on the self: "I love you because of how you make *me* feel." At the top is *agape*, a selfless, unconditional, sacrificial love. Agape is the type of love that Jesus displayed by dying on the cross. It is the love we should all aspire to.

When we talk about authenticity and the authentic self, it is intimately associated with our spiritual selves. It's living and thriving above the physical world. It's a higher plane or higher ground of living. This is another reason why there is value in looking at NDEs. They are purely spiritual experiences devoid of physical or fleshly influences because the body is dead. We should examine the idea of God rewarding us with sex or physical pleasure in heaven. It is very rare to hear any NDEr mention anything about sex or physical pleasure in an NDE. We also need to ask ourselves, "Are there examples in the Bible where sex and physical pleasure are emphasized by God or Jesus?"

As Christians, we believe that God gave us the gift of sex as a means of reproduction, but it's to be consummated within the boundaries of marriage. The sex act releases the hormone oxytocin in the blood of *both* the husband and wife. This causes us to feel more connected and engenders feelings of closeness and warmth for our spouse. It brings us closer together. That is God's idea. This also explains why adultery is so damaging. It causes those types of feelings with someone other than your spouse—not a good idea for *any* marriage or *any* family.

It's useful to think about how we see Jesus and God. Are they interested in us being rewarded with physical pleasure? It was interesting to me that Sabir Ally said "Jay, I know you want to walk with God in the garden of Eden, but eternity is a long walk. I want to walk with God for a little while, but I also want some physical pleasure."

There was only one mention of sex that I can recall in an NDE. A person was describing the sense of warmth, love, peace and joy he felt just being in the presence of God. The love this person felt was overwhelming. He said, "It was one hundred times better than sex."

Heaven promises to be much bigger, better, and more satisfying than our little brains can handle. I am not a biblical scholar, but in my humble opinion, physical pleasure and fleshly rewards in heaven seem to be ideas created by man, not God. The One Minute Apologist gives a nice little breakdown of why there won't be sex in heaven: https://oneminuteapologist.com/blog/will-there-be-sex-in-heaven.

Developing a Servant's Heart

Back to passion. When we get frustrated, discouraged, or lose our sense of enthusiasm or energy, the first thing we should look at is our servant's heart. Have we lost it? When I am most frustrated and unhappy with my own job, I tend to look at my own attitude. Am I concerned about myself first? Am I concerned about the well-being or benefit of others? This one is very tough, especially when our physical selves and our natural desires begin to creep in. We get tired, sleepy, hungry, or just plain fed up with putting other people first. We think to ourselves, "What about me?" That's a sign we may need some "downtime" to recharge our batteries. We should make sure we get plenty of sleep and real rest. We need to check that we aren't hungry or tired when we are serving others. Servants need rest and time to relax to recharge our batteries. We need to give our minds a rest. Jesus said,

> For even the Son of Man did not come to be served but to serve, and to give his life as a ransom for many.
>
> – Mark 10:45

We know that when we are serving others, we are in our physical bodies. Our bodies are weak and in a state of aging and decay as we get older. They are on the inevitable path of breaking down and getting weaker. We can slow down the process, but we can't reverse it.

The apostle Paul wrote:

> Therefore if you have any encouragement from being united with Christ, if any comfort from his love, if any common sharing in the Spirit, if any tenderness and compassion, then make my joy complete by being like-minded, having the same love, being one in spirit and of one mind. Do nothing out of selfish ambition or vain conceit. Rather, in humility value others above yourselves, not looking to your own interests but each of you to the interests of the others.
>
> In your relationships with one another, have the same mindset as Christ Jesus: Who, being in very nature God, did not consider equality with God something to be used to his own advantage; rather, he made himself nothing by taking the very nature of a servant, being made in human likeness. And being found in appearance as a man, he humbled himself by becoming obedient to death--even death on a cross!
>
> – Philippians 2:1–8

These aren't easy passages. They give us some encouragement, but to get to this level of selflessness is difficult. Why is it so tough? Because we are slowly getting older, weaker, and our physical energy is dwindling. So, what can we do? We can do our best to maximize our physical gifts, and we can devote time and energy to strengthening our spiritual selves. Keep in mind that our spiritual growth is not limited by our age—we can keep getting stronger all the way up into our nineties and beyond.

When we live, embrace, and function within the framework of our natural or physical selves, we focus on the needs, wants, and desires of that same natural self. Our brains are wired to reward, support, and focus on our physical or fleshly desires, even if we do get a sense of satisfaction and well-being from altruistic acts. When we get tired or we haven't had enough sleep, our brains will send out signals to direct us to rest. When we are hungry and it's noon and we've skipped breakfast, it is hard to concentrate on being a servant or doing something selfless. All we can think about is a nice double-meat hamburger with a big plate of fries (or a big salad for those of you in the clean-eating group). If it has been a particularly tough week, some of us are thinking about Friday afternoon happy hour with the boys (or girls), so we can sit around and have a drink and complain about the boss.

It's important to recognize that being tired, hungry, sleepy, or wanting to relax with some of your friends is a normal part of our everyday life. There is no need to beat ourselves up over being human. Paul explains in Philippians how, as always, Jesus provides the answer:

> Those who live according to the flesh have their minds set on what the flesh desires; but those who live in accordance with the Spirit have their minds set on what the Spirit desires. The mind governed by the flesh is death, but the mind governed by the Spirit is life and peace. The mind governed by the flesh is hostile to God; it does not submit to God's law, *nor can it do so*. Those who are in the realm of the flesh cannot please God.
>
> You, however, are not in the realm of the flesh but are in the realm of the Spirit, if indeed the Spirit of God lives in you. And if anyone does not have the Spirit of Christ, they

> do not belong to Christ. But if Christ is in you, then even though your body is subject to death because of sin, the Spirit gives life because of righteousness. And if the Spirit of him who raised Jesus from the dead is living in you, he who raised Christ from the dead will also give life to your mortal bodies because of his Spirit who lives in you.
>
> – Romans 8:5-11, emphasis added

The Spirit will "give life" to our mortal bodies because the Spirit of Jesus lives in us. This is a gift, and we have access to this supernatural power only if we have accepted Jesus as our savior. This is not a promise for nonbelievers.

Notice how the mind governed by the flesh is hostile to God, cannot please God, and cannot submit to God's law. Hostile and rebellious, the mind that is dominated by the flesh is angry, unwilling and unable to surrender or serve. It is controlled by and subservient to the fleshly self. That is why Jesus says the first step in following him is to deny yourself. Many times, denying self is harder than picking up our cross, but it is a prerequisite.

When we focus on the spiritual self, we tend to automatically deny the fleshly self. Our spiritual self is where the action is. Mark gives us a reminder of the critical importance of denying the self:

> Whoever wants to be my disciple must deny themselves and take up their cross and follow me. For whoever wants to save their life will lose it, but whoever loses their life for me and for the gospel will save it.
>
> – Mark 8:34–35

Here's a quick little story. The other day, I was exercising and thinking about some of these concepts, specifically about the idea of being able to hear and discern the voice of God or the Holy Spirit. We know that the primary way God speaks to us is through his Word. But we know that he reveals himself to each of us in a personal way through people, circumstances, troubles, trials, impressions, visions, and directly by a voice or whisper (remember my owl story?).

We know from NDEs that all the communication that is happening between any "being of light" and the NDEr is by voices that speak directly to their mind. That is how most of the communication occurs. In *Life after Life* Raymond Moody describes this phenomenon:

> "Hearing" in the spiritual state can apparently be called so only by analogy, and most say that they do not really hear physical voices or sounds. Rather, they seem to pick up the thoughts of the persons around them, and, as we shall see later, this same kind of direct transfer of thoughts can play an important role in the late stages of death experiences. As one NDEr puts it, "I could see people all around, and I could understand what they were saying. I didn't hear them, audibly, like I'm hearing you. It was more like knowing what they were thinking, exactly what they were thinking, but only in my mind, not in their actual vocabulary."[53]

The NDE is a purely spiritual state. Communication with God and Jesus occurs when we pray and meditate. But when we get an impression or when we hear something that could be the voice of God, how do we know? We should test it first. We test the voice or the impression and see if it lines up with the Word. That is why being in the Word and being familiar with Bible verses is so important. If I am hearing a voice tell me that I should quit my job, leave my family, and move to Los Angeles to start a music career, that is unlikely the voice of God. If I am hearing a voice that says, "You need to control your pride and learn to be more loving and patient with your wife," that sounds more like Jesus, doesn't it? Would Satan say something like that? No. He wants yelling and criticism. He despises love, patience, and kindness.

Back to my story. While I was exercising, I heard a voice say, "I am giving you my countenance." Countenance? Wait a minute. Let me just tell you that the word *countenance* is not one of my go-to words to describe *anything, ever*. I remember the word used by pastor Charles Stanley describing how if you photograph a young lady with the light adjusted in a certain way, it will change her appearance—it will change her countenance. That is the only time I could remember hearing that word. So I asked myself, "'I am giving you my countenance.' What the heck does that mean?"

The thing about that statement was not whether it lined up with God's Word, it was just that it was a mistake in how the word *countenance* was being used. I told myself, "Countenance? Yeah, that came from you, brother. God would never say, 'I am giving you my appearance.' That just sounds stupid. God don't make mistakes, bud, so you came up with that stupid idea yourself. Now it's time for some cardio, Mr. Countenance. Keep moving. You aren't even sweating yet." I started doing some cardio, my heart rate is creeping up, then here it comes again: "I am giving you my countenance." Clear as day.

Someone once asked Charles Stanley if he hears God speaking to him in a normal speaking voice. He responded, "No, he speaks way louder than that." You may know what he is talking about. This was one of those louder-than-a-speaking-voice moments for me.

From my own experience of spiritual journal writing and listening and trying to get guidance (which, by the way, I pray for every day before I type one word), one common theme is *repetition.* Repetition is important. If you keep hearing the same thing over and over and it lines up with the Word of God and with what Jesus taught, *pay attention.* Very likely it is the still, small voice of the Holy Spirit, especially if he wants you to deal with something in your life that is interfering with your relationship with Jesus. Many times, we know exactly what we need to get rid of in our own lives. It's just that we want to do things our way.

One thing I learned is that obedience releases power. Sometimes a voice can be prompting you to do something that will move you closer to Jesus and your authentic self. Whatever it is, just do it—like the Nike commercial. Clearly, we can release power by acquiring habits that get us closer to Jesus. We can also release power by getting rid of habits that move us away from Jesus. Either way, obedience yields power. We must be honest with ourselves and do the things we need to do and avoid the things we know we need to avoid. As always, the Word is our guide.

So, what did I do about this countenance thing? I went over to a computer in my workout room and looked up *countenance.* Like I said, it's not part of my normal set of go-to words to describe anything.

Countenance

1. a person's face or facial expression.
2. support.

Synonyms: permit, allow, agree to, consent to, give one's blessing to

A ha. Boom. Thank you, Lord. I'll try my best not to let you down.

14

THE CONTINUUM OF LOVE, POWER, AND PASSION

Now we come to the crux of the matter. We have enough background ideas, so it's time to roll up our sleeves and get down to business. We are going to start a running list of our power sources to keep tabs and add new ideas as we go along.

We have talked about our spirits and the supernatural, and we have talked about authenticity. In the realm of the physical, we have discussed the drive we acquire when we set goals. The physical aspect of goal setting is writing it down. It is something we must do, not something we are born with. We must physically act to fulfill or achieve goals. We acquire affirmation, strength, and confidence when we reach a goal.

Let's look at this search for authenticity and introduce the idea of the power, energy, and universality of love. Notice it is number one on the list under supernatural power. That's because God is love and he's always number one.

Supernatural power	**Physical power and energy**
1. Love 2. Holy Spirit 3. Authentic self	1. Goal setting

When we are looking at passion, purpose, our assignment of energy, and our assignment of love, these principles should lead to one thing: serving others. Our purpose, as well as our passion, is intimately tied to the service of others. When we get an "assignment" of love and energy, those assets, like passion, are to be used for the benefit of others. The highest use of life is to serve others and lay down our lives for Jesus and the good news, the gospel.

This doesn't mean we should go up to the pastor, priest, or other clergy at church services and tap them on the shoulder and say, "Uh, can you sit down for a second? I have some really good ideas I want to share with the congregation." Just like anything else, we start with what we are the most familiar with: our own families. We can serve and love our own children and our spouses and begin to add Jesus into the conversation if we aren't doing that already. The opportunities to talk about Jesus and the principles of learning to love and serve others come up every day.

I look at this as something of a continuum, like a line leading from one point to another. If you look at your own line, you can get an idea of where you are. On the left side is the natural or fleshly self. That self is totally concerned with pleasing its own flesh and has no concern for other people. When we go to the extreme left, we can characterize or identify this fleshly self by the behavior the fleshly self is engaged in. From Galatians:

> The acts of the flesh are obvious: sexual immorality, impurity and debauchery; idolatry and witchcraft; hatred, discord, jealousy, fits of rage, selfish ambition, dissensions, factions and envy; drunkenness, orgies, and the like. I warn you, as I did before, that those who live like this will not inherit the kingdom of God.
>
> – Galatians 5:19–21

This is a good list of activities associated with the inauthentic or natural self. Idolatry is very easy to identify, as it is all around us and evidenced by rampant materialism and the love of money. The acts of the flesh are totally tied to the pleasure, comfort, and support of our fleshly or natural selves. Jealousy and envy. Selfish ambition. Drunkenness. Just look at some of the blowups on "reality" television. Here is a quick experiment. The next time you see a commercial for a popular reality television show, watch for someone yelling. Someone will always be screaming. Why? Because if there is no jealousy, anger, hatred, discord, or drunkenness, there are no eyeballs watching the show. We can see all of this in advertising, movies, the internet, social media, and even coming out of the mouths of some of our politicians. Hatred, discord, and dissension have become part of our culture. I read something about Twitter the other day that caught my attention: "I don't get on Twitter at all. All I see is arguing."

From a perspective of power, passion, and purpose, if you are engaged in more than one of the above activities, you have limited access to energy and love. NDErs have told us there is an emphasis on learning how to love, with many references to a "being of light" and the love that emanates from this light. This is totally consistent with what we read in the Bible:

> Beloved, let us love one another, for love is from God, and whoever loves has been born of God and knows God. Anyone who does not love does not know God, because God is love. In this the love of God was made manifest among us, that God sent his only Son into the world, so that we might live through him. In this is love, not that we have loved God but that he loved us and sent his Son to be the propitiation for our sins. Beloved, if God so loved us, we also ought to love one another. No one has ever seen God; if we love one another, God abides in us and his love is perfected in us.
>
> – 1 John 4:7–12 (ESV)

Can you see love in any of the activities associated with the flesh? Sexual immorality—no love. Impurity and debauchery—no love. Idolatry and witchcraft—no love. Hatred, discord, and jealousy are all devoid of love. Fits of rage, selfish ambition, dissension—no love found anywhere. Factions and envy, drunkenness and orgies—not a drop of love.

On the spectrum or continuum of authenticity, if we are far over to the left, we are totally devoid of love. If anyone is spending a large amount of their time focused on these activities, they have very little love in their life. We need to understand that when there is very little love, there is very little power and energy. *God is love.*

Our Greatest Source

So, it would behoove us to get closer to our authentic selves, which live closer to the right side of the continuum. Guess who is over there smiling and waving at us, arms wide open and emanating pure love and encouragement? It's our best friend, Jesus. He is telling us that if we seek Him and grow closer to Him, we become more in tune with our spirit. This is when things get interesting and exciting. Spiritual revelations are fascinating and serve to drive us forward on our journey toward authenticity. Plus, they lead to power, peace, and fulfillment. One of the characteristics of passion is excitement. We all have a spirit, but when we are on the left side of the authenticity line, we ignore our spiritual selves and focus on our fleshly selves. When we are on the right side of the spectrum, we ignore our fleshly selves and focus on our spiritual selves. There are many advantages to working, growing, and striving to move toward our spiritual selves and true authenticity:

> But the fruit of the Spirit is love, joy, peace, forbearance, kindness, goodness, faithfulness, gentleness and self-control. Against such things there is no law. Those who belong to Christ Jesus have crucified the flesh with its passions and desires. Since we live by the Spirit, let us keep in step with the Spirit. Let us not become conceited, provoking and envying each other.
>
> – Galatians 5:22–26

Notice that last line, "Provoking and envying each other." That comes from comparing. Cooperation is a better approach (we will get to that). If we are interested in power and energy, this is where we should be striving to get to: our authentic self, our spiritual self, the self that is infused with power—the power of love.

Look at the fruit available to us. Peace, forbearance, and forgiveness are infused with love. We are more at peace and more forgiving when we allow imperfection. Jesus allows imperfection in us, so we allow imperfection in others. That brings peace and forgiveness. Kindness, goodness, and faithfulness are all driven by love. Gentleness and self-control are totally saturated with love. Self-control comes from loving ourselves—our authentic selves. When we live in true authenticity, we live by the Spirit and in step with the Spirit. We have access to power, energy, and love. When we speak about our passion, that passion that is unique to us, it is discovered, developed, and manifested only within the confines of our spiritual selves. Look at what was revealed to this NDEr when he had his experience with God:

> The entire encounter was about God, the ultimate power of God, and God's forgiveness. The message was "Love is the greatest power in the universe."[54]

Boom! There it is. The fruit of the Spirit are infused and permeated with love. As we seek to move in the direction of Jesus by taking on new habits and getting in tune with our spiritual selves, we have more love, peace, joy, kindness, goodness, and self-control. Is it easy? Of course not. There's always *one* big problem, one huge obstacle getting in the way of us moving toward Jesus and love: *us*—you and me. We are our biggest problem. We are spirit, but we are residing in this fleshly body that is constantly crying, whining, and fighting for the idols of pleasure, ease, and comfort.

Our brains are hard wired for the pleasure of sex, food, excitement, entertainment, and any other form of comfort we can think of. It isn't easy moving to the right, especially if you can think of yourself on the continuum, and the line is covered with oil or grease. You are slipping and sliding and trying not to fall. The only thing holding you up is two ropes tied to your arms. You have Jesus gently trying to pull you toward Him, toward love and authenticity. On the other side is the world, the flesh, and Satan. They are pulling you away from your spiritual self and enticing you to focus on fleshly or worldly desires.

From experience, I know this whole process is very difficult. Jesus was talking about me when He told the disciples in the garden of Gethsemane, "Watch and pray so that you will not fall into temptation. The spirit is willing, but the flesh is weak" (Matthew 26:41). I used to stand on the greased, slick, oily line of authenticity with roller skates on.

> Stand firm then, with the belt of truth buckled around your waist, with the breastplate of righteousness in place, and with your feet fitted with the readiness that comes from the gospel of peace.
>
> – Ephesians 6:14–15

I'm a little more stable now because I study the "gospel of peace." But I'm just a regular dude being pulled along the continuum trying to get closer to my authentic self and to Jesus. Let's make this very clear. We are all in this together. We need to help each other on this continuum. We have the Word and our relationship to Jesus and the Holy Spirit to help us, but there are powerful forces working against us, some of them within our own bodies. And the world, our culture, social media, and advertising are all pulling us to value and pursue fleshly rewards. It's tough.

How the heck do we win this battle? Well, we are not alone. Plus, we have weapons. If you want real power, start with love. Start with your closest inner circle: your spouse, your children, your mom and dad. Start with you. Use the mirror exercise, and ask yourself, "Am I being the most loving, kind, patient, selfless husband or wife I can be? Mother or father? Friend, son, daughter, brother, or co-worker?"

Our family and friends are gifts who help us learn how to love. They help us learn to be patient, kind, and gentle in difficult or trying circumstances. Sometimes the people closest to us make it hard to love, and just as often, we make it difficult for people to love us. Does this describe you? We can all act in ways that make others' jaws drop. This is where patience, kindness, and understanding come into play. We should develop a tolerance for imperfection in ourselves and in others. Allowing for imperfection in our own families and at the same time asking that they allow us to be imperfect make our relationships easier and more fulfilling. There is no shame in asking our families to be patient with our imperfections because we all know that no one is perfect. We can assure them that we are trying to be better, but the most convincing proof is in our actions. Can our family members see the spiritual habits of Bible study, prayer, and meditation? Are we walking the talk?

Love Connects Everything

Love is the goal for each of us and, in fact, is the primary goal of our existence on earth. In his book *God and the Afterlife*, Jeffrey Long documents an experience of one NDEr:

> All this time I was accelerating toward the light, and unfolding like a flower, although I had no body. As I unfolded I felt it—the Love, which was like nothing I have ever experienced before. Even now I cry when I talk about it. I feel like I'm going to overload from just the memory. I was enveloped by light and felt one with everything—all-seeing, all-knowing. This experience gave new meaning to that saying, "God is Love." The love was like an energy that connected every molecule in the universe.[55]

If we have faith, "God is love" is not just a saying, it becomes a fact. Love is the energy and the power and connects every molecule as it draws each of us closer. We are all connected by love; it is the most powerful force in the universe. How do I know this? Because God is love and He is the most powerful force in the universe.

In the movie *Star Wars*, Obi-Wan Kenobi describes the "Force" as "an energy field created by all living things. It surrounds us, penetrates us, and binds the galaxy together."[56] The Force is imaginary, but love is real. God is love. Love wasn't created because God wasn't created. Love has always been because God has always been. God is "I Am" (Ex. 3:14). That is what He called himself. This can be difficult for us to wrap our heads around, but that is the whole point. We are not meant to understand everything. The interesting thing is that we have access to the greatest power in the universe, the love of God. It's our responsibility to recognize, value, and appreciate this love that is available through Jesus to every single one of us. Here is another quote from an NDEr:

> The only things that are worthwhile are those that reinforce one's connection to God. The things that humans pursue on earth are mostly pointless and meaningless.[57]

This is an important concept, and it is worth remembering so we can know we are pursuing true value. Our connection to God is paramount, supreme, of utmost importance. What this NDEr is telling us is powerful and eye-opening. The sooner that we recognize the truth of this statement, the sooner we will begin to see with spiritual vision and clarity. I believe this is exactly what Jesus had in mind when He said:

> The Spirit gives life; the flesh counts for nothing. The words I have spoken to you—they are full of the Spirit and life.
>
> – John 6:63

The idea that "the flesh counts for nothing" has much value. I am not sure I can make it any clearer: fleshly activities are low value. The "things that humans pursue on earth are mostly pointless and meaningless" is consistent with the idea that humans are human. We waste time, energy, and effort on activities that have little to no value. If we desire to develop our own spiritual vision, we must be able to be objective observers. That is, we need to look at situations, circumstances, and our behavior in an objective way.

If we can look to our standard—Jesus—then we have a way to objectively look at our own activity and see if we are pursuing high- or low-value objectives. The easiest way to do that is look at the continuum. Ask yourself how you are spending your time. Honestly evaluate one by one the activities you are involved in. Ask questions like:

- Does this activity move me along the authenticity continuum toward Jesus or away from Jesus?
- Am I growing in love when I am engaged in this activity?
- Is anyone around me benefiting from this?
- Is anyone being served by this activity, or am I the only one who is getting something out of this?

Remember, love is the ultimate power in the universe. God is love.

We never lose when we focus on love. There is no downside.

If you are moving toward the flesh and the world, you are moving away from love, and you should not be surprised if you have no energy. Why would you have energy if you are moving toward hatred, discord, dissension, envy, drunkenness, fits of rage, or jealousy? Think about the morning after some big party or celebration when you have had too much to drink. Did you feel like getting up the next morning for a five-mile run and then spending time working in the yard? Probably not. You would not have had the energy.

I was recently having a conversation with someone, and they'd said something mean about another person. I asked what motivated them to say something so hateful. Their response was "Well, that is just the way that I am. God made me this way." Immediately, I thought of Jesus when he spoke of the easy and the hard road. We know that God is love, and that he made us because of love and as an object of his love. From the Bible and the life of Jesus, we know that God wants us to learn how to love him. We know from NDEs that our primary purpose in life is to learn how to love: love God and love other people. So, hatefulness and mean-spirited behavior is a choice, the product of our sin nature at war with our Creator. The most difficult thing to do in this life is to love the unlovely. It's very hard to be kind to the unkind. It's not easy to be patient with the impatient. We often choose to be hateful, mean, or ugly to others simply because it's easier. It is much less work to be rude and mean to someone who is rude or mean or who you feel is trying to take advantage of you. Jesus said,

> Enter through the narrow gate. For wide is the gate and broad is the road that leads to destruction, and many enter through it. But small is the gate and narrow the road that leads to life, and only a few find it.
>
> – Matthew 7:13–14

This is why there are so many critics in the world. It's easier to tear someone down than it is to build them up. The critical tend to briefly feel better about themselves while tearing someone else down. It's a sure sign of insecurity and immaturity. We are to give affirmation and lift each other up.

Do you want to feel more secure and confident about yourself? Move toward Jesus. Move toward love. Remember, wherever there is love, there is value and power. But how do we make loving others easier? Practice. When you do something over and over, it gets easier. Start with your family. Give compliments. Tell your husband he looks handsome today, even if you aren't thinking it. Tell your wife she looks as good as the day you met her. Tell her the smartest thing you ever did was marry her. Tell your daughter you like the new outfit she just bought. Tell someone at work that you enjoy and appreciate them. Of course, don't be insincere, but place the emphasis on loving others, and make it the central focus of your day. It will be the wisest, most valuable, and most important investment of your time. Your time is never wasted when you pursue love.

Let's go back to the examples of leadership in the first chapter. Here is the quote again,

> Great leaders are able to inspire people to act. Those who are able to inspire give people a sense of purpose or belonging that has little to do with any external incentive or benefit to be gained. Those who truly lead are able to create a following of people who act not because they were swayed, but because they were inspired. Those who are able to inspire will create a following of people-supporters, voters, customers, co-workers- who act for the good of the whole not because they have to, but because they want to.

Bill Gates, Martin Luther King Jr., and Steve Jobs all had goals, dreams, and pursuits that were totally for the benefit of others. They had goals and aspirations that would benefit the world. Martin Luther King Jr. had a vision:

> I refuse to accept the view that mankind is so tragically bound to the starless midnight of racism and war that the bright daybreak of peace and brotherhood can never become a reality... I believe that unarmed truth and unconditional love will have the final word.[58]

Bill Gates had a vision for empowering individuals with a "computer on every desktop." It was a dream for the entire world.

Steve Jobs had a vision to create products that had an impact. He said, "I want to put a ding into the universe," and, "Your time is limited, so don't waste it living someone else's life. Don't be trapped by dogma—which is living with the results of other people's thinking."[59]

The idea of not living someone else's life is totally consistent with the concept of living an authentic life. We really have an innate yearning for authenticity. It's deep within us. It's our choice to ignore it or pursue it. These three men were visionaries and leaders, and if we look at their success, we will find it fully infused with the notion of selflessness. Their vision and power were above the simple and misguided pursuit of selfish and meaningless activity.

Before we move on, let me reiterate a few vital points to consider while on your quest for passion, purpose, and meaning. When attempting to pursue an activity that has true value, we should expect troubles and trials. Count on it. Bet on it. The best approach is to mentally prepare. Before we begin, we should spend time on building a mindset of toughness. We should tell ourselves, *This is going to be really hard—requiring resilience, determination, and mental fortitude—which is why I must find my passion first.*

What's more, there is always concomitant sacrifice. Without it, there is no real selflessness. We give of ourselves—our time, our money, our energy—for this purpose. You can give without loving, but you can't love without giving. That quote has been attributed to several people, but it really doesn't matter who said it. The point is that there is truth in it.

So, we know we will encounter various difficulties, snags, and obstacles as well as opportunities for sacrifice when we are striving to move toward authenticity and our spiritual selves. It may seem daunting, but there is something greater we have working for us in the midst of the struggle: supernatural power—that is, love.

15

THE POWER WITHIN US

You are only powerless if you believe you are powerless.

The above was a line spoken by Little John in the 2018 version of *Robin Hood.* In my book, *Brave the Wave*, we looked at how we think, what we believe, what we value, and what we know. In this book, we are going to think about our sources of power. If we focus on those sources, we begin to see that we can assimilate that power into our lives and come to *know* that we have power. This is when things begin to change, but it is going to require action.

On the continuum, moving to the right—closer to our spiritual selves—tends to give us more insight and clarity. Getting closer to authenticity gives us clues to our passion, so spending time, effort, and energy on that task yields huge benefits. In other words, discovery brings more direction and more light. But the light is to the right, and it takes effort to get there.

The best-selling book *The Secret* has some ideas about power and how we can "control" the universe with our thoughts. Emily Yoffe, an editor at *Atlantic*, writes in one of her columns:

> There's no secret to *The Secret.* The book and movie simply state that your thoughts control the universe. Through this "law of attraction" you "manifest" your desires. "It is exactly like placing an order from a catalogue. ... You must know that what you want is yours the moment you ask." "See yourself living in abundance, and you will attract it. It works every time, with every person." The appeal is obvious. Forget education, effort, performance. Everything you want—money, power, comfortable shoes—is yours simply by wanting it enough.[60]

Our thoughts are some of the most dangerous things that we will ever encounter, so if we believe our thoughts control the universe, we're in trouble. The problem with our thoughts is that they're *ours*. Remember that all sin starts with a thought. Sometimes our thoughts are just plain wrong. How many times have you asked yourself, *What the heck was I thinking?* Sometimes our thoughts lead us down a dangerous path.

So, if we are not controlling the universe with our thoughts, what or who is in control? The truth is that God controls the universe. He is sovereign. This is one of the most powerful weapons we have to fight fear and discover passion. We are human, and we make mistakes. God doesn't. That is a wise approach to your thoughts.

Have you ever said something, and as the words are coming out of your mouth, in your mind you're screaming, "Oh nooooo!!!" Me too, kind of like Mr. Bill from *Saturday Night Live* in the late seventies. Usually there is emotion like anger or frustration involved. When we allow these thoughts and emotions to control our lives, it leads to an abundance of bad decisions, bad outcomes, and pain—the kind of pain that yields no insight, clarity, or vision. This kind of pain also opens the door to fear, pride, anxiety, and a big helping of valueless activities that waste one of our most valuable assets, time. Time is one thing we can't buy. We won't get a second more than what God allows us to have.

Not all our thoughts are useless, but unless they are lined up with wisdom, they are not likely to have much value. Our thoughts should be tested and evaluated to see if they line up with how God thinks and what he has revealed in his Word.

Learning how to *control* your thoughts, as opposed to waiting for your thoughts to control the universe, is a smarter way to approach life. Sometimes our thoughts are dominated by the lies that were injected by people from our past who may have told us that we were worthless, had no future, and would never amount to anything. All those statements are lies.

Sometimes we are lying to ourselves. The biggest lies we tell are the ones we tell ourselves. Remember that Satan injects thoughts and suggestions into your head all the time. He can't make us do anything, but he sure can suggest things meant to destroy you and steal your joy. One of the most fundamental truths that you can embrace is that any negative thoughts suggesting that you are hopeless, helpless, or worthless are never from God. They're all lies.

Think about the biggest mistakes you have made in your life. You can probably single out a bad thought that was the primary cause. When we begin to understand that our thoughts are not a source of power but can be a source of bad decisions, then we are on a wise path. Many times, we are focused on thoughts related to selfish goals or personal pleasure.

If you think you are powerful enough to control the universe, you can put this book down. The rest of us realize we need help. We need each other, and we need Jesus. This is a thought infused with power and wisdom.

Examine every thought and see if it lines up with wisdom—with how God thinks. It is *his thoughts* that control the universe. If you can grab hold of that idea and allow it to "stick," then you are on the path to wisdom, power, and energy. If your thinking lines up with how God thinks and with what He thinks is important, you're on the path that yields what has the most value: love, peace, joy, kindness, patience, goodness—in short, true riches.

A Two-Way Street

In chapter 3, we talked about spending time watching other people's lives and how this is not helpful for our growth. It doesn't bring anything to the table in our quest to discover our passion and power. If we look at time as an investment into our future, then we need to invest in it wisely, considering our activities and how we are spending our limited time. We must examine our lives and see where we are on the continuum of authenticity. We can focus on how much time, money, and effort we are spending on getting closer to our authentic or spiritual selves.

Following a bunch of people on social media or watching the lives of others as a form of entertainment is a one-way street. We are focusing on someone else, but we aren't receiving anything in the transaction. We aren't learning how to love, and no one is being served. We aren't growing or developing our personal relationship with Jesus. We aren't giving or receiving real love.

If we focus on developing our relationships with Jesus and with those closest to us, our immediate family and our friends, it's a two-way street. We are giving and receiving real love, learning to serve those around us, and growing closer to Jesus. Every one of these activities has eternal value and is never a waste of our precious time. But we also get closer to our authentic selves and are more in tune with our spirits. And when we are more in tune with our spirits, we have access to spiritual insight and spiritual power, almost like a switch that has been turned on. Jesus said:

> Very truly I tell you, no one can see the kingdom of God unless they are born again.
>
> – John 3:3

This is an interesting idea that is crucial to understand when seeking passion and power. John Piper describes being born again this way:

> What happens in the new birth?... (1) What happens in the new birth is not getting new religion but getting new life. (2) What happens in the new birth is not merely affirming the supernatural in Jesus but experiencing the supernatural in yourself. (3) What happens in the new birth is not the improvement of your old human nature but the creation of a new human nature — a nature that is really *you*, and is forgiven and cleansed; and a nature that is really *new*, and is being formed by the indwelling Spirit of God.[61]

This describes the authentic self in a clear way. The change occurs within us. The spiritual world surrounds us, but the ability to recognize it and tap into that power comes after the switch has been turned on. That is only accomplished by the power of the Holy Spirit. People mistakenly believe that becoming a Christian, limits you, it's actually the opposite. It opens up many avenues and possibilities. All driven by spiritual power.

Every human walking the planet is made up of living flesh. Our cells are alive—heart muscle cells, liver cells, kidney cells, all alive. We are comprised of living flesh. Not every human, though, is walking in the power of the living Spirit. This is where the action is. The power becomes available to us when our spirits have been switched on.

Pastor Charles Stanley tells a story of picking up missionary Bertha Smith from the airport. As they were leaving the airport, this ninety-year-old woman was walking so fast the pastor had to rush just to keep up with her. He asked her, "Bertha, how do you have so much energy?" She didn't look up at him or hesitate one second: "I'm walking in the power of the Spirit." He shares another story about Bertha that can help us in our own search for truth and power:

> Bertha Smith, a missionary to China, once pronounced some of the most discouraging words I'd ever heard: "Charles, I want to tell you that you're as good as you'll ever be. You're as good as you've ever been, and you won't ever be any better than you are."
>
> I had grown up believing a falsehood—that believers were to pour effort into turning their flesh around and doing right all the time. Thankfully, Bertha wasn't finished. "God never intended for you to get better, because you can't improve flesh," she said. "But the Holy Spirit, who is living inside you, will enable and live through you."
>
> She was right. My flesh hasn't changed one bit. But as the Holy Spirit releases His supernatural power in my life, I find myself going beyond what is *inherent to the nature of man*. And the indwelling Spirit intends to do the same with every follower of God.
>
> Although the works of the Holy Spirit are many, four are basic to the life of faith: The Spirit illumines the mind, enabling believers to understand the things of God; He

> energizes physical bodies to serve the Lord; He enables the will to follow through on doing what is right; and He quickens emotions to feel and express the fruit of the spirit (Gal. 5:22-23)."[62]

A couple of things to mention here. First, if we want to go beyond or live above what is inherent to the nature of man, we need supernatural power—we need the Holy Spirit. Second, no matter how much we grow and develop in our relationship to Jesus, there will never be an escape from that pull to the left. Not while we are still alive in our physical bodies. We cannot "improve flesh," but we can grow spiritually. Here are the words of Jesus once more:

> The Spirit gives life; the flesh counts for nothing. The words I have spoken to you—they are full of Spirit and life. Yet there are some of you who do not believe.
>
> – John 6:63-64

When we move toward Jesus on the continuum, we not only receive power from the Spirit, we receive life. We gain insight and vision by moving toward Jesus. Dr. Stanley goes over four benefits of the Holy Spirit:

1. *The Spirit illumines the mind.* This is clarity, vision, and discernment. God speaks through his Spirit to our spirit. That is how the communication occurs. One of the reasons we use NDEs in this book is that, for the most part, they are purely spiritual experiences. They are unencumbered by the body, so we have enhanced vision and clarity. Spiritual experiences are revelations from God that enable us to capture a glimpse of what it's like in the spiritual realm. God will allow an experience of the Holy Spirit to strengthen and solidify our faith.

2. *The Holy Spirit energizes our physical bodies to serve the Lord.* The Bible gives many examples of the power of the Holy Spirit being released. As we get closer to our authentic selves and more in tune with our spirits, we begin to have an "experience" with the Holy Spirit, and we become energized and excited. We develop an infectious enthusiasm. As we go further on the path, Jesus promises to reveal himself to us, and we have the added benefit of spiritual power. Jesus said:

> "Those who accept my commandments and obey them are the ones who love me. And because they love me, my Father will love them. And I will love them and reveal myself to each of them."
>
> John 14:21 (NLT)

Sometimes, as we are seeking spiritual insight and wisdom, we are given an impression, a glimpse of something spiritual in nature, something we can spiritually see. Impressions are revelations that God will allow to provide us with a kind of direction or a point of reference to work toward. They give us an idea of what is possible, though it doesn't mean that God is showing us the future or we can foretell the future. When I wrote *Brave the Wave*, I was given an impression of what was possible. But there were thousands of tiny steps to take to bring that into reality. So, we need to seek guidance for every step.

Spiritual revelations help us because they allow for clarity, discernment, and vision. When there is clear vision, you have a better idea of direction. Using the raft in the ocean analogy, when we have a compass or a set direction clearly outlined for us, we can concentrate and focus our energy on high-value activities that drive us toward that goal. That means less wasted energy on useless pursuits.

3. *The Holy Spirit enables the "will to follow through on doing what is right."* This is an aligning of the will with the will of God. When you go through this life focusing on your will or your plan for your life, it leads to mistakes, fear, wasted time, anxiety, and chaos. Jesus said: "Your kingdom come, your will be done, on earth as it is in heaven" (Matthew 6:10). God's will is being done in heaven at all times. The will of the Father is above everything. Jesus told us:

> "Who is my mother, and who are my brothers?" Pointing to his disciples, he said, "Here are my mother and my brothers. For whoever does the will of my Father in heaven is my brother and sister and mother."
>
> – Matthew 12:48–50

Who wouldn't want to be seen by Jesus as a brother or sister or mother? Talk about high value. Can you think of anything that has more value than that? Jesus gives us another example when he was under the most stress in his life:

> He went on a little farther and bowed with his face to the ground, praying, "My Father! If it is possible, let this cup of suffering be taken away from me. Yet I want your will to be done, not mine."
>
> – Matthew 26:39 (NLT)

Getting back to the idea of energy, Jesus also said:

> "My food," said Jesus, "is to do the will of him who sent me and to finish his work."

– John 4:34 NIV

We can see that doing the will of God is a high-value activity that supplies us with the spiritual food and energy we require. It allows us to be connected in the family of Jesus as his brother or sister, and it prepares us for our work in eternity, which is doing the "will of the Father."

We need to understand one critical concept: God's will for our lives is always the best plan. That is why Jesus emphasized it so much. God has a universal will that applies to every believer. He wants every one of us to become more like Jesus. We need to start there and then seek his will for our lives. His will and plan for each of us fits like a glove. It is as unique to us as our fingerprints or our one-of-a-kind allotment of gifts, talents, and passions. So, the third "work" of the Holy Spirit is to align our will with the power and energy-releasing perfect will of God. Seeking God's specific will for our lives is one of the wisest investments of our time.

4. *The Holy Spirit "quickens emotions to feel and express the fruit of the Spirit."* Emotion—ah, the vagaries, quandaries, benefits, and pitfalls of emotion. Emotions are a double-edged sword. They have benefit, but they also can be a hindrance as we move along. We want power and energy, so the Holy Spirit will quicken our emotions so that we can "feel and express" the fruit of the Spirit. When we look at "quickening" our emotions, we want stimulation, excitement, arousal, inspiration, and activation. In short, we want "infectious enthusiasm."

We talked about inspiration when we mentioned Bill Gates and Martin Luther King Jr. What are you excited, stirred up, or inspired about? We discussed in chapter 2 that a simple way to help you discover the answer is to pay attention to what you talk about. When you are thinking about and focused on particular ideas, troubles, or passion, harmonious or otherwise, you tend to talk about them a lot, and most of the time you aren't even aware of it. Start observing what you tend to discuss with others, and you'll notice that you subconsciously shift the conversation to those topics that are on your mind the most.

Personally, I enjoy talking about ideas, and that's a good thing. Eleanor Roosevelt said, "Great minds discuss ideas. Average minds discuss events. Small minds discuss people." I'll be honest. When someone around me starts talking about some celebrity or "famous" person, my eyes start to glaze over. I am not saying that I have a "great mind"; I'm just saying those topics are not stimulating nor do they inspire me or rouse any real emotion. The lives of complete strangers are not interesting to me because I am focused on what God's will for my life is and trying to help others find their passion and purpose.

God won't ask us about anyone else's life or compare each of us to someone else, even a celebrity. He won't say, "Why weren't you more like him or her?" If we believe what NDErs are telling us, God will say, "Why weren't you more like *you*, the authentic you, the *you* I created and gave all these gifts and talents to? Why did you bury and waste all the gifts I gave you by ignoring them and by pursuing activities with *no value*?"

This comes down to self-awareness and to our willingness to look in the mirror. As you examine yourself, if you can't see excitement, inspiration, or "infectious enthusiasm" in any area of your life, you may want to consider where you are on this continuum of authenticity. Are you moving toward Jesus or toward the world? Power and energy come from the Holy Spirit, the will of the Father, and from a growing, thriving relationship with Jesus. We waste valuable time trying to convince ourselves otherwise.

Objective Gratitude

Let me digress for one second to give you an example of an idea that has helped me from the book *The Obstacle is The Way* by Ryan Holiday related to the idea that there should be a distinction between observation and perception. Sometimes we let our emotions get the best of us, which results in poor decision-making. If we can step back, take ourselves out of a situation, and see it for what it really is, we can be more effective. Extracting ourselves from the situation, even for just a little bit, helps us to make better decisions since we can be more objective.

Recently, I was given a blessing, but all I could think about was how this blessing had no impact on what I really wanted as far as my work situation or career. Nothing really changed for me in a way that I had been hoping and praying for. I wasn't seeing the situation for what it was. God blessed me in a powerful way, yet I could only think about how it didn't really change my day-to-day work life. My response was one of selfish thanklessness. Once I got my eyes off myself and began to look at things objectively, I was able see this blessing for what it truly was. I understood that being immensely grateful was a much more appropriate, powerful, and useful attitude regarding this blessing. Many times when we look at our lives with an objective eye, our only response should be gratitude.

Being grateful brings peace and joy. Learning to be grateful, and the ability to see the grace that God has bestowed on each of us, has a direct impact on that peace and joy. If we are so busy looking at other people's lives and comparing ourselves to others, we lose the clarity and vision that come from recognizing God's blessings *in our own lives*. We lose perspective as well as the chance to get closer to authenticity, peace, and joy. If we keep focusing on what we don't have, we are setting ourselves up for disappointment, bitterness, and anger, which are the root and the fruit of unmet expectations. It is a vicious circle, a death spiral, that feeds on itself and leads us away from the truth and from spiritual power.

Acquiring Love and Power

Now it's time to keep tabs on this growing list of our "Sources of Power."

1. Love
2. Holy Spirit
3. Authentic Self (this is here because the closer we get, we receive love *and* the power of the Spirit

These are sources of supernatural or spiritual power. They exist in the realm of the unseen. We know that love is the central force of the universe and that it binds, connects, and gives us access to the central power of the universe, God. Why? Because God is love. You want love? Get closer to Jesus. You want power? Engage in activities that bring you closer to Jesus. Let's look at another example from an NDE about how our relationship to God and Jesus is of the utmost importance:

> The purpose of religion is to help you have a personal relationship with God. Religion is only a means to find God. Religion is not the destination. True religion is the love of God in every word, thought and deed of the person.

> God loves all people and is pleased by religions that seek him in spirit and in truth.[63]

Loving God in every word, thought, and deed pleases Him. When we seek Him in "spirit and in truth," we're engaging in high-value activities. Anything we do that brings us closer to Jesus or that we do in a loving or selfless manner for the benefit of others is a high-value activity.

We get power and inner strength through God's spirit. His love keeps us strong. We should do everything we can to understand and experience the width, height, and depth of the love of Jesus, knowing that no matter how hard we try, we will never be able to understand it fully. Experiencing that love makes us complete in the fullness of life and power that comes from God, which should encourage us as we seek to do our part to gain access to this "fullness of life and power."

The next time you are getting together with your friends and family, look around. Be an observer. Who has passion? Who gets excited, has energy, and is highly motivated or gets animated when they are talking about a subject? What about you? Do you get excited about anything? Do you get animated or energetic when you are talking about a project, task, or idea? If not, why not?

There may be passions in your life you aren't even aware of. If you don't go looking for treasure, you'll never find it. It's time to get in the game.

16

TAPPING THE POWER WITHIN

We are spirits surrounded by physical bodies, not bodies who happen to have a spirit. When you go on a spiritual journey seeking power, vision, and clarity, you must take your body with you while on this earth. We must not only develop our spiritual selves; we need to also take care of our physical bodies. We are obliged to have as much physical energy as we possibly can, which means exercise, plenty of sleep, and eating right. Our body is a gift from God, and we have a responsibility to take care of it so that we can be useful in his kingdom. Without it, we can't execute and implement our unique purpose.

Exercise Boosts Power

We all know exercise is good for us, yet 80 percent of the population does not get the minimum recommended amount of cardio and strength-training exercise.[64] Below is a partial list of the many benefits of regular exercise from a review article on the health benefits of exercise.[65]

We know that exercise:

1. Reduces blood pressure
2. Reduces cholesterol levels

3. Increases the concentration of high-density lipoprotein (HDL or "good" cholesterol in the blood)
4. Reduces chances for coronary heart disease
5. Increases efficiency of heart and lowers resting heart rate
6. Makes heart muscles stronger
7. Improves contractile function of the heart
8. Improves pulmonary efficiency
9. Improves respiratory function
10. Improves cardiovascular endurance
11. Provides more oxygen to body, including organs and muscles
12. Provides more nutrient supply to the body
13. Reduces risk of stroke
14. Improves vascular tone
15. Increases metabolic rate
16. Reduces risk of colon cancer
17. Strengthens and develops muscle
18. Improves various indexes of psychological functioning
19. Enhances brain functioning by increasing the amount of oxygen available to it
20. Increases sense of well-being
21. Increases resistance to pain because endorphin levels are elevated
22. Increases sense of excitement because hormone epinephrine is elevated
23. Enhances mood
24. Reduces anxiety
25. Boosts energy
26. Helps control anger
27. Reduces depression more effective than short or long-term psychotherapy
28. Enhances coordination, power, timing and balance

29. Boosts immune system functioning
30. Burns calories
31. Causes body to use calories more efficiently
32. Causes weight loss
33. Allows one to keep lost weight from returning
34. Can act as an appetite suppressant
35. Decreases fat tissue
36. Improves bone density and prevents osteoporosis
37. Reduces joint discomfort
38. Help manage arthritis
39. Prevents or manages type 2 diabetes
40. Helps insulin work better, lowering blood sugar
41. Can add years to one's life
42. Improves glycogen storage
43. Reduces risk of developing certain types of cancers of the colon, prostate, uterine lining, and breast
44. Regulates hormones

If you slowly read over each of those benefits, you are considering including more exercise in your life. If you rapidly scrolled to the bottom, you have already made up your mind that exercise is not an option for you. Sometimes we have valid reasons for not engaging in any exercise, as in the case of being immobile due to injury or illness. But here is where brutal honesty comes into play. If you are capable of exercise and you choose to reject it, you may be rejecting a key source of physical power and energy.

The benefits of regular exercise are overwhelming. So why do so many *not* exercise? Time is not the actual issue—if half the population can get in some cardio exercise two to three times a week, it stands to reason that the other half of the population should be able to fit exercise into their schedule as well. Do all people who exercise regularly love it? Nope, no way. We all know people who hate to exercise. But they do it anyway because they know and understand the benefits (even if, for them, that benefit is how they might look in those new blue jeans).

I'd argue that the foremost reason people avoid exercise has to do with one thing—which is the same thing that hampers our spiritual growth: It comes down to perception of need. People don't really change their habits or behavior until they see an immediate need—not some benefit down the road, but something that is happening right now.

As mentioned earlier, the things that get our attention are either unique, threatening, or valuable. So, try a unique workout that seems fun to you, like Zumba, rock climbing, or martial arts. Or search the internet for something new.

Unfortunately, if nothing new or unique grabs your attention, then you need something threatening. People usually change their behavior and start exercising or eating healthier after a heart attack or a new diagnosis of high blood pressure. Mortality and the idea of impending death tends to get people moving. There's a perception of need, but it's also immediate: "If I don't start exercising now, I may die within a few months!"

Then the last one is value. Exercise takes time, effort, discipline, and sacrifice. There is a payoff, but not an instant one. When my son was younger, I recommended that he start lifting weights. Honestly, I would highly recommend that *everyone* incorporate some type of weight training into their exercise regimen. Young or old, male or female, everyone should do some resistance training, starting in our early teens and continuing even into our nineties. The evidence to support the health benefits is not debatable. I discussed all of this with my son, who was playing sports. Strength training is a significant part of any sport because of the impact it has on performance. He resisted, of course, because of the effort and energy required. It's way more fun and entertaining to play video games. Then I got an idea. One bright morning I said, "You know, you are going through puberty now, and you are getting higher and higher levels of growth hormone and steroids in your body like testosterone." I showed him graphs of rising levels of testosterone and growth hormone in young males going through puberty. Then I dropped the hook, "NFL players are being fined and penalized for illegally using these same hormones to get bigger and stronger. They would kill for the hormones you are getting naturally. If you don't lift weights and exercise, you are wasting all those natural God-given hormones." Well, it took about two weeks with a trainer, and he started to see results. He was hooked. He liked the way his stronger, leaner, more muscular body looked and how it made him feel. (Plus, he saw the attention he started to get from the girls in his class.) He saw the value.

It's hard to make exercise unique. And if there is no threat, people aren't going to be motivated to exercise. So, there must be some type of value for people to make the sacrifice. When it comes to energy power and health, there is plenty of value that can be found in the above list.

In our younger years, we want to look good to make ourselves attractive to the opposite sex. After we get married, some of us kind of "let ourselves go." We are satisfied. As we get older and understand the value of having more energy and being healthy for our families, we will spend the time and effort to incorporate exercise back into our daily routines. I often give my kids advice on "never hurts, never helps"—so much so, they're probably sick of hearing it. Exercise? Never hurts you. Weightlifting? Never hurts you. The benefits are myriad. Eating healthy foods? Never hurts you. Drinking alcohol? Never helps you. Taking drugs? Never helps you.

In relation to finding our purpose and discovering our passion, we can see now that exercise is a tool, just like goal setting. Regular exercise has many benefits—too many to ignore—when it comes to energy and power. For purpose, we need confidence and a good attitude, and exercise helps with mental health far more than we understood twenty or thirty years ago. Regular exercisers have more confidence and experience less depression and anxiety. This is useful because it allows for more energy and makes it easier for us to interact with others.

If we believe there is value in finding and implementing God's purpose for our lives, we will spend time searching for our innate passion. If we value the energy boost, confidence, and the relief of anxiety that come with regular exercise, we will incorporate it into our daily routine. If we don't value those benefits or see them as a need, we will ignore them.

There is no denying the benefits of regular exercise to our mind and body. It's easy to spot anxiety, depression, and hopelessness in our society. One useful approach is to increase our level of activity. We know that today young and old alike are experiencing heightened levels of depression and feelings of worthlessness and hopelessness. We all need confidence, energy, and a boost to our self-esteem. If we make exercise, with some combination of cardio and weightlifting, a part of our daily routine, we are the ones who benefit most, but our entire family will reap reward as well. Confidence, peace, energy, and a positive attitude can spread to others as we consistently engage in exercise. There is real value and power there.

Rise Early, Find Power

Another habit that will help with both spiritual growth and physical energy is the habit of waking up early.

> Very early in the morning, while it was still dark, Jesus got up, left the house and went off to a solitary place, where he prayed.
>
> – Mark 1:35

This is the one habit that I get the most resistance on when I suggest it to my patients. They always respond, "I'm a night owl," or "I'm not a morning person."

Ignoring all the physical and emotional benefits of getting up early for just one second, let's focus on a quiet time in prayer, meditation, and Bible reading. The most important thing we do every day is spend time with God. Nothing is more important than that. It starts your day out the right way because you start with thanksgiving, prayer, and asking for guidance. Prayer is the most high-value activity that you can do with your time. Every second spent with Jesus in prayer, study, and meditation is never wasted and always has value. So, your first dose of energy is spiritual and supernatural.

This is the one habit that has had the most impact on my life. When I skip a day or two because of travel or another reason, I feel it. It's like walking around with a two-hundred-pound barbell across my back. If you want to get more energy, start by getting up early and spending time with Jesus in the Word and in prayer. Rising early to have a quiet time with Jesus centers your life and anchors it to a solid foundation. It may be hard to do at the beginning, but the benefits are tangible, impacting your life in a very powerful way—and there are no negatives.

Many people stay up late watching sports or binge-watching Netflix. It's hard for them to even consider going to bed early and this habit may be difficult to change. When you get up an hour earlier, it is a very good idea to go to sleep an hour earlier. If you can't do that, start with thirty minutes and build yourself up to it.

Anything we do when it comes to spiritual growth is going to require some sacrifice. But once we are engaged in this habitual behavior, we get energy, mood improvement, and clarity. If you combine that with incorporating exercise into your regular pattern of behavior, you get a double whammy of energy. Remember to start new habits one at a time. Let's look at some of the benefits of getting up early from an article in Forbes:

1. If you are a student, you get better grades. In a 2008 Texas University study, college students who identified themselves as "morning people" earned a full point higher on their GPAs than those who were "night owls" (3.5 vs. 2.5). Good grades help students secure better career opportunities.
2. It makes you more goal oriented and proactive. Harvard biologist Christoph Randler discovered in 2008 that early risers are more proactive. They were more likely to agree with statements like "I spend time identifying long-range goals for myself" and "I feel in charge of making things happen."
3. You are more likely to formulate a plan to reach your goal. Early risers report using their morning quiet time for organization, goal setting, and planning out their days and weeks ahead.
4. If you incorporate exercise into the habit of getting up early, that is a double energy dose. Many successful businesspeople get up early to exercise (before the family is awake and their

official workday starts). Regular exercise boosts mood and fitness, provides energy on the job, and helps create deeper sleep cycles.

5. You get better sleep. That is a big one. Better sleep means more energy. Period. Sleep experts say that if you go to bed earlier and wake up earlier, your body will be more in tune with the earth's circadian rhythms, which offers more restorative sleep.
6. Being positive is huge when it comes to having energy. Various studies have shown that morning people exhibit character traits like optimism, being agreeable, satisfaction, and conscien-tiousness. Night owls, while linked with creativity and intelligence, are more likely to exhibit traits like depression, pessimism, and being neurotic.[66]

Some examples of successful people who rise early, taken from *The Power of Positive Thinking*:

- Jack Dorsey, co-founder of Twitter, wakes up at 5:30 in the morning.
- Disney CEO, Bob Igor, gets up at 4:30 in the morning.
- Richard Branson, founder and chairman of the Virgin Group, wakes up at 5:45 every morning.
- Apple CEO, Tim Cook, wakes up at 3:45 every morning. (Yes, every morning!)67

There is one guarantee I will fully stand behind: You will never see anything in this book being highly recommended for which I have zero experience or is not a part of my daily routine. If I get up at 3:45 a.m., I'm sleeping late.

Some of these ideas and suggestions will be disruptive to a lifestyle you have grown accustomed to. You're comfortable, and you have your routine. One thing we all should realize is that comfort can be an idol. There are no verses in the Bible promising comfort and ease as we are going about our lives fulfilling our purpose.

Making the shift to getting up early will be tough at first. But once we recognize the value of a rich relationship with Jesus, that is when the change takes place. The spiritual benefits gained include vision, clarity, discernment, and intimacy with Jesus. There is nothing more valuable and no activity more high value than spending time with Jesus, prayer, and meditating on the Word. These bring power and peace.

> "No one who can rise before dawn 360 days a year fails to make his family rich."
>
> – Chinese proverb

Making our family rich in love, joy, peace, kindness, wisdom, and goodness is very good advice. Waking up early provides plenty of benefits, as we can see from the above list. Regular exercise, setting goals, sleeping better, and being positive are enough to power *anyone through anything*. We get a motor for our life raft as well as direction and navigation. But we are just getting started.

Our quiet time with Jesus in prayer, listening for his voice, reading the Bible, and meditating on the Word, will be the best GPS navigation system we can have. There is no better guidance on the planet. But that is not all. We also access the supernatural power that is available to us, especially if our superordinate goal is to grow and move toward our authentic selves, the selves we were created to be.

17

THE PATH TO YOUR UNIQUE PASSION

Life is either a daring adventure or nothing at all.

–Helen Keller

Let's review our sources of power and energy. Where should we list passion? Is it supernatural or physical? It comes from within us. If it comes from our heart, we would have to say it's supernatural because it is given to us by God. It is unique to us. Sometimes it must be discovered or unearthed because it may be buried so deeply that we aren't even aware of it.

Supernatural power	**Physical power and energy**
1. Love	1. Goal setting
2. Holy Spirit	2. Getting up early
3. Authentic self	3. Better sleep
4. Passion	4. Exercise

Self-examination is key here. We must ask ourselves, *Is there adventure in my life? Am I being daring? Am I trying new things and engaging in new experiences? Was I created for more*? We should try to nurture a passion for adventure and new experiences. God made the planet for us to enjoy, explore, and discover. We should all experience different cultures and meet different people. New experiences bring new ideas and new people into your life.

However, one of the biggest obstacles to living our own lives of passion and adventure is fear. Many times, we get comfortable in our ways, and we make that comfort and safety an idol. And here is where honesty comes into play. We should be able to recognize our own level of comfort in where we are now. You may have picked up this book because you're looking for power or energy. But to acquire new habits and abandon old ones may mean leaving our comfort zone.

Ask yourself, *Am I pursuing, discovering, or developing my passion?* Here is a list of clues to help identify your passions, many of which we have already discussed.

1. Early on, even in childhood, you noticed you were better at something than other people (e.g., drawing, painting, singing, dancing, poetry, writing, debate, public speaking).
2. You can pinpoint the time of day, where you were, or exactly what you were doing when you said to yourself, "Hey, I'm good at this," or "I really like this" (like when I heard Jimi Hendrix for the first time).
3. Something comes easy to you, you perform well at it, and you don't even have to think about it.
4. Time seems to pass quickly when you're engaged in a certain activity.

5. You realize that the activity you are engaging in improves your mood or your sense of well-being. *This is an important indicator* because it ties into goal setting and harmonious passion, both of which improve you own sense of well-being. When you are doing what you were created to do, it feels right. It feels good.
6. You enjoy learning about this activity, such as watching documentaries or YouTube videos or reading about it. You relish the process of getting better at that activity. In fact, the *process* becomes just as fun as the results. Tom Brady admits he could watch film of his opponents for hours. He loves it.
7. When you're unable to do that activity because of illness, injury, or other circumstances, you're disappointed. It also has a negative impact on our mood.
8. No one needs to push you or remind you to do the activity. In other words, it's loaded with self-motivation. You don't mind getting up early for it, and you don't need to set an alarm in the morning. You do it even if you don't feel like it.
9. You make sacrifices and plan your day so you have free time to engage in this activity.
10. Your find your thoughts drifting toward this activity even when you're not engaged in it.
11. You talk about this activity frequently.
12. You enjoy the company of other people who also take pleasure in this activity.

Now, looking at this list of the characteristics, we can begin to think about our unique passion. Let's break down the definition of *passion* into parts for a mini list:

1. A strong inclination
2. Self-defining activity

3. Activity that we like or even love
4. Find the activity important
5. Invest time and energy
6. Engage in on a regular basis

Putting it all together, we have:

A strong inclination toward a self-defining activity that one likes (or even loves), finds important, and in which one invests time and energy on a regular basis.

Combining those two lists gives you a powerful road map or treasure map to help find your passion. If we remember that self-motivation is a critical component, then we're in business. No one is going to come around to your side of the bed and say "Hey, it's time to get up. You have work to do. You are wasting your life on low-value activities. You were created for much more." That motivation and drive to do something of value *must* come from within. It should come from passion, and it's ultimately linked to purpose.

I get up early and spend time on my passions *because there's no other choice*. While they are vital to reaching my authentic self, these activities are also within the realm of "can't not." They have made the transition from things that I can do to things that I *must* do—a powerful clue for anyone that they are engaged in their passion.

Because of your distinctive gifts, experiences, talents, and passions, your purpose is custom designed for you. No one else can fulfill this purpose because only you have acquired the insight, clarity, and knowledge as you grow closer to your authentic self. These attributes are all unique to you, and until you believe that, you won't invest the time and effort required to discover your passion.

One characteristic of your own passion and purpose that should be crystal clear is that *no one else cares as much as you do*. A prime example would be Noah building the ark. Everyone thought he was nuts. He just kept on working. In the end, he was right.

If you are engaging in your passion, it may be helpful to be around like-minded people. When it comes to spiritual growth and learning, a small-group Bible study helps by giving us an avenue to discuss spiritual ideas. Not only can we learn a great deal, but it provides the added benefit of a supportive and caring environment to share our trials, triumphs, and life events. We were meant to do life together in support of one another.

In my Bible study group, we lift each other up and support and love one another. I highly recommend you become a part of a small Bible study group. It's a very powerful tool for spiritual growth, and it engenders the resilience required to move toward our purpose.

As we discussed earlier, self-motivation is a key to completing your purpose. No one is going to prod us and move us along to carry out our purpose. Everyone has their own unique purpose and passion to attend to. With every professional or personal success I have had, there was no one pushing me to get up early or finish this task or carry out that project. Self-motivation and self-discipline were essential.

Identity

Now, look at this description of passion as it relates to identity:

> The issue of identity is important. In fact, passionate activities come to be so self-defining that they represent central features of one's identity. For instance, those who have a passion for playing basketball or songwriting do not merely engage in these activities. They see themselves as "basketball players" or "songwriters." In sum, a passionate activity is not simply an activity that one loves dearly,

> values highly, and engages in on a regular basis. It is also something that comes to define oneself. The activity becomes an inherent part of who the person is.[68]

Identity is a source of power and energy, especially if it is closely associated with your passion. It is an interesting concept because our identity is bound to our self-awareness and self-analysis. We should evaluate and consider carefully how we see ourselves.

What is your identity? Some people say, "Primarily, I am a mom." Or, "Primarily, I am a wife." A recent documentary on Nancy Reagan made mention that Mrs. Reagan saw herself as "Ronald Reagan's wife." That was her primary, or alpha, identity. It was first on her list, and she was proud of it.

Discovering your own primary or alpha identity is powerful because it can be tapped to help drive you to fulfill your purpose. For example, some husbands and fathers see themselves as the providers of the family. They are the "big daddies" of the family who take care of business and provide for their wife and children. The problem arises when "big daddy" no longer goes to work, which makes him feel uncomfortable and could be a source of *identity dissonance*, a sort of disconnect between what you see as your identity and the activities you are engaging in. If you aren't devoting time, energy, and effort into activities that are harmonious with your identity, this leads to anxiety, frustration, anger, loss of energy or vigor, depression, isolation, fear, and unmet expectations. To sum all that up, you develop a total lack of well-being.

Your own alpha identity is a source of strength, power, boldness, and enthusiasm. Can you identify any of these characteristics in anything you are currently engaged in?

I myself have some measure of the provider identity. If I don't take care of my family, who will? No one is going to have the passion and concern about my family that I have. That's a source of power. If we can know and understand our identity, it helps us to discover and develop our passion. But our identity also helps us to take ownership of our role. It's the attitude of "It's on me."

Moms feel like they are the ones who take care of and nurture their children. They own the responsibility when their kids get sick or are up with a fever and coughing all night. Moms see themselves as the primary caretakers and so identify primarily with "being a mom," taking ownership of that role. When they are tired and want to get some rest, that alpha identity energy kicks in and says, "If I don't get up to take care of my child, who will? I know 'big daddy' won't."

Before anyone starts talking about how, in their family, mom is the primary provider and dad is the primary caretaker, these are just examples to help us to decipher and recognize our own alpha or primary identity. It's useful for evaluating our own passion and purpose.

Social Identity

Social identity involves our membership in a group and is typically based on race, gender, age, social class, or religion. Tajfel in 1979 proposed the idea that people developed an idea of who they were based on membership in a particular group:

> Tajfel and Turner's social identity theory explains that part of a person's concept of self comes from the groups to which that person belongs. An individual does not just have a personal selfhood, but multiple selves and identities associated with their affiliated groups. A person might act differently in varying social contexts according to the

> groups they belong to, which might include a sports team they follow, their family, their country of nationality, and the neighborhood they live in, among many other possibilities.[69]

Some socialization identities clearly allow us to function in groups, but how much impact do they have on our individual passion? If you are an artist, an athlete, or a musician and have this innate passion that is harmonious, do any of those group identity markers have any bearing on your passion? I was listening to a question and answer forum, and one of the speakers made a very interesting comment. He said, "If you get a group of one hundred people, and each of them is becoming more like Jesus as they begin to grow spiritually, they become less and less like each other as they move forward." This idea is fascinating because it's the essence of authenticity.

If we take this idea and expand on it, we can conclude that when we are focused on pursuing a false or inauthentic self, we become more and more like *everyone else*. We move toward the world on the continuum. We easily assimilate into a group of people that think and act exactly alike—usually pursuing the same kinds of worldly, fleshly goals and, in the end, have little value. We become clones.

We know we are moving in that direction when we start to ask questions like "Is this all there is?" But when we are engaged in our passion and moving in that power toward purpose, we are more likely to ask, "Okay God, I finished that task, what is next for me on the agenda?" There is no shortage of things to do.

Some people see their social identity as their primary or alpha identity. They are a member of a race, for example, and they identify with and focus all their time and energy on that identity. They then adopt a passion that is expected by that group. When we are seeking our unique passion that is linked to our unique alpha identity, we have no need to adopt a passion associated with a group. Our passion is already there, waiting to be discovered, grown, and nurtured.

Defining Ourselves by Our Passion

Let's go over our definition of passion again.

A strong inclination toward a self-defining activity that one likes (or even loves), finds important, and in which one invests time and energy on a regular basis.

The issue of identity is important here because passionate activities come to be so self-defining that they represent central features of one's identity. For instance, those who have a passion for playing basketball or writing songs do not merely engage in these activities. They see themselves as "basketball players" or "songwriters." In sum, a passionate activity is not simply an activity that one loves dearly, values highly, and engages in on a regular basis, it's also something that comes to define oneself. The activity becomes an inherent part of who the person is.

NDEs can offer clarity for us here. We talked about authenticity and our authentic selves and introduced the idea of social or group identity. If we examine our own passion and our own identity, we can see if we are engaging in any activity that benefits other people. We can be aware of this if we can be honest and ask, "Who is the one benefiting from this activity? Is anyone being served or encouraged and supported by this passion?" This is summed up very nicely in a quote from Dr. Kenneth Ring in *Lessons from the Light*:

> In examining the lives of the NDErs we have met in this chapter, do you not feel that all of them, to various degrees, have been aided to live more authentic lives,

> much more in keeping with their previously dormant gifts and propensities, and emboldened to throw off the social shackles, where necessary, that previously constrained them? The Light told Peggy, in effect, that she should "follow her love" and that yielding herself to it was, in fact, to do the most unselfish and constructive thing in the world. The Light seems to be telling us, each of us, that we have a unique gift, an offering to make to the world, and that our happiness and the world's happiness are both served when we live in such a way as to realize that gift, which is no less than our purpose in life.[70]

When we are making an "offering to the world," is that offering limited to the group we are a member of? When it comes to our spiritual family, that group is a supernatural group. Some would argue that it's a group based on beliefs or doctrines, but it is actually a supernatural group because we have the Holy Spirit inside of us. Physical characteristics are irrelevant.

Look at the group-defining characteristics again: race, gender, age, social class, or religion. Someone may be protesting, "Hey, isn't Christianity a religion? Isn't that being a part of a group?" I would argue that Christianity is a relationship—a relationship with Jesus *and* other believers. We are part of the body of Christ, the church. When we receive the Holy Spirit and worship in truth and in spirit, we are a part of a group with supernatural characteristics. We focus on love and the Spirit and growing in love. Look at what the apostle Paul is telling us:

> Therefore, as we have opportunity, let us do good to all people, especially to those who belong to the family of believers.

– Galatians 6:10

Why does the family of believers get special treatment? Because our love for each other is our best and most effective witness to an unbelieving world. This group is supernatural and lasts forever. Being a member of a group based on race, gender, age, social class, or sexual orientation dies when we die—cancelled at our funeral. The only membership that lasts forever is the membership in the "family of believers." That is the membership that has true and lasting value. But membership in this group requires being *born again.*

> Jesus answered, "Truly, truly, I say to you, unless one is born of water and the Spirit, he cannot enter the kingdom of God. That which is born of the flesh is flesh, and that which is born of the Spirit is spirit. Do not marvel that I said to you, 'You must be born again.'
>
> – John 3:5–7 (ESV)

Remember how John Piper sums it up:

> What happens in the new birth is not merely affirming the supernatural in Jesus but experiencing the supernatural in yourself. What happens in the new birth is not the improvement of your old human nature but the creation of a new human nature — **a nature that is really you.**

This is the essence of the authentic self. We need to think in terms of temporary versus eternal when it comes to identity and groups.

This idea was further entrenched into my thinking when I began to reflect on my own vocation. I remember taking care of a patient while doing my residency. He was someone very well known to the emergency room staff. He frequently came in by ambulance after a fall or after being assaulted. One day he was brought in after an assault, and he had a large gash in his scalp. He was also extremely intoxicated. After cleaning his wound, I stapled the large laceration together. About six months later, he was brought in dead on arrival after being hit by a car. When I looked at his head, he still had the staples I put in six months earlier. Thinking about that event made me realize that even if I save someone's life and they have no relationship with Christ with no spiritual inclination whatsoever, I'm making no difference in their eternity. All I'm doing is prolonging their time on earth. In some instances, all they are doing is going back to self-destructive, time-wasting activities.

But what if I introduce someone to Jesus? What if I introduce someone to the wonderful benefits of joining the family of believers? Those benefits last forever. Nothing we can do for someone else has more value. Even a cure for cancer would be a small thing in comparison.

A Ministry and a Mission

Getting back to social identity, we need to understand and realize which groups will last forever. If I am a member of the American Medical Association, is that group going to last forever? Rick Warren wrote:

> God is at work in the world, and He wants you to join Him. This assignment is called your mission, and it is different from your ministry. Your ministry is your service to believers in the Body of Christ, while your mission is your service to unbelievers in the world. God created you for both.

> Your life mission is both shared and specific. One part of it is a responsibility you share with every other Christian, and the other part is an assignment that is unique to you.[71]

We each have a ministry and a mission. This assertion is strongly supported by Scripture. Our ministry is our service to believers in the body of Christ. Serving others in the body is a high-value activity because this group lasts forever. Look at these verses:

> In the same way that You gave Me a mission in the world, I give them a mission in the world.
>
> – John 17:18 (MSG)

> The most important thing is that I complete my mission, the work that the Lord Jesus gave me.
>
> – Acts 20:24 (NCV)

We also have a mission, which is our service to unbelievers and includes bringing the knowledge of the truth of the gospel to them. We should share our faith and be witnesses to the benefits of our faith.

When we break this down and start to consider how we think, then we can see that this is clearly a physical versus spiritual concept. Social identity can be broken down by age, race, gender, or social class. Our identities as believers—our spiritual identities—are linked to service to believers and un-believers. Those are the two groups we are interested in. Here it is again:

> Therefore, as we have opportunity, **let us do good to all people**, especially to those who belong to the family of believers.
>
> – Galatians 6:10

"All people" means everyone but especially those who belong to the family of believers. God loves everyone, not just people who are members of our "group." We're to serve everyone.

We tend to get bogged down in social identity because it's comfortable and easy. We move with ease and comfort in the groups we belong to. However, we have a contribution to make to the happiness of the world, not just the happiness of our group. At the same time, being a member of a group based on the attributes we have discussed gives us an opportunity to share our life experiences and our testimony regarding Jesus. There is nothing that makes Jesus happier than to have a lost sheep come back into the fold. Jesus said:

> In the same way, there is more joy in heaven over one lost sinner who repents and returns to God than over ninety-nine others who are righteous and haven't strayed away!"
>
> – Luke 15:7 (NLT)

Can you imagine having an impact on how things are in heaven?

Harmonious Passion or Obsession

We talked a lot about harmonious passion in chapter 6. Now let's break down harmonious and obsessive passion into their components so we can evaluate where we are currently aligned:

Harmonious passion

1. freely accepted (autonomous) our own free will
2. no contingencies attached
3. acceptance provides motivation
4. contributes to our sense of well-being
5. nondisruptive to our lives or relationships
6. does not overpower our identity

7. in harmony with the rest of our lives and contributes to our overall happiness

Obsessive passion

1. feel compelled to engage in this passion
2. intrapersonal or interpersonal pressure drives it
3. contingencies involved (some reward to the self)
4. self-esteem or social acceptance are the overriding goal of the passion
5. sense of excitement derived from the activity is uncontrollable
6. feel compelled to engage in the activity because these contingencies (self-esteem, social acceptance) begin to control and drive the person
7. tends to run its course as it begins to control the person
8. does not contribute to sense of well-being
9. loss of control leads to overpowering of identity
10. leads to disruption of relationships and disharmony (identity dissonance)

If we observe the behavior of others, we will be able to easily see people who are engaged in obsessive passions while simultaneously ignoring their purpose.

When it comes to harmonious passion, I want to look at *autonomous internalization*. This idea is important because there are no "contingencies" attached, no immediate rewards to the self. In other words, we aren't getting something out of it for our own benefit. The act is its own reward. The songwriter or the artist wants others to enjoy the fruits of their labors, but the songwriter wouldn't stop writing songs if no one ever downloaded a song, and the artist would continue to paint even if they never sold a painting. The process, the act itself, is what they enjoy most.

We talked about process and results-oriented people, like football player Tom Brady. Tom Brady loves watching game film of opponents. He loves practice and preparation. The game on Sunday is the icing on the cake. Another example is guitarist Eddie Van Halen. Eddie used to practice eight hours a day for years. These are two examples of passion. For them, the process or the activity is where the joy is, and *the activity is its own reward.* They freely choose to do the activity because they enjoy it so much, so they have self-motivation and self-discipline. No one is looking over their shoulders or pushing them to fulfill their purpose.

Now contrast that with obsessive passion. This internalization of the activity originates from the interpersonal or intrapersonal pressure of the contingencies that come from that activity. A sense of excitement or distraction derived from the activity becomes like an addiction, and those engaging in obsessive passions feel compelled to be involved because of how it makes them feel.

The video game *Fortnight* is currently all the rage. I just asked somebody I know if they play the game, and he responded, "Yeah, but I had to stop. I was playing until four or five in the morning. I lost all sense of time." See how video games involve a "sense of excitement and distraction" from our daily lives?

Can you see how this is totally in line with the authentic self-continuum? Think about the power of love in the universe. If we are the only one benefiting from this passion, then we are moving away from love and authenticity. When we are playing a video game, we are only concerned with our excitement and entertainment, our own amusement. It's okay to play these games for entertainment or to watch a television show for some mindless distraction occasionally. But if you spend hours and hours on the distraction or the entertainment while ignoring family and loved ones, and you ignore your harmonious passion that benefits others, consider taking a break.

Remember the examples of Bill Gates and Martin Luther King Jr? Sure, they got accolades, and Bill Gates is always mentioned as one of the world's wealthiest people, but was that his initial vision or intent? No. He had a vision of a computer on every desktop, something that would benefit the individual. Martin Luther King Jr. had a dream that everyone would be treated by the content of their character, not the color of their skin. Yes, he was focused on the injustice facing black America, but his vision was for everyone.

Can you say the same about your passion?

18

FEAR AND THE BLANKET OF COMFORT

The unexamined life is not worth living.

– Socrates

When we are being our authentic selves and living our passion, we are free to make an offering to the world that contributes to both our happiness and the world's. But when we are involved with obsessive passions, the benefits are limited to how it makes *us* feel or how it impacts the people around us and their *perception of us*.

For example, working toward being a great football or basketball player may take time and energy for us to become the best we can be in the sport, but if we end up focusing on the wrong things that come with being engaged in that activity—how it makes us feel (pride) or how much we enjoy the attention, accolades, or money—we're no longer pursuing a harmonious passion. But what if we used our fame or money as a platform for change and for service or we give back to the community?

It's also important to remember that harmonious passions will occupy a significant but not overpowering space in our identity. It will be in harmony with other aspects of our lives. We can be engaged in this passion in our jobs or outside of our jobs, but it is not disruptive to our family or work life.

Here we must go back to the mirror and the idea of brutal honesty with ourselves. The mirror is where most change begins, and some of that change is painful. No one wants to see their flaws, of course, but we shouldn't be afraid to look at our imperfections—because everyone has them. It's no big deal. The people who are willing to examine their flaws and who try to improve are those who will get closer to their authentic selves. Not only that, but self-awareness and honesty, combined with a genuine desire to improve, benefits everyone around you, especially those you love. Those unwilling to audit themselves will miss out. They become "old infants," never growing spiritually and totally obsessed with their own needs.

We can still appreciate the beauty in a garden with flowers and trees even if there are a few weeds. But to keep the garden healthy and thriving, we do need to minimize the weeds. They steal water (time) and nutrients (energy) from the flowering trees that bear fruit. If we look at our own lives as a garden, we want to bloom in a way that reflects our authentic selves. This brings me to the story Howard Storm relates in an interview about the conversation he had with Jesus in his NDE. Jesus told Howard:

> The world is like God's garden, where God made everyone to bloom and to be beautiful—with each person unique and special, to be beautiful in their own way.[72]

To gain power, you must develop the skills of self-awareness and self-examination. Look around. It's easy to see politicians, celebrities, friends, and family who don't have the skill of self-awareness or personal accountability. We have the power to engage in spiritual habits, discover our passion, and pursue our purpose. We can inspire others by our actions and by how we interact with them. Loving those around us in selfless, kind, and giving ways is one way to help others around us be more cognizant of their own behavior.

A word of caution here: We don't have the power to change anyone. It is impossible to force someone to look at themselves honestly and make changes in their behavior. If you're trying to do that, be ready to be disappointed and frustrated. Only the Holy Spirit can change a person's heart.

Fear Hinders Progress

So we see that real growth comes from shedding inauthentic or obsessive passions. If we can discard those anchors and focus on passions that are harmonious with the rest of our lives, we are then progressing toward authenticity. From my own experience, being involved in a passion that is harmonious with the rest of my life and is fully integrated with my authentic self is the best way to live. It brings peace, joy, and fulfillment, along with energy and a sense of well-being.

But one huge obstacle to harmonious passion and the path to authenticity is fear. I would have to say *fear wrapped in a blanket of comfort*:

> **Fear**: The biggest reason for unfulfilled potential, unrealized dreams, and living the end of our lives under the constant weight of regret and unrelenting thoughts of what might have been.
>
> – Johnny Cavazos (I just made this up, but it's truth)

"Do not be afraid" is mentioned 119 times in the Bible. You think that's a coincidence? Every major success in my life has had the absolute requirement of moving against fear or doubt. Every dream or goal that I have reached required determination and a willingness to work and move against fear. Fear and comfort. Both are involved.

One idea that is helpful is that *our God-given purpose is greater than our comfort, circumstances, obstacles, trials, or fears.* There is power in that statement if we can turn it into our personal life message. It also protects us from the sting of criticism and from wasting valuable time. Passion and purpose are protective. We are going to address this idea in the chapters ahead. Passion and purpose also act as guides as we move toward our authentic selves. They are absolutely required on the path.

As we are moving toward passion and purpose, the best and most useful approach is to expect obstacles, trials, and difficult circumstances. These are absolutely required. Why? How else can we grow our faith? Faith is more valuable than gold. It allows us to reach our full potential and helps us overcome challenges that we would have never even thought possible. Our God is a BIG God. Pastor Mark Batterson says, "If your prayers aren't impossible to you, they are insulting to God." There is no reason to pray for something that you can accomplish in your own power.

God expects us to move against our fear because that is a powerful means to learn to trust him. Let me go over an idea about comfort and discomfort to help us as we are going about trying to fulfill our purpose. Someone once told me a story about an elderly priest who was in the ICU. He was in his late eighties or early nineties and, because of his illness, knew he would die soon. The interesting part of the story was that he was being visited by another priest, and they were laughing and joking like they were waiting in line for a ride at Disneyland. The priest who was dying even made a comment to his visitor, “Ha, I am going to see Jesus before you!!” And they both started laughing. They were both happy, almost joyous. The dying priest was at the end of his life, and he was at maximum comfort, on the verge of being in the presence of Jesus. He most likely spent most of his life being uncomfortable going about the business of doing God’s work.

Now we contrast that with a story that a hospice nurse shared with me. She told me about a very wealthy patient she was taking care of. She visited him on his yacht twice per week. Most of the time he had a team of advisors and family in the room while she checked his vital signs and examined him. One day he asked that everyone leave the room because he wanted to talk to her alone. She said that he called her over and told her, “Look, I have plenty of money. I can write a check for whatever you want. There must be some cure for my type of cancer that is not available to everyone. Just let me write you a check so that I can get better.”

Thinking about those two scenarios made me realize something. The wealthy man was at maximum discomfort. He was on the edge of the unknown. He was doing everything he could to stay in his life of comfort, luxury, and ease. This life was the closest thing to heaven for him.

We should not be discouraged by trials, storms, and tribulations because they are the circumstances that God allows in our lives for our spiritual growth. Growth often comes through these means. If we can understand and embrace the idea that comfort is not part of God’s plan for our lives, it will be easier to handle all the difficulties we are inevitably going to face. As a bonus, feelings of being uncomfortable or fearful when we are being asked to take on a task are a good sign that we are headed in the right direction. God wants our faith to grow. Untested faith is not very useful. *Our faith will be tested.* You can bet on that.

As I am writing this, I am involved in another uncomfortable and unforeseen circumstance that hit me in the face. One impression that I constantly get as I am working through these ideas is that I can't write about something I know nothing about. It's dishonest. I can't write about attempts to climb Mount Everest or the wonderful spiritual experiences I've had in Jerusalem because I've never been to those places. (Though visiting Jerusalem is on my list of things to do.) I *can* write about my passion. Writing is my passion currently. No one wakes me up at three in the morning to work on my edits. It fits into the "can't not" category. Or the "only I" category. Those two categories are key points when evaluating passion and purpose.

Doing anything for the faith, such as introducing others to Jesus, is going to put us right in the crosshairs of Satan. It's like getting a tattoo of a bullseye right on our chests. We should always remember that Satan hates us. Satan has two major passions: hate and lies. That is who he is. We, as believers, are the enemy. We fight him using the *love* of Jesus and the *truth* he brings to the table. Satan hates love and truth, but with them we can overcome any obstacle.

When we begin to take the Christian life seriously, understand our purpose, and try to implement God's plan for our lives, we shouldn't expect things to go smoothly. In fact, we should be prepared for war. Every choice we make as we go about pursuing passion and purpose is really an act of war. We are engaging in battle. We can be encouraged in the fact that we aren't wasting our time or our lives. There is real power and energy there.

One of the topics I feel comfortable writing about is spiritual warfare. It's something I have experience with. If you are working on purpose and it involves bringing others to Jesus, expect some disruptions and problems, trials and waves, spiritual turmoil and strife. Those flaming arrows just keep coming. That's why I am not surprised by the wave or trial that I am currently undergoing. It's disrupting my family, my home life, and my finances, but it isn't very surprising when we can understand and accept that we are in a battle. That is when things actually start to become easier. It also helps when we can look at our struggle as an honor and a privilege. We are fighting alongside the Holy Spirit and Jesus. There is no greater use of our time.

Think about a group of soldiers in war. Would they be shocked if the enemy mounted a surprise attack in the middle of the night? Would they say, "Hey, that's not fair; we were sleeping and totally unprepared!" No. Just like in the movie *Platoon*, they set up tripwires and claymores and made sure someone was on guard duty to watch for the enemy. We should also expect the unexpected. When we can learn to anticipate trials, troubles, and turmoil, then we can have peace. Our fear diminishes. Peter tells us:

> Dear friends, do not be surprised at the fiery ordeal that has come on you to test you, as though something strange were happening to you.
>
> – 1 Peter 4:12

We know it's coming, and when it does, we can say, "Oh, Satan. Here you are again trying to disrupt what I'm doing. Look, this passion and purpose thing? It's going to get done. You may as well move on to something else. I know the good Lord will take care of me." And we have the words of Jesus to help and guide us when we face spiritual warfare. Here is a very powerful Scripture text to use when you are facing it:

> The seventy-two returned with joy and said, "Lord, even the demons submit to us in your name."
> He replied,"I saw Satan fall like lightning from heaven. *I have given you authority to trample on snakes and scorpions and to overcome all the power of the enemy; nothing will harm you.* However, do not rejoice that the spirits submit to you, but rejoice that your names are written in heaven."
>
> – Luke 10:17–20 (NLT)

Here we can see that we have the authority to overcome all the power of the enemy. We can feel encouraged, confident, and optimistic. One powerful concept is that we already know the outcome of the war. By his resurrection, Christ has redeemed the world. There is power in that idea. Here is another powerful quote from C.S. Lewis:

> Christianity, if false, is of no importance, and if true, of infinite importance. The only thing it cannot be is moderately important.

Many people are living their lives as if Christianity is of moderate importance. They are ignoring their passion and their purpose. We should live our lives in pursuit of passion and purpose. Why? Because it is of infinite importance. It is clear that we are in a war and nothing is *more* important.

Battles will rage on this earth, and we will be involved in spiritual warfare, but we already know the outcomes. Jesus conquered sin once and for all, and he is coming back. We know this. Jesus had his battles, and he won. Now we must engage in ours.

Satan knows his fate, and he is trying to take as many people down with him as he can. If we're going through a tough time right now and we're tempted to be scared or anxious, we can fall back on Scripture and the words of Jesus:

> I have told you these things, so that in me you may have peace. In this world you will have trouble. But take heart! I have overcome the world.
>
> – John 16:33

Jesus has overcome the world. Our best bet is to align ourselves with him. When we do, we move to the right on the continuum.

Life is supposed to be hard. And it is more difficult for the Christian because we are being tested. But this should not be a surprise to us. If we are furthering God's kingdom as we are moving toward our God-given purpose, we are involved in spiritual warfare. It's real. Don't kid yourself.

We are in a war, and Jesus says we need soldiers. Right now. It's an honor and a privilege to serve in this war. It's also the best use of our time while here on this earth. It's time that's never wasted. I hold out every hope and prayer that someone reading this will be inspired or moved to do something valuable with their lives and join in this fight for love and authenticity.

Accept the Challenge

Now that I have scared the bleep out of you, you may be asking, "So what should I do?" I'm glad you asked. It is important to realize that every single one of us has a role to play. We have an assignment of energy or an assignment of love. The first thing we should do is take that assignment very seriously. We are going to be asked about this assignment when we stand before Jesus after we die. A common question NDErs are asked is *What do you have to show me that you have done with your life?*

What we do with our lives, gifts, talents, and passions are all very important. Jesus talked about it in the parable of the talents, and NDErs tell us that we will be asked about what we did with our lives. Remember the idea that what you do in the next twenty or thirty years will have a major impact on the next twenty or thirty billion years. If you believe that idea and it "sticks," you will act. If you don't believe it, you will probably do nothing. The good news is that when you are operating under the guidance and direction of the Holy Spirit and the power of the Word, you have supernatural power, spiritual power.

While I was writing my first book, I investigated the publishing world and read that the odds were a million to one against me. That was the likelihood that my book would get noticed. Just recently, I read an article about self-publishing, and the article stated that Amazon has 32 million books available for purchase. When I read that, I said to myself, "This is ridiculous. There is no way my book will get noticed." Then I said to Jesus, "Lord, how the heck am I going to do this? This is an impossible task." Less than one tenth of a second later came the response, "You just worry about your part. You write the book and learn everything you need to learn about spreading this message. I'll take care of the rest"—conveyed to me in a way almost like "Quit whining, and ***do your job***. Stop squawking like a chicken."

As I am writing this, my first book is going through the editing process. It may be a total disaster, but it won't be because I didn't try and because I didn't put time, money, and effort into the project. Even if it is a failure, I'm encouraged by an excerpt I read by a nun named Sister Faustina. While I was researching the spiritual principles of suffering and the purpose of pain, her diary kept coming up in my searches. Sister Faustina had multiple encounters with Jesus in the mid-1930s. In her diary she wrote:

> One day, I saw interiorly how much my confessor would have to suffer: friends will desert you while everyone will rise up against you and your physical strength will diminish. I saw you as a bunch of grapes chosen by the Lord and thrown into the press of suffering. Your soul, Father, will at times be filled with doubts about this work and about me. I saw that God himself seemed to be opposing [her mentor Father Spocko], and I asked the Lord why He was acting in this way toward [Father Spocko], as though He were placing obstacles in the way of his doing what He himself had asked him to do. And the Lord said, "I am acting thus with him to give testimony that this work is Mine. Tell [Father Spocko] not to fear anything; My gaze is on him day and night. There will be as many crowns to form his crown as there will be souls saved by this work. *It is not for the success of a work, but for the suffering that I give reward.*[73]

Look at that last line. The success of a work is not what Jesus is looking at. This brings us to a common idea. If you are confronted by a task or some other goal that is making you uncomfortable or afraid, a good question to ask yourself is *What would I do if I had no fear?* I would also take it further: *What would I do if I knew that the "success of a work" is not important?* What if you knew that as far as reward for a work, what is important is the suffering endured in taking the work to completion?

Any time, effort, energy, or money spent on furthering the kingdom of God or for the message of the gospel is never wasted, especially if carried out under the auspices of serving others in love and selflessness. Whenever a goal or purpose is selfless, there you will find power.

Affirmation

When you are going about discovering passion and purpose, you need affirmation to confirm that passion. You need other people around you or circumstances that affirm your passion. That within itself is a source of power. Usually that happens when we are younger. If you have a talent or a gift, maybe in music, academics, or sports, this is confirmed by parents, coaches, teachers, or friends. Others affirm your gift to let you know you are headed in the right direction. This is how Eddie Van Halen responded to a question about his guitar playing:

> Q: I take it you took to the guitar fairly easily?
>
> A: Not to sound-ego-out, but I was a natural. My father has been a professional musician all his life, and he said, "Kid you've got it." Some people have got it and some people don't. Even people who don't have it can practice long enough to get it down to a point. But there's always a difference between a person who has the feel and those who don't.[74]

Notice that he qualifies the affirmation. It came from his father, "a professional musician all his life." The affirmation must come from experience and objectivity. If Aunt Ellie tells you that you have the singing talent to become a star, it doesn't carry as much weight as say, Simon Cowell or music producer Clive Davis. These guys are renowned talent evaluators with long histories of finding and developing musical talent.

Affirmation within itself is a source of power because it gives you the confidence you need to go along this path toward your authentic, harmonious passion. It's a great motivator. But where does it fall in our table? When it comes to affirmation, this is when we are going to need the opinion of others. Someone other than ourselves who has some experience in this type of passion. Someone who can be objective.

Supernatural power	**Physical power and energy**
1. Love 2. Holy Spirit 3. Authentic self 4. Harmonious passion	1. Goal setting 2. Getting up early 3. Better sleep 4. Exercise 5. Affirmation

As I am writing this, LeBron James has created a bit of a stir for talking about his greatness as a player. He called himself the greatest of all time. Talk about uproar and controversy. When it comes to our passion, our purpose, and affirmation, it *must* come from outside ourselves. Other people. Look at this verse from Proverbs:

> Let someone else praise you, and not your own mouth; an outsider, and not your own lips.
>
> – Proverbs 27:2

An Impact for Eternity

Sometimes we get discouraged in trying to do something because we think we don't have the intelligence, the gifts, or the wherewithal to get it done. But the Bible, and history itself, records that much of what was accomplished was done by ordinary people doing extraordinary things. God used average, flawed people to do extraordinary things for the kingdom of God.

I remember watching a show about people trying to break into the music business. Fifteen people were in this contest/reality show, and one of the things required of the group was to go get coffee or cheesecake or whatever the "producer" asked them to do. What does going to a coffee shop or the bakery have to do with being a recording artist? That's not the point. The point was were they willing to do everything in their power to get to the next level and fulfill their dream? You could ask yourself the same question. Is there anything that could possibly stand in the way of you achieving your purpose? Those are the kinds of questions we need to be asking ourselves.

The whole idea regarding our role in the kingdom of God is not if we are worthy but if we are willing. That is the kind of attitude that God blesses. The attitude and the mindset we should have is to wake up and spend time in the Word and in prayer with God, then come to him and ask, "What can I do for you today, Jesus?" The flawed characters in the Bible had the same attitude. Samuel says:

> The Lord came and stood there, calling as at the other times, "Samuel! Samuel!" Then Samuel said, "Speak, for your servant is listening."
>
> – 1 Samuel 3:10

How often do you ask that question first thing in the morning? We may say a prayer, but I bet we say, "Listen, Lord, your servant is speaking." A humble, teachable, and willing-to-serve attitude is one of the best ways to get on the right track for our day. When we discover our passion, the next step is to ask God how we are to use this passion in fulfilling our purpose. Carrying out God's plan for our lives is the way he intended for us to live.

Looking at these ideas has brought me to the conclusion that there are only a few reasons why people aren't seeking to fulfill God's plan for their lives. One is ignorance. They just don't know what they don't know. Or they may have an inkling or sketchy idea that they have a passion or a purpose, but it isn't high on the list when it comes to value. They are focused on other goals or passions that are obsessive in nature, passions that benefit themselves. They are "majoring in the minors." If you think about that phrase, it's consistent with the high-value or low-value idea. Majoring in the minors means you are spending the majority of your time on activities with little or no value.

One clear useful indicator to help us figure out the value of any activity we are engaged in is the eternity meter. Ask yourself if the activity you are working on will have an impact on eternity. You may come to realize that much of what you are spending your valuable time on is worthless in light of eternity. Three activities we know have eternal value: loving God, loving others, and furthering the kingdom. Are you engaging your passion while participating in these activities?

Another reason people don't seek to fulfill the plan that God has for their lives is fear. The fear of failure is a big, daunting elephant in the room that prevents people from getting out the door. It's always better to follow and fail than fail to follow because Jesus takes our effort and our attempt into account. He knows what's in our hearts, so we should be confident and daring when it comes to fulfilling our purpose, if our intent is pure. If we get criticized, that is a *good* thing.

> Blessed are you when people insult you, persecute you and falsely say all kinds of evil against you because of me.
>
> – Matthew 5:11

I'm not saying we should seek criticism, but we shouldn't be discouraged by it, because we know that for every insult or evil word spoken against us, we will be blessed—for each insult, a blessing. Our attitude should be "Insult away!" There will always be critics because it requires zero effort, and most people choose the easy path. There is no such thing as a sweaty, hard-working critic. We should remember that it's impossible to do work for the kingdom of God and not be rewarded for it. The difficulty is in examining our motives. It takes complete and ruthless honesty to survey our hearts to see if our actions or goals are self-serving or if our motive is to serve God by serving others. When we have purity of intent and love is at the core of our actions, we know we are walking on solid ground. We are closer to our authentic selves.

"When we stop fearing failure, we start being artists."

-Ann Voskamp

19

THE ARTIST WITHIN

"A good man brings good things out of the good stored up in his heart"
Luke 6:45

You have an artist lurking somewhere within you—a passion, purpose, reason, and plan. It is bubbling inside of you. This whole book came about because of just one question: *What is your passion?* The responses I received when I posed that question to a group of friends—who all got a deer in the headlights look in their eyes—were the impetus for this book.

Do you have a clue what your passion is? Some people that I posed this question to simply dismissed it as irrelevant or unimportant. If we don't think our unique passion is important and we choose to ignore it, that's a huge mistake we could regret for eternity.

Shaquille O'Neal in an interview said at the end of his career he was chasing championships. Then someone told him, "Your book is already set. You can maybe add some index pages, but you can't add too much to your book." That's a good lesson for us. Shaquille was talking about his "book" regarding basketball. He is doing other things in business and is keeping busy. The question we should be asking ourselves is are we finished with our "book"? Are there chapters that we should be working on? Is there any task that needs to be completed? There are people who wrote short stories who could have easily added three or four more chapters to their "book."

The word *retirement* isn't in the Bible. Many people have the dream of being able to relax, travel, and enjoy grandchildren in their golden years, and I am one of them. But I believe that God wants us engaging in our passion and pursuing our purpose even after we retire from our jobs. Ask Jesus how important our passion is. Remember what he said,

> "His master replied, 'You wicked, lazy servant! So you knew that I harvest where I have not sown and gather where I have not scattered seed? Well then, you should have put my money on deposit with the bankers, so that when I returned I would have received it back with interest. "⍰'So take the bag of gold from him and give it to the one who has ten bags. For whoever has will be given more, and they will have an abundance. Whoever does not have, even what they have will be taken from them. And throw that worthless servant outside, into the darkness, where there will be weeping and gnashing of teeth.
>
> – Matthew 25:26-30 (NLT)

Look at the emotion in this verse. Many times, when I'm reading the Bible, stopping to visualize the scene where Jesus is emphasizing a point helps me to focus on what he considers to be the most important ideas he is trying to convey. Try to imagine how he is talking to his disciples. Is he standing or is he sitting? Is it night or during the day? Is he outside or in someone's home? In this verse, it's hard to visualize Jesus lying or reclining on a cushion just talking. It seems more likely that he is standing up and motioning with his arms, moving around and getting into the face of His apostles. It's loaded with energy and emotion because it's a warning.

This verse really comes down to a choice. We're either going to believe Jesus and take him seriously or we aren't. It's very simple. Jesus is telling us in this parable that our talents and gifts are infinitely important to our purpose. They aren't moderately important or irrelevant.

Read the above verse a few times. This passion, purpose stuff is no joke.

You may have no energy, or you are anxious or unfulfilled in your job. Don't be discouraged. There is still time to discover and try new things. It's an adventure. You may be a bird in the water or a fish in the air. You aren't in the right place. You don't have access to power because you are out of your element. Passion and energy are inside of you, bubbling and churning, waiting to be released. It's part and parcel of the essence of your authenticity. Developing and engaging this passion gets you closer to your spiritual self. When you can get a glimpse of your authenticity and engage in your passion while working toward your purpose, you are in contact with your spiritual self. The unseen. A whole new world opens up to you. It's living the spiritual life. It's way more exciting and fascinating than spending time looking at someone you don't know do something that has nothing to do with your life or your purpose. Remember they may also be expending time and energy on passions and a purpose that is totally inconsistent with who they were created to be.

Ask yourself "what happens if I'm blind and I'm being led by the hand by another blind person?" Both of you will fall into a ditch. Wisdom comes from letting Jesus lead. You have one-hundred different paths in front of you. Only he knows what is at the end of every single one of those paths. We humans don't have a clue.

Remember that we are ALL spirits. Getting closer to your spiritual self is one key component to discovering your passion as you work to fulfill your purpose. The crucial first step is spending time with Jesus and learning how to enjoy his presence. There is power, vision, and clarity in that experience. You begin to experience life in a richer and fuller way. You have access to clearer vision and a sensitivity to spiritual experiences and ideas. You are more aware of the unseen spiritual world around you, plus the natural world like birds, trees, and animals seem to take on a different type of appearance.

I remember being in a Bible study and someone mentioned that when they came into a relationship with Jesus, everything looked different. The sky, trees, birds, flowers, everything. I've had a similar experience. Going back to near-death experiences, many people say that when they come back, things look different in the world and they have an enhanced appreciation of the "joys and majestic power of nature."

When we look at post-NDE behavior or psychological changes, we can see that there are many changes that occur in people's lives that can be linked to passion and purpose. Let's look at some of these changes and point out how they can help with *our* unique passion and purpose. We should remember that NDEs are an educational experience for the person undergoing the NDE. They are meant to guide people to their true, authentic selves. These are some after-effects of NDEs.

- Self-acceptance (more self-confident and outgoing): absolutely required to fulfill our purpose. We need confidence to overcome fear

- Increased concern for others: very important because we know our purpose involves others
- Anti-materialism: life centered on acquisition and materialistic values seen as empty or pointless. This is useful in identifying harmful obsessive passions.
- Anti-competitiveness: NDErs no longer follow common socially approved pathways that require us to compete with others for material rewards. Impressing others ceases to be important. NDEs help us to value cooperation with others in fulfilling our purpose. It's absolutely required. Competition is inauthentic.
- Spirituality: a universal or inclusive spirituality. Remember the continuum. Moving toward Jesus, and love yields spiritual power. We need that power to fulfill our purpose.
- Knowledge: many NDErs are imbued with a tremendous thirst for knowledge. You are going to have to learn and acquire knowledge to develop your passion and fulfill your purpose. Passion doesn't come fully developed.
- Purpose: Life is meaningful, and there is a *sacred purpose* to everyone's life. Many feel that the task of post-NDE life is to discover their own spiritual *raison d'etre*, or reason for existence.
- Belief in God: They have a deep, confident inner certitude that God exists. Power comes from love primarily. God is love.[75]

If we look at the NDE as a purely spiritual experience outside of the body, it's like taking a space shuttle at light speed to true authenticity. It's a giant leap toward the right along the continuum of love and authenticity.

Many NDErs get to experience the all-encompassing power of the love of God. They feel this firsthand. But many benefits come from those experiences. Look at the above list and think about how much power and energy come from each one of these psychological and behavioral changes. These are all available to us when we grow in our relationship to Jesus. We don't necessarily get a space shuttle ride to that level of authenticity. The rest of us must work at growing our spiritual senses and vision, and it takes time and effort. However, the thing about this quest is that as soon as you see some light and have been granted insight or revelation, you want more.

People who have had near-death experiences seems to always mention how everything is connected. We are all bound together, and that binding energy or force is love, which is intertwined and inherent in all the ideas mentioned above. Love brings:

1. *self-acceptance and confidence*. It's rooted in love and self-appreciation.
2. *a concern for others*. It comes from a selfless, more mature approach to life.
3. *anti-materialism and anti-competitiveness*. This has more to do with an idea of cooperation rather than competitiveness.
4. *spirituality and knowledge*. Getting a glimpse of our spiritual selves helps us to see the value of living more in tune with our spirits as we seek knowledge and truth.
5. *an understanding that we have a sacred purpose*. The pure experience of love is enlightening. We understand we have a sacred purpose and we desire a more meaningful relationship with God.

This is a nice road map to see where you are on this path to passion and purpose. Peruse this list and see if you have any of these characteristics. Do you accept yourself? Do you have concern for others? Can you see that materialism is pointless? Are you in tune with your spirit? Do you have a tremendous thirst for knowledge? Are you seeking your purpose?

Don't be discouraged if you feel like you don't have many of these characteristics; they take time to develop. But they can be acquired by acknowledging and developing our relationship with Jesus. And it starts with love.

True, some of these come about due to difficult circumstances that bring pain and discomfort. That's part of the process. Believe it or not, pain brings power. It's not what we would expect. This could easily be listed on our sources of supernatural power, but this topic is reserved for another book in the *Authentic Self* series. (Shameless plug.)

These changes don't come easy, and they aren't free. The difficulty is that it takes time, effort, and patience to be connected with our spiritual selves. It takes time to develop our spiritual senses. But the value that comes from connecting with our spiritual and authentic selves is priceless.

The guidance, discernment, and clarity of vision to see and decipher our passion and our purpose has a tremendous impact on our daily lives. These changes benefit each of us and everyone around us for the better. If we want to connect to the physical or natural realm, we can sit on a recliner and just be. Connecting to our spiritual selves and opening the eyes of our hearts will require time and effort. We know that we are to take this growth very seriously:

> Therefore, my dear friends, as you have always obeyed—not only in my presence, but now much more in my absence—continue to work out your salvation with fear

> and trembling, for it is God who works in you to will and to act in order to fulfill his good purpose.
>
> –Philippians 2:12-13

The Right of Imperfection

Things become a little easier if we cut ourselves some slack. We should allow ourselves the right of imperfection. We as humans are born with that right. Every human is imperfect. You may have looked at that list above and began to feel discouraged or down about yourself. Remember one thing: the people who underwent an NDE had a pure spiritual experience. Their spirits left their bodies. When we are going along on this path, we can't escape our bodies. Our spirits are trapped. We have those thoughts that are fleshly, and our brains are hardwired for rewards from physical pleasures such as sex or the satisfaction of eating our favorite meal. We also get feelings of pride or excitement when we buy something new or someone notices us in a new car.

This isn't a laid-back journey on the continuum toward love, joy, and peace. But there is no value in critiquing or criticizing ourselves if we feel we aren't measuring up. We should remember that no one is. That is not the point. The point is being able to look in the mirror and be honest with ourselves. The power comes from asking the questions, "Can I do better? Can I be better? Was I created for more?" Finding your passion while moving toward your purpose will get you closer to "better." The rewards and benefits are undeniable.

We already know that everyone walking on the face of the earth can be better or do better. The only one who had no room for improvement while living on earth was Jesus. He fulfilled his purpose. His last words were "It is finished" (John 19:30).

When we work to move toward our authentic selves, we benefit and everyone around us benefits. There really is a payoff, one that lasts for eternity.

A Hunger for Knowledge

We learned that NDErs consistently gain a thirst for knowledge. Truthfully, we should have a passion for pursuing knowledge, wisdom, and truth no matter what our purpose is. Many of you have heard the slogan "Knowledge is power." That is true, and so we should strive to be as powerful as possible. The Bible has referenced wisdom and knowledge for thousands of years:

> A wise person is hungry for knowledge, while the fool feeds on trash.
>
> – Proverbs 15:14 (NLT)

Notice that in order to be wise we must hunger for knowledge. Does that describe you?

> A wise man is strong, And a man of knowledge increases power.
>
> – Proverbs 24:5 (NASB)

> Good sense is a fountain of life to him who has it, but the instruction of fools is folly.
>
> – Proverbs 16:22 (ESV)

> Let the wise hear and increase in learning, and the one who understands obtain guidance.
>
> – Proverbs 1:5 (ESV)

> For the protection of wisdom is like the protection of money, and the advantage of knowledge is that wisdom preserves the life of him who has it.
>
> – Ecclesiastes 7:12 (ESV)

> If any of you lacks wisdom, let him ask God, who gives generously to all without reproach, and it will be given him.
>
> – James 1:5 (ESV)

Now look at all those statements above, and tell yourself one thing. "Those verses are about me. I'm the one pursuing knowledge and wisdom right now." No one put a gun to your head and made you buy this book. You're self-motivated. You're seeking wisdom. You're saying to yourself by your actions, "I can do better." This is affirmation coming from outside yourself. If you think about it for a second, you're already better than when you started this book. You probably know more, especially when it comes to passion and purpose. If you began to incorporate any of the suggestions mentioned, you have more power and energy. Already you are better and stronger than when you started the book.

But if you haven't started yet, that's okay too. If you begin to take some of these suggestions seriously and begin to act, there is no question you will have more energy, confidence, power, and peace. Plus, you will have the satisfaction of knowing that you are closer to your authentic self, the self that God had in mind when he created you.

Let's see what NDEs tell us about the pursuit of knowledge. Raymond Moody talks about this in *Life after Life*:

> Some of those I interviewed claim that, while they cannot adequately explain it, everything they had ever done was

> there in this review (what has been described as a life review) from the most insignificant to the most meaningful. Others explain that what they saw were mainly highlights of their lives. Some people characterize this as an **educational effort** on the part of the being of light. As they witness the display (of their life review), the beings seem to stress the importance of two things in life: Learning to love other people and acquiring knowledge.[76]

Let's look more closely at this idea. There's an "educational effort on the part of the being of light." It seems that these experiences are about education. Learning. Wisdom. Knowledge. We have talked about how the "being of light" points out a fictional or false self as a point of learning and growth. It is essentially telling people, "Hey, look, you are living a lie, and you are wasting your time." My argument is that we don't have to die to find out we're living a lie.

In his book *Lessons from the Light*, Kenneth Ring summarizes some important ideas that we can gain from the NDE, knowledge being one of them:

- Life does not begin with birth nor end with death
- Life is precious—live it to the fullest.
- The body and its senses are tremendous gifts—appreciate them.
- **What matters most in life is love** (this is a biggie because God is love).
- Living a life oriented toward materialistic acquisition is missing the point.
- Cooperation rather than competition makes for a better world.
- Being a big success in life is not all it is cracked up to be.

- **Seeking knowledge is important—you take that with you.**[77]

Love and knowledge. Boom. End of story. If we stop and think about our unique experiences and our unique gifts, those can be linked to knowledge. Discovering our passion is actually a very important part of "knowing" ourselves. When combined with the genuine desire to serve and love others selflessly, that releases power and energy.

Now we can go back to our list with one new addition, *knowledge*:

Supernatural power	Physical power and energy
1. Love 2. Holy Spirit 3. Authentic self 4. Harmonious passion 5. Knowledge	1. Goal setting 2. Getting up early 3. Better sleep 4. Exercise 5. Affirmation

So, what does this all mean for us as individuals as we pursue authenticity, passion, and purpose? When we are working on our passion, we are going to have to do some learning. Eddie Van Halen had natural talent, but it took years of practicing eight hours a day to get to that level of skill. It takes knowledge, effort, and discipline to develop that passion.

Even Picasso had to spend years in training to perfect his artistic skill. You may have heard the following story about him. Picasso was sitting in a café sketching a drawing on a napkin and was about to throw it away when a patron in the cafe sitting next to him asked if he could have it. Picasso replied, "Yes, for twenty thousand dollars." The man was shocked and said, "That is ridiculous. It took you one minute to draw out that sketch." Picasso replied, "No, it took my whole life."

That is the combination of passion, discipline, and knowledge. Picasso diligently studied many other artists before developing his own unique style. When you are developing your passion, you must invest time and effort, and you must acquire knowledge about whatever pursuit you are going to be engaging in. Honestly, there are no other options. Plus, it's a clear indicator for you to know that you are on the right track because learning about your passion and studying it is fun and enjoyable. You don't feel that you are wasting your time when you are pursuing knowledge related to your passion. Eddie Van Halen says he never took a lesson, but he studied every note that guitarist Eric Clapton played.

We should develop a passion for learning, a passion for acquiring wisdom, especially if we can embrace the idea that wisdom is thinking the way God thinks. If we focus on love and knowledge, we're already thinking along the same lines. We should begin by being curious and asking questions. The most important inventions and innovations came about by simply asking the question, "What if?"

Develop a mindset of adventure. Seek new experiences. Learn new things. God made the planet for us to enjoy, explore, and discover. Experience different cultures and meet different people. These activities bring new ideas and new people into your life.

The pinnacle of adventure is engaging in our unique passion while working to fulfill our unique purpose. Living the way God intended for us to live brings us closer to authenticity and fulfillment. You're discovering things about yourself that you didn't know or understand before. You are going to have to dig and explore to uncover the artist within. There are many hidden interests, passions, and talents sitting there waiting to be discovered. As you start to get serious about looking for these passions, you may be asking, "Where do I start?" Well, if you have been paying attention, you start early in the morning. If you spend time in prayer, listening to God's voice, and reading the Word, you are headed in the right direction.

The Will of the Father

God created you, and he has a dream for your life that is intimately associated with your purpose. Believe it or not, there may be more than one purpose God has in mind. That's why I am writing this book. I believe that a part of my purpose has been realized by my vocation. It is just one thing that God had in mind for me. But there are seasons of passion as we grow that are unique to circumstances, maturity, experiences, spiritual visions, and revelations. I'm in a new season now.

This is related to the idea that purpose is an "only I" proposition. Only you can engage your unique passion, tap into that "assigned energy," and pursue and fulfill your God-given purpose. Your experiences, talents, and gifts are unique to you, and your purpose is an "only I" endeavor. Only you can fulfill your purpose in the way that God has in mind.

This reminds me of a time when my son was playing a baseball game one cool, spring evening. He was probably around nine years old at the time. His team was losing by one run, and it was the bottom of the ninth inning. My son came up to bat. There was one runner on base. My son hit a hard line-drive into center field. The runner on base scored. The game was tied! My son made it around second and was rounding toward home. The outfielder had trouble getting the ball but relayed it to second base. My son was rounding third! The second baseman threw the ball toward the catcher right as he was reaching home, but it grazed his glove. Infield home run! I was screaming and yelling and making a fool out of myself. "Infield home run! Infield home run! He won! He won!" That was huge for a dad. The pride and joy I felt were absolutely amazing, even though in the grand scheme of things, it was tiny.

Right now, as I'm writing this, Tom Brady just won his sixth Super Bowl ring. Can you imagine the pride that Tom Brady's dad feels? Do you think God or Jesus are any different? Don't you think they smile when we are doing exactly what we were designed to do? Rick Warren says the smile of God is the goal of life. God smiles when we are engaging in our passion and fulfilling the purpose that he designed for us when he created us.

When your love for God and Jesus grows and you develop a strong sense of their presence in your life, you live your life with gratitude and a willingness to do what pleases them. Being you—the genuine you, the organic you, the authentic you—is what pleases Jesus. But the critical thing to realize is that you are the one who benefits most along with everyone you love and care about. There is real power in that idea.

When it comes to purpose, there could be more than one purpose that would be consistent with what God has in mind for you. We know from NDEs that people are told they must go back to their bodies because it wasn't "their time." Unfinished business must be completed—tasks to do, things to learn, love to give.

Chances are likely that you and I won't have a near-death experience, but that doesn't mean we are absolved from taking care of our business. We as Christians are in the love business, and business should be booming. We have an obligation to complete our tasks, use our talents, and discover and develop our passions.

When we learn to love and serve others and can appreciate and understand the vastness of the love of Jesus for each of us, we're automatically closer to our authentic selves. When we discover and develop our passions and we unlock the power to fulfill our purpose, we become more in tune with our spiritual selves. This is when the fun begins.

20

THE POWER OF THE WORD

The Bible was not given to increase our knowledge
but to change our lives.
– D.L. Moody

We have talked about the supernatural power of the Word as the primary way that God speaks to us. The chief way to test if the voice you are hearing is the Holy Spirit is by comparing it to what is said in the Bible. The benefits of spending time in God's Word are overwhelming. This is a list of some of the more obvious examples:

- We learn the mind of God.
- Knowledge of the Bible helps us defend our faith.
- We spend time getting to know Jesus.
- We grow our faith by understanding God's promises.
- We acquire wisdom.
- It helps us see and understand true spiritual warfare.
- We can easily find guidance for every situation.
- God's Word gives us the weapons to fight in spiritual warfare.
- Memorized Bible verses help us stay on track.

- We are helped in our interactions with other people.
- Memorized Bible verses help us defeat temptation.
- God's Word helps us in our finances and business dealings.
- It helps us to see worldly values as empty
- It helps us in our marriages.
- It allows us to focus on eternal values
- It helps us in our role as parents.
- We begin to see the spiritual world more clearly
- We better understand the sacrifices that Jesus made for us
- We acquire discernment, which opens up the Word even more. The more we learn, the more we learn.
- It inspires us to be more like our early church leaders such as the apostle Paul.
- It helps us to recognize the importance of Truth
- It gives us the best insight into the very nature and person of Jesus.
- Our hearts begin to grow and create space for Christ's love
- We can identify with different people in the Bible, such as David, Paul, Peter, Mary Magdalene, Martha, Ruth.
- It points out our flaws so we can see where we can improve.
- It gives us a cursory idea of the nature of heaven and hell.
- It gives us a clearer picture of the nature of Satan and the reality of spiritual warfare
- It gives us a greater appreciation and love for Jesus.
- It helps us to recognize God's will for our lives.
- Spending time in God's Word will change your life

When we are discussing power and access to power from a spiritual standpoint, we can't ignore the Word of God. It's that simple. It's just too important. There is supernatural power in the Word, and we receive too many benefits from Bible study to leave it out of our daily lives.

Clarity of Vision

As you progress along this path or continuum toward your authentic spiritual self, be ready to encounter battles. We all have three enemies or obstacles on this journey toward our authentic selves, and they have power while we are on this planet. We fight Satan, the world, and our fleshly or natural selves as we pursue spiritual goals. As we strive to get closer to Jesus, love, and authenticity, three ropes pull us toward worldly desires, fleshly pleasure, and toward sin.

However, seeing the spiritual world more clearly has value. If you go into battle, it's always good to be able to see your enemy. But when our spiritual vision becomes clearer, we can not only recognize the hand of God in everyday circumstances but discern the demonic forces working against us. We need to be aware that there are spiritual battles constantly going on all around us.

The following is an excerpt from an article written by one pastor regarding Rick Warren's *Purpose Driven Life* on the subject of clarity of vision:

> Warren says: "You know you are maturing when you begin to see the hand of God in the random, baffling, and seemingly pointless circumstances of life."
> Here is where the danger lies. People assume that the "hand of God" is involved in everything going on in their lives. They have no evidence that this is the case. It's just assumed. Rather than being pro-active in resolving problems and making informed decisions, people will lie back and wait for God to work things out. When nothing

> happens, they become disillusioned with God and begin to draw back from Him.[78]

Let's dissect this a bit. First of all, Rick Warren is speaking the truth about seeing the hand of God in random, baffling circumstances that go on around you. The closer you get to your true and authentic self, the *more* you see. The further away from Jesus you are, the darker things become. The spiritual world is more real than the physical world. I spend a lot of time in *Brave the Wave* talking about how NDErs could see more when they were separated from their bodies. The whole point of this spiritual maturity and vision is being able to decipher and discern those circumstances that have a spiritual component to them. They are there.

I would venture to say that most everyone who is reading this probably *does not* "assume that the hand of God is involved in everything going on in their lives." That statement takes out the idea that you are an intelligent human being who has reason. To say that we would "lie back and wait for God to work things out" should be insulting to us personally because we are reading, working, and acting at this very moment in time. If you weren't, you wouldn't have bought this book. You are spending two of the most important assets you have: time and money. That is not *lying back.*

Look at the time, effort, and energy we have devoted to the idea of getting up and moving. We are comfortable with this principle because the Bible has many examples of people acting first and then God releasing his power. Stepping forward in faith is a consistent principle seen throughout the Bible.

Sometimes we wait for God to act, but usually that's after we've taken a step of faith or a step toward obedience. The whole point regarding spiritual maturity is that we can see events that are spiritual in nature. We can see circumstances in our own lives, and we begin to see the hand of God in them. He will open the "eyes of our heart," but that vision is gained through action and movement.

One fascinating idea that we can add is that when your vision becomes clearer and you're moving closer to authenticity, you begin to see the hand of God in events that happened in your life *decades ago*. Now that is something that I can attest to personally.

God never promises full understanding of everything that goes on around you, but he does grant revelations. Jesus promised us that he would reveal himself:

> Those who accept my commandments and obey them are the ones who love me. And because they love me, my Father will love them. And I will love them and reveal myself to each of them.
>
> – John 14:21 (NLT)

Revelations are real, and they bring power, but they begin in the Word. They are one of the most rewarding aspects of moving toward our authentic selves. Spiritual growth and spiritual revelations make life on this earth exciting, challenging, and fascinating—absolutely mesmerizing. We need them as we move along pursuing our purpose. This is exactly how God wants us to live, with the vision and clarity of spiritual guidance and in the power of the Holy Spirit. Spiritual revelations give us vision, power, confidence, and insight. The tangible benefits they bring are empowering. Ignoring them leaves power and vision on the table. We may never have a near-death experience, but spiritual revelations and impressions are available to all believers.

When it comes to the relational aspects of our spiritual growth, we know that loving God and loving others are both critical and of supreme importance. The Bible is our guidebook, instruction manual, and our open door to the love of God. His words have power and are totally imbued with love. Remember how the apostle John described Jesus:

> In the beginning was the Word, and the Word was with God, and the Word was God. He was in the beginning with God. All things were made through him, and without him was not anything made that was made.
>
> – John 1:1–3

How can we love God without loving the Word if the Word is God? You want power? There it is. Think about the fact that 70 percent of those who consider themselves to be believers don't read the Bible regularly. The Word is the primary way that God speaks to us as a family of believers and as individuals. Jesus said:

> It is the Spirit who gives life; the flesh counts for nothing. The words that I have spoken to you are spirit and life.
>
> – John 6:63

Can you see and feel the power in what he is saying? The idea that the flesh counts for nothing is an astounding idea. He tells us that his words are "spirit and life." As we move toward Jesus, we step in the direction of our authentic selves and toward love, spirit, and life—which, again, brings joy and peace, kindness and goodness, patience and self-control.

Our Spiritual Mirror

So, we've established the immense power God's Word has to give us discernment and revelation. Another way it brings change into our lives is by allowing us to see ourselves more clearly. Therefore, the Bible is described as a spiritual mirror. When we examine our lives objectively and compare them to the image projected through the Word of God, we get closer to our objective, authentic selves and the person God had in mind when he made us. As we look intently in the mirror of Scripture, we will begin to notice the image of Jesus superimposed on our image, and that is where there is real power. Our goal is to conform our lives and our behavior in a way that reflects Christ. Remember mirror neurons?

The power doesn't stop there. Not only does the Word help us see ourselves more clearly, it helps us see others in the way God wants us to see them. One of the most useful things we can do is learn to see people the way Jesus does. When we can master this skill, it brings special insight and spiritual vision into our relationships. It brings about the special gift of empathy, the ability to enter into the pain of others. Many NDErs talk about how, when they came back to their lives here on earth, they were able to recognize in themselves an increased sensitivity to the pain and suffering others were experiencing. When we are able to enter into and experience the pain of others and have compassion for them, this helps us love them. When you inject empathy into a marriage or into a family, it is much easier to love others and be selfless. Our marriages are strengthened, and we become better parents. It empowers us to be better brothers and sisters or sons and daughters. Empathy is a special gift of spiritual insight that we acquire as we move toward authenticity. Spending time in the Word and with Jesus are the habits we need to acquire in order to move toward empathy.

So, what is the opposite? Apathy. Experienced marriage counselors agree that a marriage is doomed when there is apathy in both partners. Apathy is the opposite of love, and it is apathy or indifference that kills families, marriages, and most relationships. We can see that many people don't have a thriving, growing, intimate relationship with Jesus, not because of hate but because of apathy.

As we continue to delve into the Word and move toward authenticity, we acquire spiritual fruits that, by their very nature, help us deepen our relationships. Here is where we introduce the idea of other people. As we are learning to love and begin to acquire a sense of empathy and compassion, we need people around us. Loving and serving others while being patient and kind are skills we develop in our interactions with others. We can't learn love, kindness, and goodness by ourselves meditating in a cave. We need to be around others. Want to learn patience? Just throw a teenager into any household. We need others to help us as we are going about trying to develop joy and peace—no question about it. Think joy and peace would be helpful if your husband or wife is having a bad day?

These skills are also to be used in the service of others. Learning to love others requires that we engage with people. Sometimes those around us can be rude, angry, bitter, or mean. Why start with social media trolls, jaw-droppers, and love testers? Because if you can learn to love, empathize with, and be kind and patient to the people who are in these groups, everything else is a downhill ride.

We know that our purpose and our passion are intimately tied to other people. Relationships are important, but people can be unloving, mean, and critical. When we can learn to love the unlovable, be kind to the unkind, and patient with the impatient, that is strong evidence that we are growing in maturity.

Am I good at being kind to the unkind or loving to the rude and obnoxious? Absolutely not. Let me give you an example of a love tester from an experience I had seeing a patient just two days ago. This patient came in to be seen and to get pain medication for a toothache because she could not get in to see her dentist. When I walked in, she was on her cell phone talking. When I asked to see her bad tooth, she stopped talking, opened her mouth for me to see, then closed it and kept talking. She never looked at me or spoke a word to me.

To be sure, this scenario is a rare occurrence. Usually when I walk into a room to see a patient and they are on their cell phones, they will immediately say, "Oh, the doctor just walked in, let me call you back. Hi, doc! How are you?" That's just normal, cordial, polite interaction. Those are the easy ones. Those people are the ones who keep me going and make my job worthwhile. If that describes you, thanks—I love you. You give me energy and power. *Ding. Ding.* There's a clue. Energy and power. Honestly, those words just typed themselves out. That is an example of how other people give us energy and power through encouragement and support of each other.

People can be a source of power and energy, or they can steal the oxygen from the room and make it hard to breathe. It's easy to love those who are kind and polite to you. It's the love testers, jaw droppers, and oxygen stealers that are the problem. They suck the life, love, and energy out of us.

Jesus talks about this:

> But to you who are willing to listen, I say, love your enemies! Do good to those who hate you. Bless those who curse you. Pray for those who hurt you. If someone slaps you on one cheek, offer the other cheek also. If someone demands your coat, offer your shirt also. Give to anyone who asks; and when things are taken away from you, don't try to get them back. Do to others as you would like them to do to you.

> If you love only those who love you, why should you get credit for that? Even sinners love those who love them! And if you do good only to those who do good to you, why should you get credit? Even sinners do that much! And if you lend money only to those who can repay you, why should you get credit? Even sinners will lend to other sinners for a full return.
>
> Love your enemies! Do good to them. Lend to them without expecting to be repaid. Then your reward from heaven will be very great, and you will truly be acting as children of the Most High, for he is kind to those who are unthankful and wicked. You must be compassionate, just as your Father is compassionate.
>
> – Luke 6:27–36 (NLT)

I've been working on loving the unloving and being kind to the rude and mean for decades. It is one of the toughest things we do in this life. If we can get better at this one command from Jesus, we are closer to the kind of love he wants us to get to: *agape*. Agape love is the kind of love Jesus showed us on the cross—selfless, sacrificial love. It's the mother or father who would run into a burning house to save a child. No fear of death, just pure love. If we can be patient with the rude and impatient, then we are becoming more like Jesus. But being around other people is the absolute requirement.

Sometimes, though, we have to be careful because other people may want to take advantage of us or harm us. Jesus doesn't neglect this idea either. This is why the Bible is so important. Many warnings help guide us on the path. Jesus himself warns about not being gullible or naive. He tells us:

> I am sending you out like sheep among wolves. Therefore, be as shrewd as snakes and as innocent as doves.
>
> – Matthew 10:16

Jesus said in Matthew 7:6 (ESV), "Do not give dogs what is holy, and do not throw your pearls before pigs, lest they trample them underfoot and turn to attack you." Jesus knows about the love testers and jaw droppers. We are to love and serve others, but we are also to be wary of the world. We are to be as shrewd as snakes because we are like sheep among wolves. We shouldn't be worldly, but we should be familiar with how the world operates and what the world values. We must remember that Satan roams the world and that he is the father of lies.

Jesus said that all the laws of the prophets can be summed up by loving God and loving our neighbors. We can't be involved in our purpose or passion without the presence of others. Someone else must be served. We start with the skills of love and empathy, then we add patience and kindness. We develop and begin to use those skills when interacting with our spouse or our children. Who deserves our love and empathy more than our spouse? When there is kindness, love, and empathy in a marriage, it serves to strengthen the entire family. We can learn how to love in a way that is selfless when we start the day by asking our spouse, "What can I do for you today?" When we begin our day focused on loving others, we have to learn to put their needs before our own. That is the first step toward authenticity; we must "deny the self." This mindset releases power.

There is value in being able to see love testers and jaw droppers as sources of power. Also, as we are growing in our vision, we can begin to see Jesus in the faces of those closest to us. That skill yields power. It's easier to love those who are loving and kind.

Learning patience in dealing with my teenagers reminds me of my own behavior when I was their age. My standard smart-aleck response to my dad when he was on my case about something was, "Well dad, you know something? You don't have to be old to be wise." That was the title of a song by the heavy metal band Judas Priest, and it is an excellent example of the wisdom of a fifteen-year-old. The payback for that comment is still going on today, and deservedly so. The problem with that is that most young people don't have the experience of many years of bad decisions and poor choices, which is how wisdom is acquired.

A successful businessperson was asked how he became so successful, and his response was "Good decisions." When asked how he learned how to make good decisions, he replied, "By making bad ones." That is a crucial part of wisdom—making mistakes and **learning from them**. The reality is that you have to be old to be wise. Sorry kids.

Wisdom is thinking the way God thinks. We learn his mind by spending time in the Word. You never go wrong when you can think that way.

Music and Meditation

Now let's briefly discuss two additions when it comes to physical power: music and meditation. Both are extremely useful to give us the energy boost we need. Meditation, rumination, and contemplation of the Word gives us power and strength. The benefits of meditation are myriad, and there are many resources to look at when it comes to that one topic.

And science supports the idea that you will exercise with more vigor and, on average, you will work out longer when you incorporate music into your workout regimen. It also helps to improve mood.[79] From my own experience, I don't even bother working out without music.

Conclusion

So here we are with three new additions to our list. Our one addition on the supernatural side is the Word of God. The Word has supernatural power because it is the primary way that God speaks to us. If we value our relationship with Jesus, we will communicate with him daily by reading, studying, and meditating on the Word.

The other additions to the physical power side are other people and music/meditation. We need each other to complete the tasks that God has in mind for us. When it comes to the physical, I am listing music/meditation because they are both helpful when it comes to releasing physical energy. Let's look at how our lists are shaping up:

Supernatural power	**Physical power and energy**
1. Love	1. Goal setting
2. Holy Spirit	2. Getting up early
3. Authentic self	3. Better sleep
4. Harmonious passion	4. Exercise
5. Knowledge	5. Affirmation
6. The Word of God	6. Other people
	7. Music/meditation

21

IDENTIFICATION OF THE FALSE SELF

The deadliest attitude of the Pharisees that we exhibit today is not hypocrisy but that which comes from unconsciously living a lie.
– Oswald Chambers

One of the scariest and most worrisome pursuits we could be involved in is living a lie. Oswald Chambers wrote the above quote in his book, *My Utmost for His Highest*.[80] The word *unconscious* means senseless, comatose, unaware. Self-examination is critical for outlining and discovering the false self. We have described people who have a total lack of self-awareness, the "jaw droppers." We are all capable of acting in a jaw-dropping manner. We should spend time putting our observer glasses on, to see with our spiritual vision and endeavor to see with the "eyes of our hearts," viewing the world and its pursuits as they truly are. We should try to look at the people around us to see if they are self-aware or are living a lie. This is not an exercise in finger-pointing or judgmentalism but mainly an opportunity to sharpen our vision. We need this skill so we can be honest about our own behavior.

Real power comes from self-examination or self-awareness because it is absolutely essential for spiritual growth and to make changes for the better. If done in the spirit of confidence and self-love, self-awareness is not that difficult. Are we unconsciously living a lie? One of the most powerful ideas gleaned from the study of NDEs has been the idea that the "Being of Light" was pointing out an inauthentic self or an inauthentic life. That was the goal of the NDE:

> "I have talked about this authentic or true self as something that is the Light's function to disclose to the individual. How does it do that? The answer is, often by first showing the NDEr his or her false or socially conditioned self." He continues, "In other instances, however, the NDEr is given a direct perception into the nature of the false self and is thereby allowed intuitively to understand that the person one has identified with and habitually thought of as one's essential self was nothing more than fiction."[81]

I quoted this in chapter 4 when we briefly introduced the false self, but I've repeated it here for a reason. NDEs are supernatural experiences that powerfully point out the false self. But, more than likely, you and I won't have the advantage of such a dramatic encounter here on earth. We will have to do this for ourselves, so this is where self-examination comes into play. The Word and studying books on passion and purpose like this one will help us to see aspects of our lives that are taking us toward a false or fictional self. It will take some time and effort on our part, but this can definitely be classified as a high-value activity.

It also involves extricating ourselves from what the world values. When I came to the knowledge of the truth, I realized that no value can be found in accumulating things. Jesus talked about this in the Sermon on the Mount:

> Do not lay up for yourselves treasures on earth, where moth and rust destroy and where thieves break in and steal, but lay up for yourselves treasures in heaven, where neither moth nor rust destroys and where thieves do not break in and steal. For where your treasure is, there your heart will be also.
>
> – Matthew 6:19–21 (ESV)

And here again, in one of my favorite verses:

> Yes, a person is a fool to store up earthly wealth but not have a rich relationship with God.
>
> – Luke 12:21 (NLT)

Accumulating wealth is a pursuit that will most likely keep you from reaching your authentic self, which yields joy, love, peace, gentleness, kindness, and patience. These spiritual riches are not available to us if we are chasing after superficial or worldly goals.

These aren't my ideas. They belong to Jesus. We should be willing to develop our spiritual selves. If we believe he is telling the truth and we trust in him, we must look at our own behavior. We don't compare ourselves to others; we compare our values, pursuits, and our goals with the words of Jesus. Do our goals and our pursuits line up with what Jesus thinks is important? His standard is *the standard.*

Powerful Truth

That brings us to the next source of power on our list, truth. Truth is power. Jesus doesn't point and say, "Here is some truth," or "Over there is truth." Instead, Jesus declared:

> I am the way and the truth and the life. No one comes to the Father except through me.
>
> – John 14:6

The Father is love. Love is power, but truth also leads to power. We should seek truth just as fervently and diligently as we seek knowledge. The power of studying NDEs comes from truth. These experiences exist entirely within the spiritual realm, the realm we can't see. That is where most of the action is occurring. It is the Grammys after-party everyone wants an invite to. NDErs also emphasize the principles that Jesus focused on: love, service, relationships, knowledge, spiritual riches. These are real truth. Truth by itself is infused with power. It tends to reveal itself bubbling its way to the surface. But we should still seek it.

Truth is the way things really are. Truth is "that which is in accordance with fact or reality." If you have a Christian worldview, you believe in spiritual truths. You believe that you are a spirit. One of the most important ideas we can embrace is that most of our power to accomplish anything of value lies in the realm of our spiritual selves.

When we pursue authenticity, we spend time engaging in spiritual endeavors and growing in our relationship to Jesus. These spiritual pursuits point us in the direction of truth and love. Jesus told us we are to worship God in spirit and truth (John 4:24).

The problem comes when we aren't conscious of a lie we're living. To become aware of this, we are going to have to open the eyes of our heart and get in tune with the spiritual side of who we are. It requires the discovery and pursuit of authenticity that may be lurking underneath the superficial dreams of the natural self. The natural self is only concerned with the here and now. It is obsessed with short-term pleasures like sex, food, money, materialism, entertainment or comfort, which are outside the realm of the spiritual world and blind us to the reality of our authentic selves. These pursuits rob us of the joy, love, and peace of fulfilling our real and true purpose. When we devote our time and effort to goals or idols that we think will make us happy or fulfill us, we get sidetracked and frustrated. We lose heart.

Finding Heart

Lose heart? If we can lose heart, we should be able to find heart also. You are perfectly capable of finding your own passion. There is power in your passion. When you've lost heart, you've lost passion.

Let me give you a quick illustration of finding heart in unexpected places. This can help us with self-examination and looking for our individual passion. I was watching a documentary the other day about the actor Harrison Ford. In the documentary, Harrison mentions that he has a passion for aviation and flying airplanes, which started when he was in his twenties. He couldn't afford to do much flying back then, so he rekindled that passion again in his early fifties. He talked about how he "reinvented" his life at the age of fifty-two. He has six airplanes and two helicopters and engages in his passion frequently because he enjoys it so much. An interesting fact I wasn't previously aware of was that he was involved in the rescue of two people—a young boy who had gotten lost in Yosemite and a young girl injured in the mountains of Montana.

This is a useful illustration when it comes to finding our passion. Harrison Ford knew he loved flying, but he didn't engage in that passion for over thirty years. Once he started to rekindle that passion, he says that he "reinvented" his life. He loves flying and spends time and money on aviation, but he uses those skills in the service of other people. Flying is not his vocation, and it has nothing to do with what he does for a living. He supports himself by acting, but he nurtured and rediscovered a passion that had always been there, and he has used that passion in serving others. This is a real-world example of finding your heart and passion linked with purpose.

Losing heart means to become discouraged, to be sad or depressed or no longer interested in pursuing a goal. Your real passion is part of your authentic self. It is organic. When we think of something *organic*, we tend to think of produce, all-natural, and free of chemicals and pesticides. In the same way, we are God-made, not man-made. We're all natural and pure. It takes effort to free ourselves from the chemicals and pesticides of worldly, cultural, or social influences. It's not easy, but it's possible. That is exactly how you can describe your passion: It's pure, organic, God made, and an innate part of you.

When we pursue a false or inauthentic self, most likely it was man-made. You're more concerned with fleshly or worldly desires, like money, sex, comfort, luxury, and ease. When you create an inauthentic self, you create a false idol. It circumvents the path to your purpose, and it bypasses the pure, supernatural, Spirit-driven power that is available to you.

The most miserable people I know are the people who have selected a job or a career just to make a lot of money. Their idol is money, and they tend to use people, treating others as tools or pawns in the game to get what they want. When we love money, we are inclined to use people. But when we learn to use money and love people, we are on the path to authenticity.

We have an idea from NDEs that when we get to the end of our lives, we will be asked a question with regard to our purpose:

> The second question that arises for people who are near death is more complex than the first. Yet, there is still an amazing amount of agreement as to what is basically being asked. Roughly translated, the second question is, "How well did you use your gifts to live your unique life purpose?" Implied in this question is that we each have some specific contribution to make. Our mission, should we decide to accept it, is to figure out what our particular gifts are, and how we can use them to better the world.[82]

This is always asked within the purview of serving and loving others, learning how to love. If we have it right and we are pursuing our passion and purpose in the way God intended, we are loving people and using money, and not the other way around. It is a measure of our spiritual growth.

So, we have discovered our passion. We have searched, examined, observed, read, and studied, and we found it, like a sports car in the garage with a dusty canvas cover over it. Remove the cover, and the car is shiny, sparkling, and filled with gas. It's ready and raring to go. Passion is useless if you don't take it out of the garage for a drive on a beautiful Sunday afternoon. It is meant to be expressed, released, and taken out for a spin.

If you are one of the seventy-five million people out there who would change careers if you had the choice, do the thing that revs up your heart as often as you can. If you are stuck in an unrewarding or unfulfilling job, engaging in your passion will add vigor and energy to everyday life. It is God given, and we should never be ashamed to be engaged in our passion, especially if there is some type of service to others being expressed. It's a gift.

God's purpose for our lives is inextricably linked with our passion. Our purpose is to use the gifts, skills, and talents we have in the service of others. We have talked extensively about the one question that is asked of NDErs—What have you done with your life to show me?—and we continue to emphasize this. It should be like a tape loop running consistently in the foreground of our lives. If this question is consistently asked of people during an NDE, it clearly has significance and should be taken seriously. Jeffrey Long in his book, *God and the Afterlife*, notes: "The message given to NDErs is that we are here for a purpose and that love is very important to the meaning and purpose of our earthly lives."[83]

As usual, love is the central focus. Love is at the center of your passion and love is at the center of your purpose.

To close out this chapter, let's add two more sources of power to our list on the supernatural side: truth and self-awareness.

Supernatural power	**Physical power and energy**
1. Love	1. Goal setting
2. Holy Spirit	2. Getting up early
3. Authentic self	3. Better sleep
4. Harmonious passion	4. Exercise
5. Knowledge	5. Affirmation
6. The Word of God	6. Other people
7. Self-examination (self-	7. Music/meditation

awareness) 8. Truth	

22

PASSION, POWER, PURPOSE

Most people miss the purpose that God has for their lives.
– Rick Warren

Is the above a true statement? Not much research is available to either prove or disprove it, but we can agree that it certainly is thought-provoking. What if it's true, and most of the people around us, including our loved ones, are missing the purpose God has for their lives? Isn't it incumbent on us to tell our family and friends that God has a purpose for their lives?

When we begin to see our passion and are devoting time and energy in developing that passion, we get some clarity as to how purpose is linked. Purpose is where the action is. It is supernatural because it is assigned by God. Our purpose was created by him out of love for us, but it also serves to protect us and provide a path as it simultaneously infuses us with the power we need to fulfill it. Remember that every one of us has an assignment of energy and an assignment of love. God created us and gave us gifts, talents, and attributes to fulfill our specific purpose, and pursuing it is never a waste of time—especially if there is work completed for the kingdom and glory of God. If God gets the glory, you're in business.

> Therefore, my dear brothers and sisters, stand firm. Let nothing move you. Always give yourselves fully to the work of the Lord, because you know that your labor in the Lord is not in vain.
>
> – 1 Corinthians 15:58

This is a promise, a hang-your-hat verse. Any work done for the Lord is never wasted. We can be sure we are not squandering our time or effort if our intent is to further the kingdom.

Purpose

Let's take a quick glance at our list and add one more to the *Supernatural* column:

Supernatural power	**Physical power and energy**
1. Love	1. Goal setting
2. Holy Spirit	2. Getting up early
3. Authentic self	3. Better sleep
4. Harmonious passion	4. Exercise
5. Knowledge	5. Affirmation
6. The Word of God	6. Other people
7. Self-examination (self-awareness)	7. Music/meditation
8. Truth	
9. Purpose	

Purpose is in the realm of the supernatural because it is God given. Let's again look at some thoughts from the pastor who commented on *The Purpose Driven Life*. We are discussing these ideas with regard to purpose because some people may feel the same way:

> Scripture teaches that the purpose God has for man is to facilitate reconciliation with Himself through Christ. I do not see in scripture where God has individual, specific purposes for every individual born, other than reconciliation. Yes, there are examples of people in scriptural history that were born to a specific purpose in life. John the Baptist and Paul are two such individuals. Where people have been born with a specific God ordained purpose for this physical life, they didn't have to seek God to discover their purpose. God saw to it that His purpose in them was carried out.

This contradicts what he said previously:

> People assume that the "hand of God" is involved in everything going on in their lives. They have no evidence that this is the case. It's just assumed. Rather than being pro-active in resolving problems and making informed decisions, people will lay back and wait for God to work things out. [84]

My question is *What now?* Do we let God work out his purpose for us, or do we become proactive and try to resolve problems and make informed decisions with regard to our passion or our purpose? The answer is *we never go wrong by looking to Jesus*. He is truth. Whatever he says is the right path.

This commentary is saying that we have no unique, specific purpose in this life, however, there is a *major* problem with this line of thinking in that it negates what NDEs have told us, and more importantly, it negates what Jesus told us in the parable of the talents. We need to be careful when people propose ideas contradictory to what Jesus teaches.

One of a Kind

We need to be able to see ourselves as unique, as one of a kind. That's just reality. It's truth. There is no value in believing that we are not unique, that we have no special gifts or talents. If you can't see yourself as someone uniquely created for a specific and divine purpose, much of what we have been discussing is irrelevant.

Just observing my own children, it becomes obvious that we are all unique, each with distinctive gifts. Our children are brought up in the same environment with the same rules and the same parents yet have totally different personalities and distinctive modes of behavior—unique.

Reflecting on my own childhood and teenage years, it's easy for me to see that I was different, which I knew from an early age. I'm still different. Weird. We all are. It may not be obvious to you, but if you don't work at embracing this idea, you will miss the whole purpose for which you've been created.

To think that we aren't given a unique purpose also refutes what thousands of people with NDEs have said. We have an assignment of love and an assignment of energy, and this is one of those deep truths that must be a part of you. When we incorporate these ideas into our very being, we can embrace the idea of purpose. Jesus tells us:

> What is the price of five sparrows—two copper coins? Yet God does not forget a single one of them. And the very hairs on your head are all numbered. So don't be afraid;

> you are more valuable to God than a whole flock of sparrows.
>
> – Luke 12:6–7 (NLT)

God does not forget *a single one of us*. We have value. We are unique, with different gifts and talents. We have the testimony of the people who have undergone NDEs to back this up. Let's look at some of the questions NDErs were asked by the "being of light":

- Are you prepared to die?[85]
- What have you done with your life to show me?[86]
- "Is it worth it?" And what *it* meant was, did the kind of life I had been leading up to that point seem worthwhile to me then.[87]
- "Lovest thou me?" "If you do love me, go back and complete what you began in your life."[88]
- As he took a walk through this heavenly place, Mark began to hear a voice that seemed to be "from nowhere, yet everywhere." "Mark! You must go back!" "Go back? No! No! I can't go back!" Again, the voice said, "You must return, I have given you a task, you have not finished."[89]
- I was made to understand that it was not my time, but I always had the choice, and if I chose death, I would not be experiencing a lot of the gifts that the rest of my life still held in store.[90]

Let's focus for a second on that last line, because it applies to every single one of us. We should ask ourselves the question *Are there gifts that I am missing out on because I'm ignoring my passion and my purpose?* In other words, *Are there any spiritual insights, clarity, or wonderful spiritual gifts I've chosen to forgo so I can pursue a life that is inauthentic or false?* These are the kinds of questions that should stick in our minds. If we choose to ignore our passion and our purpose, we will miss out. In addition, the people we love most will be deprived of the love, joy, and peace that are bestowed on us when we move toward authenticity. These gracious gifts are meant to be shared. When you are operating within the sphere or power of your passion, you are not the only one benefitting. Everyone who is around you and everyone you love benefits also.

All I can do is give you my testimony. From personal experience, I know that if I hadn't focused on passion and purpose, I would have missed out on wonderful experiences of clarity, vision, love, peace, and insight—plus, the most valuable added bonus, a stronger, more intimate, loving relationship with Jesus.

This comes with a warning, though. It hasn't been easy. Pain and suffering are part of the process. That is just part and parcel to spiritual growth. It's just like how Tommy Lee Jones' character answered Will Smith's when he asked, "Is it worth it?" in the movie *Men in Black*. Tommy Lee smiles as he says, "Oh yeah, if you're strong enough." We are going to need strength as we pursue our purpose. But we *know* that we have access to power—supernatural power.

We have seen this excerpt from *Lessons from the Light*, but here it is again to remind us:

> In examining the lives of the NDErs we have met in this chapter, do you not feel that all of them, to various degrees, have been aided to live more authentic lives, much more in keeping with their previously dormant gifts and propensities, and emboldened to throw off the social shackles, where necessary, that previously constrained them? The Light told Peggy, in effect, that she should "follow her love" and that yielding herself to it was, in

> fact, to do the most unselfish and constructive thing in the world. The Light seems to be telling us, each of us, that we have a unique gift, an offering to make to the world, and that our happiness and the world's happiness are both served when we live in such a way as to realize that gift, which is no less than our purpose in life.[91]

I'm a living, breathing example of this principle without the advantage of having a near-death experience. I've come to experience unique spiritual revelations, blessings, and gifts. These gifts and experiences would have never come about without the time, effort, and energy expended in growing closer to Jesus and my authentic self. No complacency here, though. Too much work left to do. It is not the pursuit of happiness that power comes through but the happiness of pursuit. We gain power, confidence, love, and fulfillment on the path toward purpose.

Living your life on purpose and in the power of your own unique passion is exactly how God intended you to live. It brings fulfillment and peace, and it's also pleasing to God, bringing a smile to his face.

However, one question should be lingering in the back of our minds: How helpful is it to convince others that they have no purpose? How helpful is it to convince someone that they are not unique or different? Think about the repercussions of convincing a large number of people to ignore what Jesus is telling us in the parable of the talents and what NDEs are telling us. How much love is being spread? How many people are being served? How many families are strengthened? How many people will come to the knowledge of the truth? If you have no unique purpose or plan for your life, then God created you to accept Jesus then to sit around and wait to die. Intuitively we know that this isn't the case. We also know that love is an action. In order to love, we must act.

We don't need more sitters—we need movers. We need more passion. No passion? No power or energy. No purpose? No power. You are special, valuable, and unique. You have love in your heart that is meant to be shared. Your purpose is unique and valuable to the kingdom of God. You know it. *You feel it.*

Here is another critique of *The Purpose Driven Life* that I want to discuss for just a second:

> While I am sure that God is accomplishing an overall plan and purpose in allowing the creation to function as it does, I don't see any reason to believe he is as active in our day-to-day lives as Warren suggests. I see life pretty much going along fortuitously with God intervening where necessary or in response to needs that we bring before him.[92]

One of the most important concepts I have come to understand as I got closer to my authentic self is the value of my relationship with Jesus. The idea that Christianity is not a religion but a relationship is a very important one. It changed my entire life. If you subscribe to this idea, you understand the value of the relationship we have with God and Jesus. We know Jesus talked about these things as a point of emphasis:

> You hypocrites! Isaiah was right when he prophesied about you:
> "These people honor me with their lips,
> but their hearts are far from me.
> They worship me in vain;
> their teachings are merely human rules."
>
> Jesus called the crowd to him and said, "Listen and understand. What goes into someone's mouth does not

> defile them, but what comes out of their mouth, that is what defiles them.
>
> Then the disciples came to him and asked, "Do you know that the Pharisees were offended when they heard this?"
>
> He replied, "Every plant that my heavenly Father has not planted will be pulled up by the roots. Leave them; they are blind guides. If the blind lead the blind, both will fall into a pit."
>
> – Matthew 15:7–14

First, let's get a good picture in our minds of Jesus's emotional state. Do you think he is happy and having a good time? How about frustrated and angry? Why was he so angry? Because he wants our hearts. He wants our love, time, and devotion. His desire is that we know and love him like we would a father, mother, son, daughter, brother, or sister. We should be asking ourselves, "Do I love Jesus in this way?" If we have a love for Jesus, and we yearn to spend time with him the way we would with a spouse or a child, that is a clear indicator that we are progressing toward our authentic self, which takes time, energy, and effort. All strong relationships have these requirements.

When someone suggests God is not active in our day-to-day lives, that suggests a one-sided relationship. It proposes no communication, no intimacy, no love. It suggests that God is like a celebrity we follow on Instagram, and he never speaks to us or invites us to spend time with him.

Think about a marriage where your wife is not active or a part of your everyday life. Do you think that's a recipe for a strong, thriving, intimate relationship? We know God desires a relationship with us, and Jesus tells us that loving God with heart, mind, spirit, and strength is the greatest commandment. How can we do this with an absentee God? That's not just my opinion; look at what the Bible says:

> The Lord's eyes scan the whole world to find those whose hearts are committed to him and to strengthen them.
>
> 2 Chronicles 16:9 (GW)

If God is scanning the whole world looking to strengthen us, do you think that is just on the weekends? Or maybe Sunday? Usually, in any strong, thriving relationship there is communication and time spent together *every day*. It is common sense that this would be a good idea. We know that the most important reason we have for existence is to grow in our love and intimacy with God. Again, we never ever fail if we look to Jesus as a model for our behavior.

Very early in the morning, while it was still dark, Jesus got up, left the house and went off to a solitary place, where he prayed.

Mark 1:35

There is mention of God moving away from us occasionally as a test of faith. That is called the *dark night of the soul*. God sometimes hides his face as he did in the book of Job, but that is the exception, not the rule.

Our passion and our purpose are unique. We know that God is involved in our daily lives. We just need to open our spiritual vision and the eyes of our hearts.

We have blessings, *and* we have trials. God allows the waves in our lives also. But as we grow and mature, we appreciate those trials. Remember Kim Kardashian and what she learned from being robbed at gunpoint? She appreciated the insight and clarity that came from that experience.

God is active and involved in our lives as individuals. Not only that, he yearns for us to spend time with him and commit to him so he can strengthen us. When we feel that we have a grasp of our passion, then we get guidance with regard to our purpose. That's our cue to act.

A clear distinction exists between people who are successful in pursuing their goals and those who aren't. People who are successful act; they move. If we are to determine our purpose, a central focus, theme, or guiding light should be in the center of that purpose, and it should be unmistakable. That light is love. There shouldn't be any guess work in this endeavor. If love is central to your purpose—and that includes loving others and growing in your love for God—that purpose is firmly grounded in truth. The most important principle when it comes to love is that love itself is an action. It is our destiny. *We must love. We must act.*

23

PURPOSE IS PROTECTIVE

All of God's people are ordinary people who have been made extraordinary by the purpose HE has given them.

– Oswald Chambers

Passion is a source of power and energy, and purpose directs and focuses that power toward a goal. Your unique purpose is bigger than you because it is God's idea for your life, not yours. As we discussed, the most interesting idea to mull over is that purpose serves more than one function in our lives. It helps us with focus, perseverance, and resilience, but it also protects and provides power. One central focus of parenting should be to instill the idea of purpose into our children. Love protects. Purpose protects.

Most people who live long lives and who live in so-called blue zones (areas associated with longevity) "have and cultivate a strong sense of purpose."[93] A sense of purpose is one of the common characteristics of the people who live long lives. They also have strong relationships with family or have strong ties with the community through faith or culture. There is a strong sense of connectedness with other people.

We have talked about real flesh-and-blood relationships and how they are helpful in surviving the everyday stress that is inherent in living out our lives. Clearly there is a cultural phenomenon of connecting electronically with social media, but we need to be aware of the negative or harmful aspects that come along with that activity. When we consider the negative aspects of social media and the criticism and bullying associated with it, it becomes clear that we have a responsibility to protect our children from the psychological trauma we discussed in previous chapters.

What we are seeing is increasing isolation due to this social experiment, and if we are being honest with ourselves, we have no clue as to the long-term repercussions. Cell phones, an artificial means of relating to one another, are increasingly replacing face-to-face interaction. Social isolation is a problem and, when coupled with bullying and a sense of not belonging, creates a powerful trifecta that leaves people feeling lonely, depressed, and saddled with low self-esteem. It has a particularly powerful impact on our youth because it leaves them with few options:

> Rising rates of youth suicide and psychiatric disorders come as the health care system has started to focus on the effect of loneliness on mental and physical health. Young people, seemingly the most connected of all through social media, are being hit hard, San Diego State University psychology professor Jean Twenge reported in a study in March.
>
> Teens whose face time with friends is mostly on their phones are the loneliest of all, but even those who mix real-world socializing with social media still are increasingly isolated, Twenge found. The share of high

> school seniors who said they often felt lonely increased from 26% in 2012 to 39% in 2017.
>
> An NBC News/Survey Monkey poll out today places much of the blame for teen mental health challenges on social media. Nearly a third of about 1,300 parents of 5- to 17-year-olds blamed social media for mental and emotional health problems in children. Bullying and stress were the next most frequently cited problems in the poll.[94]

These statistics tell us that the next generation, responsible for our future, is dealing with depression, low self-esteem, anxiety, and a sense of helplessness and worthlessness. How do we address these issues? What do we do?

When teenagers and children spend most of their time on social media, they are instilled with a vision or an idea that everyone else has a better life than they do. This is what singer and actress Selena Gomez, who has 150 million followers, said about social media:

> Gomez said too much screen time on Instagram made her "kind of depressed looking at these people who look beautiful and amazing, and it would just get me down a lot, so I just think taking breaks is really important."[95]

This is a beautiful, talented, and famous young woman. How are our teenagers supposed to feel?

Research conducted by Cigna showed that young people with the highest rates of social media use reported very similar feelings of loneliness as compared to those who barely use it. Cigna CEO David Cordani says that "meaningful, in-person interaction" was seen as key to reducing isolation, so more face-to-face conversations are needed.[96]

The antidote to loneliness and isolation is relationships—family and friends who are there for support. From thirty years of experience in emergency rooms, I can tell you that we know those patients with very limited social support—few family members, few friends—are at highest risk for another attempt of suicide after discharge from the hospital. One way to counteract this growing trend is to emphasize the importance of friendships and family.

Fortunately, there is another protection against the negative aspects of social media such as body shaming, bullying, or rejection. Research data sheds some light on what protects us when it comes to getting criticism or not receiving validation through "likes" on social media: a sense of purpose. Having purpose is a cocoon of protection against this gamut of negativity flowing out of social media and protects our children and grandchildren from the critiques and barbs thrown about by others:

> In a survey of 300 adults, Burrow and Rainone examined the relationship between Facebook likes, self-esteem, and sense of purpose. To assess sense of purpose, participants rated their agreement with six statements such as "to me, the things I do are all worthwhile" and "I have lots of reasons for living." Those who indicated that they had a great deal of purpose in life showed no relationship between Facebook likes and self-esteem. But for those who lacked purpose, the more Facebook likes they received, the better (or worse) they felt about themselves.[97]

This is crucial, valuable information in this age of social media and distraction. A sense of purpose, as well as forming healthy and thriving relationships with friends and family, helps with confidence and a healthy self-image. Talking about purpose and self-image with our children and grandchildren is a good way to get a bearing on where they are with respect to loneliness, self-esteem, and their own sense of well-being.

Purpose Brings Resilience

Most people who have lived a life of purpose or who have accomplished great things have failed in one endeavor or another before they achieved success—and the list is long. A few notable examples in no particular order: Thomas Edison, Walt Disney, Jay-Z, George Washington, Bill Gates, Stephen King, Oprah Winfrey, and Abraham Lincoln.

Examine the common denominators in that list of names. We would have to agree that passion is very high on the list; it would be silly to argue otherwise. These are people who acted. They moved. They strived. The definition of *strive* is to "make great efforts to achieve or obtain something."[98] I'm sure you would concur that great effort was expended in the lives of every one of these examples. They applied an abundance of energy in pursuit of their purpose. Perhaps most critical to their success was that they continued to persevere in the face of roadblocks and obstacles. They were relentless, tireless, and unyielding in their passion, purpose, and action. Purpose and passion drive us through obstacles, failures, and criticism.

Great people are just ordinary people with extraordinary determination. Your level of determination and perseverance in fulfilling your unique purpose will determine your own destiny. You are no different than anyone on the list above, and you must believe that in order to take action. It's good to look at the lives of people who have succeeded in one area of life or another because they can inspire us to get up and move.

I am focusing on these principles because of the pervasive complacency and lack of action in our culture. This book was written because I was shocked that so many people were clueless as to what their passion was. Not only did some have no idea what their passion was, others believed that their passion or purpose was unimportant or irrelevant to what they were doing in their daily lives. That's a man-made plan for our lives, not a God-made plan. It is also a one-way train ride to a destination of frustration, anxiety, apathy, and depression.

In looking at the power that comes from purpose and the protection afforded to us when we pursue that purpose, it's clear that we would be wise to discover our passion. It's never a waste of time to search for this powerful gift from God. It would also behoove us to share these ideas with those we love. Our passion and purpose are supernatural principles created in the mind of God. These are his ideas. We start with a relationship with Jesus. We start with the Word and learning and valuing how God thinks, which is the essence of wisdom.

Every time we remove God from our lives and seek our own plan for our purpose, we run into trouble. There is plenty of history to illustrate this concept. Remove God from the plan? Bad idea. Communism as an ideology tried that in the twentieth century. The result? One hundred million people murdered. God's plans are perfect and wise; man's—not so much.

Minimalism Kills Passion

Another thing we know from experience and observation is that many people are looking for the quickest and easiest path to whatever goal they are striving for. Just look at the advertising for weight-loss products or get-rich-quick schemes all over television and the internet. The most common words used are *quick*, *fast*, and *easy*. Here is a good time to be skeptical.

When I was in high school, one of my coaches would always say, "In this world, there are two kinds of people when it comes to completing an assignment or a task—those who do the most they can do and those who do the least they can do." Look at the list of successful people above, and try to find anyone among that group who did the least they can do.

The elephant sitting on your kitchen table is telling you to go to the bathroom right now and look in the mirror. Ask yourself, *When it comes to doing a task or striving to reach a goal, where am I on the spectrum?* Are you always trying to do the most you can do, or are you satisfied with doing the least? The mindset or ingrained habit of thinking in terms of the least we can do is the idea of minimalism. It is nowhere to be found in the Bible. When we think in terms of doing the least we can do, this devalues our passion and our purpose and absolutely derails our pursuit of the realization of our authentic selves. If we live in a swamp of minimalism, our lives will never cast but a shadow of what we were created to be.

In the Bible, John the Baptist talked about being less in order to make Jesus more:

> The bride belongs to the bridegroom. The friend who attends the bridegroom waits and listens for him, and is full of joy when he hears the bridegroom's voice. That joy is mine, and it is now complete. He must become greater; I must become less.
>
> – John 3:29–30

John the Baptist is saying, "I must become less," so that Jesus can become greater. Note that he is not saying, "I must *do* less." One of the most important tasks in this life is to glorify God and bring others to Jesus. We can't accomplish this goal if we have the mindset of doing the least we can do.

Just one week ago, my son was telling me a story about his weekend vacation with a group of about thirteen teenagers at a beach house. He said that they were making breakfast for the group, but he was shocked that only four people out of the group of thirteen were doing most of the work. Everyone else was sitting around looking at their cell phones just waiting for those four to finish breakfast for them. Talk about teeing up a ball for me to hit as a teaching point! I responded, "Son, in this life there are two types of people in the world when it comes to doing a task—those who will do the most they can do and those who will do the least they can do."

Minimalism is a killer of passion. Matthew Kelly, in his book *The Rhythm of Life*, writes:

> The litany of the minimalist is never ending. What is the least I can do and still keep my job? What is the least I can do and still get reasonable grades in school? What is the least I can do and stay physically fit? What is the least I can do and raise my children? What is the least I can do and keep my spouse from nagging me? What is the least I can do and still get to heaven? The minimalist wants the fruit of a certain toil but does not want to toil. Minimalism breeds mediocrity. It is a destroyer of passion.[99]

Passion is the opposite of minimalism. It's the pursuit of excellence in a task. One clear indicator that you are engaging in a God-given passion is that you enjoy the pursuit of excellence. It brings peace, power, and a sense of well-being.

Examining your own life for areas of minimalism or passion is a good starting point on the path to deciphering your purpose. You may find that you are engaging in minimalist behavior in only one or two areas. My life began to change when I came to the realization that I was engaging in minimalism in my role as a father and a husband. Being a good parent or husband requires sacrifice, time, effort, discipline, maturity and an attitude of selflessness. All of these are absolutely necessary.

If you can't identify any areas of passion in your life, you may be wading in the swamp of minimalism. The only thing you're going to find in that swamp are snakes and alligators—the snakes of lethargy and apathy and the alligators of anxiety, depression, low self-esteem, and a longing for fulfillment. If you have no energy and no sense of purpose or desire to act, you may be just bumping along with no goal or vision. You can see people engaging in minimalism all around you. Just take a look around at the grocery store, dental office, car wash, movie theater, restaurant, or coffee shop.

A manager of a fast-food restaurant once told me that whenever he was hired to run a new restaurant, he would bring in about thirty to forty employees and work with them for an average of two to three weeks. That's how long it took to figure out the five or six employees he was going to keep. He was weeding out the minimalists.

I've seen sizable five-hundred-bed hospitals where the entire staff, from registration clerks and nurses to security officers and doctors, all had the same pervasive attitude of apathy. I've observed cruise ship companies that have a clear dedication to customer service, and you can see it from top to bottom.

One critical principle to understand and embrace in this is that we have a choice whether we want to ignore our purpose or pursue it. No one will force us to discover our passion or try to convince or cajole us to acquire the knowledge we need to fulfill our purpose. No one will demand that we develop and nurture the skill needed to execute God's plan or purpose for our lives. It's totally on us.

24

WORK NEVER WASTED

Work hard so you can present yourself to God and receive his approval. Be a good worker, one who does not need to be ashamed and who correctly explains the word of truth.

– 2 Timothy 2:15 NLT

When we emulate Jesus, we never lose. It's a win for you and everyone around you. When you expend time, energy, and effort discovering your passion while endeavoring to fulfill your purpose, you are working alongside Jesus. It is an absolute honor and privilege to be a co-laborer with Jesus in the work that God has called us to do.

> But Jesus replied, "My Father is always working, and so am I.
>
> – John 5:17 (NLT)

We are to be beacons of light and truth in the world. We can start by being examples of love and patience in our own families. Our own personal laboratory of love. We then venture further to have a positive impact on friends and co-workers. If we put Jesus in his rightful place in our lives—the center—his love flows out of us like the ripples from a pebble thrown in a pond. When we pursue our passion and purpose, we extend that flow of love further and further outside our circles of influence.

Let's go back to the parable of the talents for a second and look at why the "wicked worthless" servant failed to act. He said, "I was afraid, and I went and hid your talent in the ground." When we have knowledge of our talent or our passion, and we're afraid to pursue purpose, we're burying that passion and purpose, keeping it hidden from the world. What's more, if we pursue that talent or purpose for our own gain or for worldly goals or pleasures, it's not consistent with what God has in mind for us. It's abusing or misusing our talent for selfish reasons.

As we begin to grow in our relationship with Jesus and in our love for him, we begin to focus on pleasing him over pleasing ourselves. Our fleshly selves become a secondary concern, a sign of spiritual growth.

In our family relationships, we love our spouses and our children, and so we enjoy doing things that make them happy. We don't want to disappoint them. When we love Jesus in the same way, we don't want to stand before him and say, "I never discovered my passion and didn't pursue my purpose because of fear. I was afraid of failing and of what people would think of me."

Here is a quote from a documentary I saw about a tech company that failed in the early '90s:

> You have to believe. You have to be proud. You have to be convinced that you are going to bend the way the world is moving and you're going to take it in a different direction. If you're always playing it safe, and you're not failing, there is a very high probability you're not doing anything that is particularly important.[100]

We don't necessarily have to believe that our purpose involves bending how the world is moving, but our purpose most likely involves shaping or moving the world directly around us. The point of the quote is that we should avoid playing it safe. We should have an impact on the world directly around us that involves work life, family life, and church life.

We all feel fear. It is a natural response to a threat. What's important is that we move against it. We don't gain power until we learn to move against that fear. A good definition of *courage* is the ability to move, act, and function in a situation that has caused you to be afraid. There is no power in refusing to move against fear or in being controlled by the opinions of other people. Burying our talent, passion, or gift is the same as ignoring it.

Creating Value

If you do any work or put any effort into discovering your passion and purpose, no matter what it is, you and everyone around you will benefit. There is absolutely no downside. You must trust that God is infinitely smarter than you are. You should trust that the plan and purpose that he has in mind for you is perfect. Not only that, God wants you to live true. Live true to you.

The overarching theme in all this is the amazing, difficult-to-grasp, all-encompassing, over-whelming, inexhaustible love that God has for each and every one of us. Why would he come up with a dream or plan for your life that would *not* be the best for you? Why would his dream and plan not be perfect and line up exactly with your gifts, talents, and passions? When you discover and develop those passions, you acquire peace, the peace that comes from knowing that: (1) God loves you, (2) he wants what's best for you, (3) his plan and dream for your life is always going to be the best plan, (4) you're doing everything in your power to fulfill your purpose, and (5) you are working to create value in your life and in the lives of others. It comes down to being a consumer or a creator. If you create value in your family and in your own life, you and everyone around you will benefit.

When you can recognize this, it brings love, joy, and peace. When we acquire those spiritual fruits, it allows for kindness, goodness, and patience. It brings calm and order because you know that you are doing your part. It lessens anxiety and breeds confidence. You are exactly where you're supposed to be, doing exactly what you're supposed to do. You're the bird flying or the fish swimming. It engenders a sense of well-being.

Even if you are expending time and energy to fulfill your purpose and it somehow fails, you will be rewarded and there will be benefit. When we act to fulfill our purpose in the power of our passion, the result of that act is none of our business—it's in the realm of *God's* business. That is the beauty of the action. We take care of our part, and he takes care of the rest.

From my own experience, some of my greatest movements toward the right on the continuum and my biggest strides in love and intimacy with Jesus have come from my biggest failures. Spiritual vision and clarity come after your eyes have been washed with tears. My greatest experiences of pain and suffering yielded the biggest spiritual rewards, growth, and vision. It goes back to braving the wave, turning and trusting. It was a bumpy, painful ride, but in the end, I was closer to Jesus. Honestly, I'm still waiting for a smidge of success as I'm pursuing passion and purpose.

Engaging in your passion as you work toward your purpose is its own reward. The joy, peace, and sense of well-being are in the process. Can you imagine the love, growth, vision, clarity, peace, and fulfillment you will get when you realize and fulfill your purpose? It's all win-win when it comes to finding your unique passion and purpose. Even the process is of benefit to you and those closest to you:

> For this reason I kneel before the Father, from whom every family in heaven and on earth derives its name. I pray that out of his glorious riches he may strengthen you with power through his Spirit in your inner being, so that Christ may dwell in your hearts through faith. And I pray that you, being rooted and established in love, may have power, together with all the Lord's holy people, to grasp how wide and long and high and deep is the love of Christ, and to know this love that surpasses knowledge—that you may be filled to the measure of all the fullness of God.
>
> – Ephesians 3:14-19

The apostle Paul tells us to look at what is available to us: strength, power, Christ in our hearts, faith rooted in love, and the ability to grasp the deep love that surpasses knowledge, which fills us with the fullness of God. These benefits are within our grasp. We should work to trust in the love of Jesus. It starts by putting him at the center of our lives. He is our greatest source of love, power, truth, and passion. He helps us fulfill our purpose.

Most people who have encountered a being of light during their NDE have a profound inability to describe the love they felt. It is so overwhelming and powerful that there is no way to describe it in human terms or human language. Is that not consistent with everything written in the New Testament? *God is love.*

The depth of your determination and the willingness to overcome fear and obstacles to fulfill your purpose determines your destiny, now and in eternity. Try repeating this line out loud to yourself a few times: *My purpose is greater than my fears, my circumstances, my troubles, or my weaknesses.* When you really believe that and you can incorporate it into your very being, that is when things change. This is a source of power, energy, and confidence.

When we have discovered our passion, and we begin to undertake the task of purpose, the best attitude to embrace is that it will never be easy. That's a simple but useful approach to pursuing purpose. We shouldn't be surprised by this because nothing in this life is ever easy. Is marriage easy? Is parenting a teenager easy? What about starting a business or getting an education while working full time? Our approach should be willingness and watchfulness. We should be watchful because God does not set us on a path and then ignore us as we stumble around. He will allow circumstances, vision, and other people to help us along the way. We should be watchful for spiritual guidance and willing to do whatever Jesus asks of us no matter the consequences. We should have an attitude of steadfastness, resilience, and determination.

When we focus on our unique purpose, we will be criticized and spiritual warfare will be involved. This is another area in which we should be watchful, especially if you are trying to bring other people to Jesus. Satan is not going to take bringing more people to the truth lying down. When soldiers go into battle, they "steel themselves" and get ready for the attack. We must maintain this determination and resilience because the consequences of these battles last forever. "What we do in this life echoes in eternity." That may sound a little romantic and idealistic, but it's true. Our purpose has meaning for ourselves, our families, and for those around us who we are serving or bringing into the kingdom. We can gain strength from the encouraging words of Jesus:

> Blessed are you when people hate you, when they exclude you and insult you and reject your name as evil, because of the Son of Man. Rejoice in that day and leap for joy, because great is your reward in heaven. For that is how their ancestors treated the prophets.
>
> Luke 6:22–23

Do you want to leap for joy? For us to be hated and insulted so "they" can "reject our name as evil," we are going to have to *do* something for the kingdom or the Son of Man, Jesus. No one is going to insult or reject or hate us if we are just sitting quietly and meekly in our kitchens. We must act. We know it's a little scary and it makes us uncomfortable, but honestly, there's no other way. We are going to have to go into battle. Spiritual warfare is a part of the process. The best battle plan is preparation.

Sometimes Failure Is the Plan

From my own experience, the best battle plans are the ones that are fluid, that can be adjusted on the fly and readjusted to fit the circumstances. A good example is what SEAL Team Six did on their mission to kill Osama Bin Laden. One of the helicopters used to raid his compound had a malfunction and had to make an emergency landing. The team made an adjustment in their battle plan on the fly (no pun intended) and in moments had a seamless and clean updated attack plan. A willingness to change our approach in the middle of the battle is a good plan. If one road is blocked, we find another while constantly asking for guidance. Jesus said:

> Suppose one of you wants to build a tower. Won't you first sit down and estimate the cost to see if you have enough money to complete it? For if you lay the foundation and are not able to finish it, everyone who sees it will ridicule you, saying, "This person began to build and wasn't able to finish."
>
> – Luke 14:28–30

It will be hard, but the rewards in this life for you and your family are totally worth it. You are getting closer to authenticity, and you will have more vision and power. You can enjoy the fruit—love, joy, peace, kindness, gentleness, and self-control—that is needed for the task that God has in mind for you. The fruits of the Spirit are blessings that are real, powerful, and useful in helping us reach our purpose within the framework of our passion. Living in the strength of our passion and driven by the power of our purpose is the best and wisest way to live. It's exactly what God has in mind for us. His plan is always perfect.

So, what does it mean to be in partnership with Jesus seeking the kingdom or doing work for the kingdom? The best way I've heard it explained is the kingdom is wherever God is king, wherever he reigns, and that means everywhere. If we believe that God is sovereign, we trust that he is in control both on earth and in heaven. He is in charge of everything, and nothing happens unless he allows it to happen. He is also in control of blessings and revelations. All are within the bounds of his grace. He decides how much or how little success he is going to allow us at any point along the path to completing our purpose. We should not be surprised if he gives us a few failures on the road. But even if we fail, we can be comforted in knowing that he is watching. Sometimes the plan *is* failure. That's when frustration and anxiety set in. He is testing our faith and building our focus and our powers of resilience. He is also testing us to see just how determined we really are.

Don't be surprised if it seems like everything is going wrong, because that is exactly what will happen. Remember what Jesus told Sister Faustina? "It is not for the success of a work but for the suffering that I give reward." Here is another bit of encouragement taken from *Jesus Calling*:

> Thus begins your journey of profound reliance on Me. It is a faith-walk, taken one step at a time, leaning on Me as much as you need. This is not a path of continual success but of multiple failures. However, each failure is followed by a growth spurt, nourished by increased reliance on Me. Enjoy the blessedness of a victorious life, through deepening your dependence on Me.[101]

What is most important is to be prepared for difficulty, trials, and obstacles. They will come, and we shouldn't be surprised by any bumps in the road when we are on our way to finding our passion and our purpose. There is value in the idea that "this is not a path of continual success but of multiple failures." This prepares us for the difficulties ahead. The Bible tells us:

> God has given each of you a gift from his great variety of spiritual gifts. Use them well to serve one another. Do you have the gift of speaking? Then speak as though God himself were speaking through you. Do you have the gift of helping others? Do it with all the strength and energy that God supplies. Then everything you do will bring glory to God through Jesus Christ. All glory and power to him forever and ever! Amen.

> Dear friends, don't be surprised at the fiery trials you are going through, as if something strange were happening to you. Instead, be very glad—for these trials make you partners with Christ in his suffering, so that you will have the wonderful joy of seeing his glory when it is revealed to all the world.
>
> 1 Peter 4:10–13 (NLT)

Now look at those last two sentences. Compare those to what Jesus told Sister Faustina. Do you see the consistency? That is why the Bible is always our ultimate source for truth. If we are ignoring the Word, we won't get the encouragement and strength we need to overcome these "fiery trials."

We trust and rely on his judgment. Sometimes we are in a season of sowing. The harvest will come; we should just keep trusting. God may be waiting for us to grow closer to authenticity. This is where you need faith and where good habits like prayer and spending a quiet time with Jesus help us. This is the time for writing down your prayers, listening for his voice, and journaling what he is saying to you. We have the words of Jesus to help us in trying times:

> And why do you worry about clothes? See how the flowers of the field grow. They do not labor or spin. Yet I tell you that not even Solomon in all his splendor was dressed like one of these. If that is how God clothes the grass of the field, which is here today and tomorrow is thrown into the fire, will he not much more clothe you—you of little faith? So do not worry, saying, "What shall we eat?" or "What shall we drink?" or "What shall we wear?" For the pagans run after all these things, and your heavenly Father knows that you need them. But seek first his kingdom and his righteousness, and all these things will be

> given to you as well. Therefore, do not worry about tomorrow, for tomorrow will worry about itself. Each day has enough trouble of its own.
>
> – Matthew 6:28–36

Obedience Releases Power

One component of power that lies within God's promises has to do with obedience. Obedience is a source of supernatural power that is available to us because it is an act of faith and love. When we obey Jesus, we are acting in a loving way. We are putting his lordship in a place that yields great power—the center of our lives. Placing Jesus at the center of our lives brings power, peace, and revelation. Think about a spinning top. If it is balanced, it is spinning as if it's still. Perfectly balanced. Peaceful. Once it loses its balance, it becomes wobbly, and its motion becomes chaotic.

That is similar to living life without Jesus at the center. Rick Warren says that when we have Jesus in the center of our lives, we worship. When he is not, we worry.

One aspect of placing Jesus at the center of our lives is revelation. He reveals himself to us and we grow in intimacy with him. We get to know him and experience his love more deeply. This brings peace, power, and confidence, the kind of confidence we need to overcome the spiritual warfare and inevitable obstacles we will face on the path to purpose.

We need to be observers of our own actions. Actions speak most powerfully as to the nature of our behavior. One of my favorite things to say is "I'm sorry, I can't hear what you're saying because your actions are screaming too loudly." Sports commentator Shannon Sharpe puts it this way: "My grandad always used to say, 'Boy, I can see better than I can hear!'" Actions reveal truth and show that we mean business. Talk is cheap. Jesus said:

> Whoever has my commandments and keeps them loves me. Whoever loves me will be loved by my Father, and I will love them and reveal myself to them.
>
> – John 14:21 (CEB)

From my own experience, personal revelations from Jesus bring power, perseverance, faith, confidence, conviction, and focus. One of the things that I came to appreciate most in my own spiritual journey was the experience of loving Jesus in such a powerful, self-affirming way, that I was fully aware that *he* was aware of my love for *him*. It's a little strange, but I realized that I know that *he* knows that I love him. This continues to bring confidence and boldness into my spirit.

A simple idea to understand is that we as humans are hardwired to give and receive real love. God created us out of love so that we could receive and give real love.

When I was in training, learning how to deliver babies, the thing that was pounded into my head was after we stimulated the newborn with a warm towel and there was a good cry, we were to place the child on the mother's chest. Thinking about my training made me realize that the first thing we all experience when we come out of the womb is discomfort. We are made to be uncomfortable so we can take a big breath and to get the blood moving in our tiny bodies. The next thing we experience is the loving comfort of our mothers, their soothing voices and their touch.

So, in this life, the first thing we feel is pain and discomfort. The second thing is love and nurturing. We are built to give and receive real love. It is important to realize that as humans built to give and receive real love, this can't be faked or be artificial. If we love someone with real love, it is impossible to hide it or fake it. It just comes pouring out of us. The opposite is also true. If we don't love someone with real love, we can't fake it or hide it; eventually the truth becomes evident in our behavior. We can't help it. We don't need to try to hide or fake anything when it comes to our love for Jesus, since he already knows:

> Yes, I am the vine; you are the branches. Those who remain in me, and I in them, will produce much fruit. For apart from me you can do nothing. Anyone who does not remain in me is thrown away like a useless branch and withers. Such branches are gathered into a pile to be burned. But if you remain in me and my words remain in you, you may ask for anything you want, and it will be granted! When you produce much fruit, you are my true disciples. This brings great glory to my Father.
>
> – John 15:5–8 (NLT)

This is one of my favorite verses because it's an absolute. There is no ambiguity. We can do nothing without Jesus. But we should start with love. We should spend time with him to develop and grow our love for him. We should spend time with him so we can get to know him. If we believe and trust Jesus, we will anchor our lives to this verse. If we remain in him and obey him, we can ask for anything we want, and it will be granted if it is consistent with God's will and if it produces much fruit. He will grant us anything as long as we remain in him, love him, obey him, value his words, and focus on the will of God. You want power? There it is. The key is obedience. Here are four references to obedience from scripture.

1. "Do not merely listen to the word, and so deceive yourselves. Do what it says." James 1:22
2. "Jesus replied, 'Anyone who loves me will obey my teaching.'" John 14:23

3. "The world and its desires pass away, but whoever does the will of God lives forever." 1 John 2:17
4. "Therefore, everyone who hears these words of mine and puts them into practice is like a wise man who built his house on the rock." Matthew 7:24

So, let's add this crucial source of power, obedience, to our list:

Supernatural power	**Physical power and energy**
1. Love	1. Goal setting
2. Holy Spirit	2. Getting up early
3. Authentic self	3. Better sleep
4. Harmonious passion	4. Exercise
5. Knowledge	5. Affirmation
6. The Word of God	6. Other people
7. Self-examination (self-awareness)	7. Music/meditation
8. Truth	
9. Purpose	
10. Obedience	

25

TAKING INVENTORY

If your prayers aren't impossible to you,

they are insulting to God.

– Mark Batterson

One of the most important lessons we can learn is that if you are being prompted to do something with your talent that makes you uncomfortable or fearful, that's almost always a sure bet you are being inspired by the Holy Spirit. Why? Because it requires faith.

Part of the reason for our very existence is to develop and grow our faith.

> In all this you greatly rejoice, though now for a little while you may have had to suffer grief in all kinds of trials. These have come so that the proven genuineness of your faith—of greater worth than gold, which perishes even though refined by fire—may result in praise, glory and honor when Jesus Christ is revealed. Though you have not seen him, you love him; and even though you do not see him now, you believe in him and are filled with an

> inexpressible and glorious joy, for you are receiving the end result of your faith, the salvation of your souls.
>
> – 1 Peter 1:6–9

Faith is a source of power. No surprise here.

Supernatural power	**Physical power and energy**
1. Love 2. Holy Spirit 3. Authentic self 4. Harmonious passion 5. Knowledge 6. The Word of God 7. Self-examination (self-awareness) 8. Truth 9. Purpose 10. Obedience 11. Faith	1. Goal setting 2. Getting up early 3. Better sleep 4. Exercise 5. Affirmation 6. Other people 7. Music/meditation

If something is easy or doesn't require you to move against any fear at all, it would be wise to question whether that is something God wants you to do. A powerful way to discern if you are being inspired by God to accomplish a task is to ask yourself, *Will this goal or this task bring me closer to Jesus or other people?* Another useful question to ask is *Do I need God's power to help me complete this goal?* That's a good indicator to help you see if you are on the right track. God wants us to learn to trust and depend on him. Taking on a purpose that absolutely requires his power for you to succeed is a bold push of the chips to the center of the table. We're saying, "I am doing my part, but I need your help to carry this to completion."

We should keep our eyes and our ears open at all times, though, because God will put people on our path who can help us. Ask for guidance and wisdom. Trust in him. We can't forget to ask, *Am I engaging my gifts, talents, and my passion as I am working on this goal or task?* There are red flags when we bury, hide, or run in fear from our assignments, but there are rewards when we face our fears and assume responsibility for the implementation of our purpose:

> For it will be like a man going on a journey, who called his servants and entrusted to them his property. To one he gave five talents, to another two, to another one, to each according to his ability. Then he went away. He who had received the five talents went at once and traded with them, and he made five talents more. So also he who had the two talents made two talents more. But he who had received the one talent went and dug in the ground and hid his master's money. Now after a long time the master of those servants came and settled accounts with them. And he who had received the five talents came forward, bringing five talents more, saying, "Master, you delivered to me five talents; here, I have made five talents more." His master said to him, "Well done, good and faithful servant. You have been faithful over a little; I will set you over much. Enter into the joy of your master."
>
> – Matthew 25:14-21 ESV)

This parable is a constant reminder to take inventory of our talents and gifts. We should also look to see if we are using those talents and gifts in a way that is fruitful. The idea of "set you over much" is important because it has repercussions for our own personal and unique eternity. What we do with our talents and gifts is unique to us because no one else has them. It also helps us to realize that the size of the gift or talent is not important, but what matters is what we do with it for the kingdom and for Jesus.

Gifts of time, energy, money, and abilities are to be used in the service of others and in the service of the kingdom. Remember some of the common ideas that NDErs say they learned from their experiences. Just for fun and for our own edification, I'm going to list a Bible verse consistent with the ideas from NDEs[102] listed below:

- There is a reason for everything that happens: Ecclesiastes 3:1–15
- Find your own purpose in life: Romans 8:28
- Do not be a slave to time: James 4:14
- Appreciate things for what they are, not for what they can give you: Romans 1:20
- Do not allow yourself to be dominated by the thoughts or expectations of others: Galatians 1:10
- Do not be concerned with what others think of you: Romans 12:2
- Remember, you are not your body: John 3:6
- Fear not (even pain and certainly not death): 119 verses in the Bible about "fear not"
- Be open to life, and live it to its fullest: Luke 24:45
- Money and material things are not important in the scheme of things: Mark 4:19
- Helping others is what counts in life: Matthew 20:28; Mark 10:45; John 13:1–17
- Do not trouble yourself with competition: 2 Corinthians 10:12

Let's review a list of changes that occurred in people who have undergone an NDE:

1. Appreciation for life, sense of gratitude increases
2. Self-acceptance, greater self-worth
3. Concern for others—most striking and consistent change
4. Reverence for life, appreciation for the planet and nature
5. Anti-materialism, acquisition of things seen as pointless and empty
6. Anti-competitiveness, impressing others not important
7. Spirituality, a more universal spirituality
8. Quest for knowledge, tremendous thirst for knowledge
9. Sense of purpose, life more meaningful, sacred purpose to everyone's life
10. Fear of death—that is vanquished forever and completely gone
11. Life after death, there is some form of existence after death
12. Belief in God, deep inner certitude God exists

There may be critics who don't believe in the phenomenon of the NDE, and that's okay. My response would be to take the time to read and learn all you can about this area so you can make wise decisions. The principles above are common themes that occur or are emphasized in addition to the major ideas of learning to love and acquiring knowledge.

Many of these individuals were not spiritual in the least before their NDE. But look at the wealth of spiritual principles being emphasized after their NDE and which are consistent with the teachings of Jesus. Why are love, service, and purpose emphasized repeatedly? May I be so bold as to suggest that it is because they are so very essential? Notice that NDErs mention purpose as being sacred. *Sacred* means connected to God. How can we find our sacred purpose without consulting God?

Whatever we accomplish in God's name and for the kingdom, we are bound and limited by his grace. This is a very important concept, because he is in control. When we have success, it was allowed by him. God is sovereign. He knows the plan. It all fits in his perfect plan for our lives and for the world.

Living Your Passion

Let's use a baseball analogy to help us visualize where we are with regard to our passion and purpose. We start by getting up to bat. If you are ignoring your passion and your purpose, you are in the dugout; you aren't in the game other than as a spectator, and you're essentially "riding the pine," as the saying goes. But if you spend time engaging in any activity that you truly love and have a true God-given passion for, that is a single. You find your passion, engage in that passion, and develop it. You get on base.

Getting on base is no easy task in the major leagues. In the movie *Money Ball*, Brad Pitt plays the general manager of a major league team, and he is explaining to the coaches why they should try to acquire an older player that most considered washed up. Brad argues that this player is desirable because... then he pauses and points to Jonah Hill, who responds, "He gets on base." There is value in getting on base. You can't score runs without base runners.

Now, what if you are pursuing or engaging in your passion and someone is being served? It could even be the members of your own family. That is a double. You are getting to do the activity you love to do and someone else is benefiting. This generates joy, love, peace, and fulfillment in your life. You benefit, and so does everyone around you. Doubles bring value in this game.

Imagine that you are engaging in your passion, someone is being served, and you are being compensated for it. That is a triple. Triples are hard. This is an example of the person who engages in their passion every day on the job. Remember that 14 percent of the population is working in their dream job. Some of those people are living in the power of their God given harmonious passion. If this describes you, be grateful and thank the good Lord.

As we discussed, there are seventy-five million people who would change their careers right now if they could. What if this is you? My recommendation is to engage in your passion in your free time. If someone else is being served, then that is good enough. This helps in developing a sense of well-being and, hopefully, will bring more joy to you in your vocation.

These ideas are especially important if you have children who are trying to decide on a career. It's important to take God's opinion into account when deciding on a career rather than simply looking at lifestyle, geography, job availability, student loan debt, and workplace environment.

It's common knowledge that a significant number of people have jobs but their passion lies outside of their everyday work life. The most fulfilled, joyful, and peaceful people are those who are engaging in their passion while they are at work. Comedian Chris Rock sums it up like this:

> Some people have jobs, some people have careers.... If you've got a career, thank God. If you've got a job, I hope you get a career one day. Because when you've got a career, there ain't enough time in the day. When you've got a career, you look at your watch, time just flies: *Whoa, it's 5:35! I gotta come in early tomorrow and work on my project!* Cause there ain't enough time, when you've got a

> career. When you've got a job? There's too much time. You look at your watch like, *9:08! You don't even trust the time when you've got a job, be like: What time you got, what time you got?*[103]

So even if you are not engaging in your passion while on the job, you can still have an impact on the lives of others by serving them outside of your job. If you are serving in the power of your passion, you are in business. You can win many games with a bunch of singles and doubles.

What's left? How about engaging in your passion, serving others, and then bringing another person to Jesus? Home run, baby. You have changed someone else's life and their eternity. You stand before Jesus when you die and you turn around and say, "Oh, and I brought her/him with me."

There is no greater act of love than introducing Jesus to someone who doesn't know him. You are telling that person about the light, love, power, and salvation that Jesus brings to the table. There is no greater use of our time, energy, and talents and no greater honor and privilege for us as believers.

Home runs aren't easy. Triples aren't easy either. It's been said that a person needs to hear the gospel message at least eleven or twelve times before they make any change in their lives. Living out your life getting some singles and doubles is plenty rewarding enough to make life fascinating, challenging, fun, and fulfilling. We must get out of the dugout and face that pitcher though. It's absolutely required.

Home runs may be the ideal scenario, but the majority of us are just trying to survive. We aren't engaging in or even seeking our passion or our purpose. You can have your job and start engaging in your passion an hour or two a day or maybe on the weekends.

Maybe someone will be encouraged to grow closer to Jesus and will make the changes needed to be a better spouse, mom, dad, son, or daughter. Start thinking about your passion. What excites you? Try new things. Seek new experiences. Grow in your relationship with Jesus. Your vision and values will become clearer, and your path will be more easily discernible. That is a promise from God.

> Trust in the Lord with all your heart;
> do not depend on your own understanding.
> Seek his will in all you do,
> and he will show you which path to take.
>
> – Proverbs 3:5–6 (NLT)

Let's look at our list and take one last inventory.

Supernatural power	**Physical power and energy**
1. Love	1. Goal setting
2. Holy Spirit	2. Getting up early
3. Authentic self	3. Better sleep
4. Harmonious passion	4. Exercise
5. Knowledge	5. Affirmation
6. The Word of God	6. Other people
7. Self-examination (self-awareness)	7. Music/meditation
8. Truth	
9. Purpose	
10. Obedience	

11. Faith	

As we can see, the supernatural component of all this has more sources. Clearly it makes sense for us to spend time moving along the continuum toward Jesus and towards our spiritual or authentic selves. That is where the love, power, excitement, fulfillment, peace, and self-discipline lie.

However, our spirits are surrounded by our physical bodies, and we can't do anything on this planet to fulfill our purpose without dragging that physical body with us. We need spiritual power and physical energy. Be willing to engage both.

When it comes to authenticity and getting closer to our authentic selves, we have access to supernatural power. Communication, direction, focus, and energy are all available when we get closer to authenticity. The attributes of supernatural power feed on themselves. Love brings truth, purpose, and obedience. Love, the Holy Spirit, passion, knowledge, and purpose make us *want* to be obedient. The Word is closely aligned with truth and love. When we move on the continuum toward truth, toward Jesus, it brings every single component of supernatural power. Every single one. *Jesus is the key.*

Great Dreams Come from God

In sports talk shows, the word *great* is thrown around innumerable times, such as "We really can't begin to appreciate his greatness until we look at his performances in the playoffs." Greatness here. Great there. When we look at some synonyms for the word *great*, we get *prominent*, *eminent*, *important*, *distinguished*, *illustrious*, *celebrated*, *honored*, *acclaimed*, *admired*, *esteemed*, *revered*. How does Jesus see the idea of being admired, esteemed, celebrated, or revered? Those don't fit anywhere in the picture. When we think about purpose, our focus is on others, and the only one who should be getting revered, honored, or celebrated is Jesus. Who deserves it more?

Purpose starts with a dream. We begin to understand that God had a dream for our lives when he created us, and he gave us all the gifts, talents, love, and energy we need to fulfill that dream. When we think about our lives and what we consider to be great, Rick Warren said it best: "Great lives are built on great dreams." But what you and I consider to be great may be different than what God considers to be great. God measures greatness by how many people you serve. There is no reverence, admiration, or celebration for us—not until we get to heaven. In the meantime, we serve so that *God gets the glory*. No one deserves it more.

You have to attach yourself to the dream to live out that dream. This is your purpose. Every dream that God has is great because it came from him. You need to attach yourself to God's dream for *your* purpose and for *your* life. This is bigger than you, and God's plan is perfect. He doesn't make mistakes. If you can discover and develop his plan, purpose, and dream for your life, you cannot lose. Sometimes you will stumble, and sometimes you will fail, but you must believe that he knows exactly what he is doing. Remember, sometimes failure *is* the plan. Most likely, the very failure that we complain and whine about will give us the attributes and experience we need for the next step on the road. These are gifts of experience and knowledge that are critical to our getting through the next task or assignment. The failure was just a needed steppingstone on the path to fulfilling our overall purpose. This is where faith comes in. We learn to trust in the love of God and Jesus.

Sometimes you will have success, spiritual triumphs, or revelations. Those spiritual experiences enhance vision and allow for a better understanding of who Jesus is and who we are. They are priceless. They are exciting, stimulating, mesmerizing, and reveal a robust spiritual world that is a harbinger of the wonderful things to come in eternity—in heaven. I can't wait.

EPILOGUE

But in your hearts revere Christ as Lord.
Always be prepared to give an answer to everyone
who asks you to give the reason for the hope you have.
But do this with gentleness and respect.
– 1 Peter 3:15

This book really just wrote itself. It all stemmed from one question, *What is your passion?* It came from an idea that perhaps most of the people we come across in our lives are not engaged in any passion at all. Maybe there is a correlation between the lack of energy we all see in the people around us and their lack of job satisfaction. The statistics tell us that very few of us are in our dream jobs. How do we address this problem? We find our passion first. This sheds the light that we need to see the path towards purpose.

We really can't fail if we have purity of intent and we genuinely want to help other people. We also know that we are not wasting our time or energy if our goal is to grow the kingdom of God and introduce others to Jesus. We know there is no downside.

This is an excerpt taken from a sermon in the movie *Ragamuffin* mentioned previously:

> On Judgment Day, the Lord Jesus will ask one question and one question only: "Did you believe that I loved you, that I desired you, that I waited for you day after day? That I longed to hear your voice?" The real believers will

> respond and say, "I believed in your love and I tried to shape my life as a response to it." Many of us are going to answer, "Well, frankly, no sir, I never really believed it." There's the difference between real believers and the nominal Christians that abound in our churches. No one can measure like a believer the depth and intensity of God's love. (Jesus says) "I know your skeletons, your sins and your feeble prayer life. I dare you to trust that I love you just as you are, not as you should be." Because none of us are as we should be.[104]

That is our challenge. We dare to believe. We dare to believe that we are loved, we are unique, and we have a God-sized dream waiting to be discovered and fully realized. That is the essence of both our passion and our purpose. We should realize that purpose also protects, nurtures, and guides us on the path. But we must act, and we must move. We are on this road together through trial after trial, struggle after struggle, painful experience after painful experience. But God also allows triumphs, victories, spiritual insight, and spiritual fruit.

We should encourage one another, especially those of us in the family of believers. When we do that, we are witnessing to the world. We are witnesses to the love of Jesus, the most powerful force in the whole universe.

Let me share an idea that I just read by Pastor Mark Driscoll in his book, *Win Your War: Fight in the Realm You Don't See for Freedom in the One You Do*. The notion that he espoused is a powerful one. I am compelled to leave this with you. As believers in Jesus, as we are pursuing our purpose in this life, the struggles, trials, and pain we encounter will be the closest we get to hell. It won't get any worse than this. Our best days are ahead of us because we look forward to an eternity in heaven. We relish the idea of spending time with Jesus in unimaginable joy, peace, and love. This is an empowering idea.

For unbelievers, this life is the closest thing to heaven that they will experience. Their best days are the ones they are living now. Everything going forward is just going to get worse than the life they experience on earth. This is a sobering idea.[105]

This reminds me of an interview I read about with atheist director Woody Allen. He admits that he wakes up terrified every day. He lives in a constant state of fear because he believes that life has no meaning. He believes that everyone is on the same train and we all end up at the same station. Once this life is over, there is nothing else. He lives in constant fear, and he deals with it by making one movie per year. "At 72, he says he still lies awake at night, terrified of the void. He cannot reconcile his strident atheism with his superstition,... but he knows why he makes movies: not because he has any grand statement to offer, but simply to take his mind off the existential horror of being alive."[106]

We find our meaning in our passion and purpose. As believers, we know that we are unique, we are loved, and we have power. We believe it. We know it.

If you enjoyed this book, I humbly ask that you please leave a review. If you know someone who you care about who is living without purpose or passion, please share it with them. If you have any feedback or critiquing that you feel compelled to share with me, you can email me at the address below. If you would like to join my email list to get blog posts and free excerpts of upcoming books just sign up on my website at bravethewave.org. If you do, you will receive a free PDF download on my website that goes over the head to toe symptoms that should prompt you to go the emergency room.

Thirty years of emergency room experience does bring some useful, practical and time saving tips.

When we are engaged in our passion and moving toward our purpose, we know that other people are involved. I know that I need your help because I'm just a nobody trying to tell everybody about somebody (Jesus) who saved my soul. Pursue passion and purpose. You will never regret it.

With love,

Johnny Cavazos, MD

bravethewaveweride@gmail.com

bravethewave.org

ENDNOTES

Introduction

[1] Reuters, "Poll Finds 80 Percent of Workers In Their 20s Want To Change Careers," Huffpost, updated August 31, 2013, https://www.huffingtonpost.com/2013/07/01/workers-change-careers_n_3530346.html.

Chapter 1

[2] Lexico, s.v. "energy," accessed February 5, 2020, https://www.lexico.com/en/definition/energy.

[3] Lexico, s.v. "dabble," accessed February 5, 2020, https://www.lexico.com/en/definition/dabble.

[4] "Dream job? Most U.S. workers want to change careers – poll," Reuters, July 1, 2013, https://www.reuters.com/article/us-usa-work/dream-job-most-u-s-workers-want-to-change-careers-poll-idUSBRE96015Z20130701.

[5] Simon Sinek, *Start with Why: How Great Leaders Inspire Everyone to Take Action* (London: Portfolio, 2011), 183.

[6] Sinek, 6.

Chapter 2

[7] Art Kohn, "Brain Science: The Forgetting Curve—the Dirty Secret of Corporate Training," Learning Solutions, March 13, 2014, https://www.learningsolutionsmag.com/articles/1379/brain-science-the-forgetting-curvethe-dirty-secret-of-corporate-training.

[8] "4 Athletes with Legendary Eyesight," LASIK Vision, January 20, 2015, https://www.lasikmd.com/blog/4-athletes-legendary-eyesight.

[9] Caleb K. Bell, "Poll: Americans love the Bible but don't read it much," Religion News, April 4, 2013, https://religionnews.com/2013/04/04/poll-americans-love-the-bible-but-dont-read-it-much.

[10] Daniele Fanelli, "How Many Scientists Fabricate and Falsify Research? A Systematic Review and Meta-Analysis of Survey Data," PLOS One, May 29, 2009, https://doi.org/10.1371/journal.pone.0005738.

[11] Kenneth Ring and Madelaine Lawrence, "Further Evidence of Veridical Perception During Near-Death Experiences" *Journal of Near-Death Studies*, 11(4) Summer 1993, 225.

Chapter 3

[12] Ravi Zacharias, "Ravi Zacharias - The Glory of God for This We Were Made," Sermons.love, Accessed March 3, 2020, https://sermons.love/ravi-zacharias/4880-ravi-zacharias-the-glory-of-god-for-this-we-were-made.html.

[13] Jeffrey Long, *God and the Afterlife: The Groundbreaking New Evidence for God and Near-Death Experience* (New York: HarperOne, 2016), 97.

[14] Kathleen Doheny, "CDC: Suicide Rates Rising Across U.S.," WebMD, Accessed March 3, 2020, https://www.webmd.com/mental-health/news/20180607/cdc-suicide-rates-rising-across-us.

[15] Clarissa Silva, "Social Media's Impact On Self-Esteem," HuffPost, Updated February 22, 2017, https://www.huffpost.com/entry/social-medias-impact-on-self-esteem_b_58ade038e4b0d818c4f0a4e4.

[16] Dan Wootton, "Ed Sheeran forced to quit Twitter after revealing vile comments bring him down," July 3, 2017, https://www.thesun.co.uk/tvandshowbiz/3939544/ed-sheeran-forced-to-quit-twitter-after-revealing-vile-comments-bring-him-down.

Chapter 4

[17] Kenneth Ring and Evelyn Elsaesser Valarino, *Lessons from the Light* (Needham,

MA: Moment Point, 2006), 54.

[18] Rick Warren, "A Life of Purpose," TED, February 2006, https://www.ted.com/talks/rick_warren_a_life_of_purpose/transcript.

Chapter 5

[19] J. Robert Vallerand and Genevieve Mageau, "On Obsessive and Harmonious Passion," *Journal of Personality and Social Psychology,* 2003, Vol. 85, 756–67.

[20] Ring, *Lessons from the Light*, 47.

[21] Ring, *Lessons from the Light*, 47.

[22] Jennifer Grasz, "National "Dream Jobs" Survey Reveals Four Out of Five U.S. Workers Are Still Searching For Their Dreams Jobs," CareerBuilder, January 25, 2007, ttps://www.careerbuilder.com/share/aboutus/pressreleasesdetail.aspx?sd=1%2F25%2F2007&id=pr347&ed=12%2F31%2F2007.

[23] Vallerand, "On Obsessive and Harmonious Passion," 757-58.

Chapter 6

[24] Vallerand, "On Obsessive and Harmonious Passion," 757–58.

[25] Vallerand, "On Obsessive and Harmonious Passion," 757.

[26] Ring, *Lessons from the Light*, 50.

[27] Vallerand, "On Obsessive and Harmonious Passion," 757.

[28] Vincent Harris, "The unlikely rebirth of David Crosby," *Charleston City Paper*, May 24, 2018, https://www.charlestoncitypaper.com/charleston/the-unlikely-rebirth-of-david-crosby/Content?oid=18824165.

[29] S.v. "Dormancy," Simple English Wikipedia, Updated June 28, 2018, https://simple.wikipedia.org/wiki/Dormancy.

[30] Greg Evans, "If music gives you goosebumps, your brain might be special," Indy100, March 11, 2017, https://www.indy100.com/article/music-goosebumps-some-people-science-research-emotions-psychology-study-harvard-7926781.

Chapter 8

[31] Caleb K. Bell, "Poll: Americans love the Bible but don't read it much," *Religion News Service*, April 4, 2013, https://religionnews.com/2013/04/04/poll-americans-love-the-bible-but-dont-read-it-much/

[32] David C. Stancil, "'Miracles in the Bible': Exodus 14:15-31," *David C. Stancil, Ph.D.* (blog), Accessed March 5, 2020, http://www.dcstancil.com/yahoo_site_admin/assets/docs/Miracles_in_the_Bible_2014.10990210.pdf.

[33] Stancil, "Miracles in the Bible," emphasis added.

[34] Lexico, s.v. "retire," Accessed February 5, 2020, https://www.lexico.com/en/definition/retire.

[35] Ring, *Lessons from the Light*, 153, 154, 158.

Chapter 9

[36] Diana Bruk, "Kim Kardashian Opens up About the Robbery in Paris That Changed Her Life," Best Life, October 22, 2018, https://bestlifeonline.com/kim-kardashian-opens-up-about-the-robbery-in-paris-that-changed-her-life.

[37] "Alabama doctor stops to give homeless man his coat," YouTube, January 15, 2018, https://www.youtube.com/watch?v=8Q5StknL4S4.

[38] Sinek, 6.

Chapter 10

[39] Ring, *Lessons from the Light*, 50.

[40] Richard Feloni, "Thomas Edison's Reaction To His Factory Burning Down Shows Why He Was So Successful," Business Insider, May 9, 2014, https://www.businessinsider.com/thomas-edison-in-the-obstacle-is-the-way-2014-5.

[41] "The Harvard MBA Business School Study on Goal Setting," Wanderlust Worker, Accessed February 20, 2020, https://www.wanderlustworker.com/the-harvard-mba-business-school-study-on-goal-setting.

[42] Kelsey Mulvey, "80% of New Year's resolutions fail by February — here's how to keep yours," Business Insider, January 3, 2017, https://www.businessinsider.com/new-years-resolutions-courses-2016-12.

[43] Nicole Spector, "2017 New Year's Resolutions: The Most Popular and How To Stick to Them," *NBC News*, Updated January 1, 2017, https://www.nbcnews.com/business/consumer/2017-new-year-s-resolutions-most-popular-how-stick-them-n701891.

[44] Ben Gilbert, "'Fortnite' just had its biggest month ever, with nearly 80 million people playing in August," Business Insider, September 21, 2018, https://www.businessinsider.com/how-many-people-play-fortnite-stats-2018-2018-9.

[45] C. Wrosch and M.F. Scheier, "Personality and quality of life: The importance of optimism and goal adjustment." *Quality of Life Research*, (2003)12, 64, emphasis mine.

[46] "Have Goals for the Future," Action for Happiness,

http://www.actionforhappiness.org/10-keys-to-happier-living/have-goals-to-look-forward-to/details.

Chapter 12

[47] "Lida NDE 2011," YouTube, November 6, 2011, https://youtu.be/0gA6lU44S_c.

[48] Sarah Gray, "A Shocking Percentage of Americans Don't Exercise Enough, CDC Says," *Fortune*, June 28, 2018, http://fortune.com/2018/06/28/americans-do-not-exercise-enough-cdc.

[49] Aaron Earis, "How Many Protestant Churchgoers Actually Read the Bible Regularly?" Facts & Trends, Lifeway, July 2, 2019, https://factsandtrends.net/2019/07/02/how-many-protestant-churchgoers-actually-read-the-bible-regularly.

[50] Dan Schawbel, "Angela Duckworth: 'A Passion Is Developed More Than It Is Discovered,'" Forbes, January 9, 2017, https://www.forbes.com/sites/danschawbel/2017/01/09/angela-duckworth-a-passion-is-developed-more-than-it-is-discovered/#44b5c7903c0b.

[51] John Piper, "What Does It Mean to 'Abide in Christ'?" Desiring God, September 22, 2017, https://www.desiringgod.org/interviews/what-does-it-mean-to-abide-in-christ.

Chapter 13

[52] "Statistic: Jesus' Teachings on Money," *Christianity Today*, Accessed February 20, 2020, https://www.preachingtoday.com/illustrations/1996/december/410.html.

[53] Raymond Moody, *Life after Life* (San Francisco: Harper One, 2015), 44.

Chapter 14

[54] Long, *God and the Afterlife*, 50.

[55] Long, *God and the Afterlife*, 57.

[56] "6 Great Quotes about the Force," *Star Wars*, July 25, 2016, https://www.starwars.com/news/6-great-quotes-about-the-force.

[57] Long, *God and the Afterlife*, 45.

[58] "Martin Luther King Jr.—Acceptance Speech," The Nobel Prize, Accessed March 9, 2020, https://www.nobelprize.org/prizes/peace/1964/king/26142-martin-luther-king-jr-acceptance-speech-1964.

[59] Shaun Anderson, "The Best Steve Jobs Quotes – Putting a Ding In The Universe," Hobo, October 6, 2011, https://www.hobo-web.co.uk/the-best-steve-jobs-quotes-putting-a-ding-in-the-universe.

Chapter 15

[60] Emily Yoffe, "I've Got the Secret," *Human Guinea Pig*, May 7, 2007,

http://www.slate.com/articles/life/human_guinea_pig/2007/05/ive_got_the_secret.html.

[61] John Piper, "What Happens in the New Birth," Desiring God, November 25, 2007, https://www.desiringgod.org/messages/what-happens-in-the-new-birth-part-1.

[62] Charles Stanley, "The Power Within," HopeLife, Accessed, March 10, 2020, http://www.hopelife.org/devotionals/intouch-the-power-within-0629/0629.

[63] Howard Storm, *My Descent into Death: My Second Chance at Life* (New York: Doubleday, 2005), 73.

Chapter 16

[64] Ryan Jaslow, "CDC: 80 percent of American adults don't get recommended exercise," CBS News, May 3, 2013, https://www.cbsnews.com/news/cdc-80-percent-of-american-adults-dont-get-recommended-exercise.

[65] Darren E. R. Warburton, Chrystal Whitney Nicol, and Shannon S. D. Bredlin, "Health benefits of physical activity: the evidence," March 14, 2006, National Center for Biotechnology Information (NCBI), https://www.ncbi.nlm.nih.gov/pmc/articles/PMC1402378.

[66] "Top 10 Advantages of Waking Up Early," *Forbes*, Accessed March 11, 2020, https://www.forbes.com/pictures/gglg45gfd/benefits-of-early-risers/#100a29b31eb7.

[67] Andrian Teodoro, *The Power of Positive Energy* (n.p., Amazon Digital Services, 2016), 29.

Chapter 17

[68] Robert J. Vallerand, "The role of passion in sustainable psychological well-being," *Psych Well-Being*, March 21, 2012, https://rdcu.be/b2P6K.

[69] J.C. Turner & H. Tajfel, "The social identity theory of intergroup behavior," *Psychology of Intergroup Relations*, (1986), 7–24.

[70] Ring, *Lessons from the Light*, 50-51.

[71] Rick Warren, "Evangelism: Made for a Mission," CBN, Accessed March 11, 2020, http://www1.cbn.com/churchandministry/evangelism-made-for-a-mission.

Chapter 18

[72] Howard Storm, "Howard Storm Part III A Million Questions," August 16, 2015, YouTube video, Cline Cinematography, https://www.youtube.com/watch?v=RwOWYtXKV6g.

[73] Maria Faustina Kowalska, *Diary of Saint Maria Faustina Kowalska: Divine Mercy in My Soul* (Stockbridge, MA: Marian, 2005).

[74] John Stix, "Eddie Van Halen Opens Up in his First Guitar World Interview From 1981, Part 1," *Guitar World*, March 5, 2102, https://www.guitarworld.com/gw-archive/eddie-van-halen-opens-his-first-guitar-world-interview-1981-part-1

Chapter 19

[75] Ring, *Lessons from the Light*, 125–27.

[76] Moody, *Life after Life*, 58.

[77] Ring, *Lessons from the Light*, 19.

Chapter 20

[78] David Kroll, "Commentary on 'Purpose Driven Life' Part Three," *Theological Perspectives* (blog), Accessed March 12, 2020, http://theologicalperspectives.com/commentary-on-the-purpose-driven-life-part-three.

[79] C. I. Karageorghis, et al., "Ergogenic and psychological effects of synchronous music during circuit-type exercise," *Psychology of Sport and Exercise*, (2010)11(6), 551-59.

Chapter 21

[80] Oswald Chambers, "The Master Will Judge: March 16," *My Utmost for His Highest*, Accessed March 13, 2020, https://utmost.org/the-master-will-judge.

[81] Ring, *Lessons from the Light*, 51.

[82] Jonathan Robinson, "These Two Questions Are The Final Exam of Our Life," *InnerSelf*, Accessed March 13, 2020, https://innerself.com/content/personal/happiness-and-self-help/life-purpose/9544-how-to-know-your-mission-in-life-the-near-death-questions.html.

[83] Long, *God and the Afterlife*, 98.

Chapter 22

[84] Kroll, "Commentary on *The Purpose Driven Life*."

[85] Moody, *Life After Life*, 53.

[86] Moody, *Life After Life*, 59.

[87] Moody, *Life After Life*, 54.

[88] Moody, *Life After Life*, 56.

[89] Long, *Evidence of the Afterlife: The Science of Near-Death Experiences* (San Francisco: HarperOne, 2011), 61.

[90] Long, *Evidence of the Afterlife*, 17.

[91] Ring, *Lessons from the Light*, 50.

[92] Kroll, "Commentary on *The Purpose Driven Life*."

Chapter 23

[93] "Secret to Longer Life is Low-Tech," Blue Zones, Accessed March 13, 2020, https://www.bluezones.com/2018/08/secret-to-longer-life-is-low-tech.

[94] Jayne O'Donnell, "Help hard to find for teens struggling with mental health, thoughts of suicide," *USA Today*, May 23, 2019, https://www.usatoday.com/story/news/health/2019/05/20/teen-suicide-depression-soar-but-treatment-hard-find/3679364002.

[95] Sara M. Moniuszko, "Selena Gomez on body changes from lupus: 'People started attacking me... that really messed me up'," *USA Today*, November 12, 2019, https://www.usatoday.com/story/entertainment/celebrities/2019/11/12/selena-gomez-lupus-body-changes-online-attacks-got-to-me-big-time/2572263001.

[96] David M. Cordani, "A Message from David M. Cordani, President and CEO of Cigna," Cigna, Accessed March 13, 2020, https://www.cigna.com/about-us/corporate-responsibility/report/ceo-letter

[97] A. L. Burrow & N. Rainone, "How many likes did I get?: Purpose moderates links between positive social media feedback and self-esteem," *Journal of Experimental Social Psychology*, 2016.

[98] Lexico, s.v. "strive," https://www.lexico.com/en/definition/strive.

[99] Matthew Kelly, *The Rhythm of Life* (New York: Beacon, 2015), 102.

Chapter 24

[100] *General Magic*, directed and produced by Sarah Kerruish, Matt Maude, released April 20, 2018, https://www.generalmagicthemovie.com.

[101] Sarah Young, *Jesus Calling* (Nashville: Thomas Nelson, 2013), 6.

Chapter 25

[102] Ring, *Lessons from the Light*, 25.

[103] Chris Rock, *Chris Rock: Kill the Messenger*, HBO Studios, January 20, 2009, DVD.

Epilogue

[104] *Ragamuffin*, directed by David Schultz, produced by David Schultz, Ryan Bodie, Matthew Tailford (Color Green Films, released January 9, 2014).

[105] Mark Driscoll, *Win Your War: Fight in the Realm You Don't See for Freedom in the One You Do* (Lake Mary, FL: Charisma, 2019), 40.

[106] Jennie Yarbroff, "Woody Allen: Still Working, Still Terrified," *Newsweek*, August 7, 2008, https://www.newsweek.com/woody-allen-still-working-still-terrified-88175.

Made in the USA
Monee, IL
25 August 2020

39282491R00193